Getting Started WITH LEGO Robotics

A Guide for K–12 Educators

Mark Gura

International Society for Technology in Education
EUGENE, OREGON • WASHINGTON, DC

Getting Started with LEGO Robotics

A Guide for K–12 Educators

Mark Gura

Director of Book Publishing: *Courtney Burkholder*
Acquisitions Editor: *Jeff V. Bolkan*
Production Editors: *Tina Wells, Lynda Gansel*
Production Coordinator: *Rachel Williams*
Graphic Designer: *Signe Landin*
Copy Editor: *Kathy Hamman*
Proofreader: *Jodie Rogers*
Indexer: *Kay Schlembach, Potomac Indexing*
Cover Design, Book Design and Production: *Kim McGovern*

Library of Congress Cataloging-in-Publication Data

Gura, Mark.
Getting started with LEGO robotics : a guide for K–12 educators / Mark Gura. — 1st ed.
p. cm.
Includes index.
ISBN 978-1-56484-298-5 (pbk.)
1. Educational technology. 2. Robotics—Study and teaching. 3. Robots—Design and construction. 4. Lego toys. I. International Society for Technology in Education. II. Title.
LB1028.3.G85 2011
371.33—dc22

2011010744

First Edition
ISBN: 978-1-56484-298-5
Printed in the United States of America

Cover Images: © Dreamstime.com: Riekefoto (robot outline), Aprescindere (LEGO blocks); Creative Commons License @ Flickr (photos): steevithak, SpecialKRB, Nic's events.
Interior Images: © iStockphoto.com: Leontura (photo p. 52), göksu emre özkan (truck), Jordan McCullough (LEGO blocks)

About ISTE

The International Society for Technology in Education (ISTE) is the trusted source for professional development, knowledge generation, advocacy, and leadership for innovation. ISTE is the premier membership association for educators and education leaders engaged in improving teaching and learning by advancing the effective use of technology in PK–12 and teacher education.

Home of the National Educational Technology Standards (NETS) and ISTE's annual conference and exposition (formerly known as NECC), ISTE represents more than 100,000 professionals worldwide. We support our members with information, networking opportunities, and guidance as they face the challenge of transforming education. To find out more about these and other ISTE initiatives, visit our website at www.iste.org.

As part of our mission, ISTE Book Publishing works with experienced educators to develop and produce practical resources for classroom teachers, teacher educators, and technology leaders. Every manuscript we select for publication is carefully peer-reviewed and professionally edited. We value your feedback on this book and other ISTE products. Email us at books@iste.org.

International Society for Technology in Education
Washington, DC, Office:
1710 Rhode Island Ave. NW, Suite 900, Washington, DC 20036–3132
Eugene, Oregon, Office:
180 West 8th Ave., Suite 300, Eugene, OR 97401–2916
Order Desk: 1.800.336.5191
Order Fax: 1.541.302.3778
Customer Service: orders@iste.org
Book Publishing: books@iste.org
Book Sales and Marketing: booksmarketing@iste.org
Web: www.iste.org

About the Author

Mark Gura has been an educator for over three decades. The former director of instructional technology of the New York City Department of Education, he began his career as a teacher, spending 18 years in elementary and middle school classrooms in Harlem. More recently, he has taught graduate education courses at Fordham University and Touro College. Gura was a staff and curriculum developer for NYC's central Division of Curriculum and Instruction before being recruited to develop and administer the first citywide instructional technology program. He has written extensively on education for the *NY Daily News*, *Converge*, and a variety of other education magazines, and has written and published numerous books on education. He is the co-producer/co-host of the popular *The Teachers' Podcast* (http://teacherspodcast.org) and *Talking Financial Literacy Podcast* (www.talkingfinlit.org). Gura has spoken on the subject of instructional technology throughout the U.S. He lives and works in both the New York City area and Palm Beach County, Florida.

Acknowledgments

The author wishes to thank the following colleagues for their time and enthusiasm in sharing their experiences and expertise:

Dwayne Abuel, *Technology Coordinator, Highlands Intermediate School, Pearl City, Hawaii*
Laura Allen, *CEO/President, Vision Education & Media, New York City*
Corbett Beder, *Student Robotics Specialist/Staff Developer, New York City*
Chris Dudin, *Public School Robotics Teacher, New York City*
Phil Firsenbaum, *Educational Consultant/Student Robotics Specialist, New York City*
Ken Johnson, *LEGO Education sales representative to schools (NJ, PA, WV)*
Isaac Kestenbaum, *Robotics Specialist, Vision Education & Media, New York City*
Mike Koumoullos, *Teacher at Aviation High School, New York City*
Luke Laurie, *Middle School Science Teacher/Coordinator RoboChallenge, Santa Maria, California*
Ian Chow Miller, *Teacher, Frontier Junior High School, Graham, Washington*
Mark Sharfshteyn, *Chairperson, New York City FIRST LEGO League Planning Committee*
Maxwell Shlansky, *High School Student/Assistant Robotics Teacher, New York City*
Evan Weinberg, *High School Science Educator, New York City Public Schools*
Keith Wynne, *Elementary Science Specialist, New York City Public Schools*

Contents

Introduction

I didn't choose LEGO Robotics; it chose me. That was nearly two decades ago. I had just moved on from the classroom after 18 years as a middle school teacher in the New York City public school system. In my new, central district job as a staff and curriculum director, I also accepted the responsibility of administering a few federal grants intended to improve the overall instructional program English language learners (ELL) received at a dozen or so schools throughout New York City. I hadn't written the grant documents or submitted the applications. I hadn't designed the programs, nor did I have any idea what was supposed to be done with the funds that had been awarded us. On my first day on the job, however, my new supervisor handed me a stack of thick documents and told me that each of them, in essence, was a promise to create something. It was my job now to see to it that the Board of Education of New York City kept that promise by making happen what was described in those documents.

One of the grants was named LEGO LEP, and it called for creating a LEGO Robotics program to serve the limited English proficient (LEP) student populations in six different middle schools. The acronym LEP has since been replaced with ELL. I was fascinated by the idea and considered myself fortunate to be put in charge of making something this cool take shape. I had heard of LEGOs, of course. Although LEGOs weren't popular when I was a kid, they had since taken the world by storm. Could students actually be taught to create robotics? And could robotics materials really be made out of LEGOs? I had never heard of this phenomenon; nor had any of my colleagues.

As it turned out, the person who had written this grant application had wisely tapped into the NYC school system's tiny LEGO Robotics community. He had written into the application half a dozen schools that already had a small robotics program up and running. These were either after-school clubs, serving 20 or fewer students or a shop class that had updated itself by adopting the LEGO Robotics resource. Back then the city still had vestiges of its old industrial arts middle school program in place, although the wood shop, ceramics shop, and print shop classes were viewed as out of date. In some of the schools, a teacher here or there had managed to shoehorn LEGO Robotics somewhere else into the regular program. The point of this grant was to build onto what was being done and to expand the program for these schools' large ELL populations, taking advantage of materials already in each school's possession and a staff member or two on site who knew something about LEGO Robotics and how to use the technology with kids. The materials, by the way, made up a not-so-different forerunner of the classic LEGO RCX Robotics kit that would become popular a few years later.

Because I hadn't known about LEGO Robotics before being drafted to run the program, the LEGO salesman from whom I purchased materials for the schools gave me a quick tutorial on what it was and how it worked. I located and drafted a couple of experienced teachers to help spearhead the program, and their insights proved invaluable. Above all, I learned about LEGO Robotics from a couple of rambunctious classes of students while observing them use the materials in an industrial arts class in a huge middle school in Elmhurst, Queens. This school was located in the heart of the recently arrived immigrant community in New York City, and the students only spoke Spanish. However, the language challenge was immaterial in this class. LEGO Robotics has its own, universal language. The students' ease in learning it, the way it motivated and filled them with exuberance, and the wonderful things they constructed with it spoke volumes.

A few words about the motivating capabilities of LEGO Robotics are in order here. The schools where I have supervised or supported groups using this material over the years, dozens and dozens of them, have principally been in the inner city. When you see that LEGO Robotics, when used appropriately, has the capacity to engage, motivate, and foster learning—even in schools marked by student apathy, low achievement, and widespread dysfunctional behavior—you realize that you are in the presence of something with the undeniable potential to contribute significantly to student learning. In schools I had known for years where keeping students on task was nearly mission impossible, I observed LEGO Robotics activities in which getting the students to stop their work and move on to the next class or to pack things up and go home was the greater challenge for the teacher.

In many schools every fall, winning the students over, getting them back on board with the program, and re-involving them with their own educational process as partners with the school are more difficult than getting them through the year's math text. What I observed with LEGO Robotics showed that it is a resource and body of practice with the potential to perform this vital function for our students and our schools. It is not just fun; it is a relevant, engaging form of learning through play—serious play.

Later on in my career, during my tenure as director of the Office of Instructional Technology, a central district division of New York City's public schools, the international program called FIRST LEGO League (FLL) was begun. As the person in charge of supporting the city's 80,000 teachers in their use of classroom technology, I was approached by FLL for support. Our office spread the word throughout the city that this was a highly worthwhile program. We purchased starter quantities of LEGO Robotics kits for citywide distribution to inform and support likely teacher-adopters of FLL throughout the city. And we engaged Vision Education & Media, a service provider, to teach a series of professional development workshops we organized, so that teachers throughout the system could get themselves up to speed on what FLL is, how it works, and how they could work with their students in order to participate.

FLL has since become a runaway smash hit. Few things have done more than FLL to make LEGO Robotics known and appreciated as a very special realm of activity for today's students. In many schools there are students benefiting from robotics activities simply because of the presence of an FLL team or two. In others, robotics eventually becomes integrated into the teaching of academic subjects because of the school's initial involvement with FLL. Participation in FLL is the reason why a school acquires its first robotics materials, staff know-how, and general familiarity with and appreciation for robotics.

In addition to the strong motivating power that LEGO Robotics has on students, it is important to note the response of teachers. LEGO Robotics does call for leaps of faith, spurts of growth, and the willingness to embrace the new and the unknown. Robotics, after all, does involve mechanics, engineering, and computer programming, skills that can at first appear frightfully technical to many teachers without backgrounds in any of these areas.

What's remarkable about the LEGO Robotics kits is that their designers have pared these rarefied skill sets and bodies of knowledge back and refined and simplified robotics into something that truly can be handled by the average upper elementary school student. Yet, the kits' creators have not dumbed down the subject matter. LEGO Robotics is real robotics; it fosters learning real physical science and real engineering. The upshot of this technology is that any teacher willing to push the envelope a little can teach genuine science and engineering concepts and applications by using the LEGO Robotics kits. This opens up vast new horizons for students, teachers, schools, and the entire field of education. With the appropriate curriculum, practices, and materials to support them, students can learn content and skills that in the past required instructional specialists with advanced expertise. Furthermore, even where such specialists have been available, their activities and ambitions often were hampered by lack of access to specialized materials and the spaces required to use them. The emergence of LEGO Robotics materials has eliminated many of these constraints.

Why Read This Book?

This book presents the broad range of educational applications of LEGO Robotics, enabling you to narrow this large, potentially confusing body of practice down to practical uses for integration into personal teaching practice. It also explains the extensive variety of LEGO Robotics materials, helping you to understand what they are, how to make use of materials already in the school's possession, or to understand them with an eye toward purchasing new ones. Furthermore, this book provides support in the areas of organizing and managing the classroom for LEGO Robotics implementation, and it gives needed background and expert advice on key instructional and assessment issues when using robotics as the basis for teaching and learning.

Robotics can be the focus and rationale for activities that have been important educational goals but for which a solid context has been elusive. For instance, journaling has long been a favored activity in language arts classes, at least in principle. And science educators often make teaching technical and descriptive nonfiction writing a goal, as they try to make communication and reflection meaningful parts of science class. Journaling, though, can devolve into a contrived item on teachers' wish lists as they and their students discover that coming up with writing subjects that offer intrinsic motivation to get them down on paper are the exceptions and not the rule. Similarly, while science teachers concede that writing is a crucial skill in the professional lives of real scientists, if they are teaching traditionally with books and plastic models as the only support materials, they are not covering every aspect of real science. Finding opportunities for real science writing can be difficult for those who are studying about science. Forcing the issue with contrived writing assignments simply doesn't help. Students engaged in robotics writing projects not only record real experiences from authentic contexts in their daily journals, but also have real reasons for keeping the journals. Taking notes on the scientific process helps them create their robots more efficiently and reinforces the learning they experience.

Generally, when we hear about a student robotics program, it is a successful one. Beyond the impressive phenomenon of student motivation and engagement, robotics offers opportunities for real learning, learning that is definable and measurable. However, it also calls for a high degree of change in the behaviors of students and teachers. Educators are often encouraged to engage students in project-based learning, alternative or portfolio assessment, authentic activities, and the like. These progressive approaches are frequently left on the implementation to-do list simply because a solid, do-able practice with real educational value is not easy to identify or implement. However, robotics gives tangible form to that real, value-laden body of practice. Realistic expectations are keys to success in this rapidly growing area. I have taken pains to present projects that teachers can realistically expect students to carry out successfully. Included are rubrics and practitioner reflections on evaluating what students have accomplished through their robotics activities.

Here, I would like to discuss 21st-century skills. Not technology skills per se, 21st-century skills are new skills emerging from the ways learning and the work of the intellect are changing due to the impact of technologies. These new skills involve collaboration, and student robotics is generally taught as a collaborative learning experience. Unlike other practices that are adapted to allow for collaboration, robotics is inherently collaborative. Robotics projects work best when students divide labor, share ideas, and build on one another's contributions to a group effort. This is important because it parallels work in the real world. Student robotics projects are one of the most authentic and natural ways to model and teach this.

In "Student Robotics, a Model for 21st Century Learning," a chapter in the book *Classroom Robotics: Case Stories of 21st Century Instruction for Millennial Students*, which includes a long list of progressive education practices and 21st-century learning goals, such as authentic activities, individualized and collaborative learning, addressing multiple intelligences, applied learning, and so on, I discussed at length the power of student robotics to actualize the practices of 21st-century learning. Robotics often involves the following elements:

- Changes in classroom organization in which the roles of teacher and learner are shifted from traditional teacher control to student control with teacher support
- Learning that is cross disciplinary because robotics is a cross-disciplinary field, as opposed to traditional learning that often conforms to separate disciplines
- A change in the order of learning because of the experimental nature of robotics, in which play and exploration produce results that are understood after construction, not before

When you consider the points above and understand that LEGO Robotics—a reasonably priced, user-friendly, classroom-compatible resource set and body of practice—makes implementation eminently doable in the average school, you begin to see the power and potential of it. While a sizable body of practice and professional reflection has already been accumulated, much of it mined for this book, we have just begun to scratch the surface of this rich variety of education we can provide today's students.

It's not surprising, therefore, that over the past two decades, student robotics has evolved from being a curiosity, a special program found in a handful of schools, to a form of learning that is exploding in popularity. Though student robotics is not offered in every school, robotics programs are no longer rare. And the ubiquitous presence of robotics in our schools is no longer hard to imagine. This is true for a couple of reasons. One, our nation continues to prioritize STEM (science, technology, engineering, and math) education, and student robotics is perhaps the most perfect practice available to teachers and students that embodies all four subject areas. And two, students love it. To whatever extent the choices and desires of our young people determine what's offered in our schools, they are directly responsible for the proliferation of student robotics.

Another reason for the rapid adoption of student robotics in our schools is the emergence of LEGO Robotics materials. Most educators find that LEGO Robotics materials are reasonably priced, readily available, and easy to work with. They also are durable, compatible with effective classroom management practices, and appropriate for high-value instructional activities. While LEGO Robotics materials are certainly not the only student robotics materials available, they have become a favored choice by a great many teachers. They not only have been adopted by teachers and schools globally, but also figure in important international programs and competitions, such as the annual FIRST LEGO League competition and the RoboCup Junior international events.

A startling thing about LEGO Robotics materials is that while they are marketed and used as instructional material for students as young as the middle elementary grades, the very same materials are used in robotics courses in high schools and universities as well as by research groups like NASA and in industry. While these materials can be understood and used by young students, they by no means are merely toys.

Because there is so much interest in LEGO Robotics, teachers everywhere are considering using it as a motivational tool for STEM instruction. Some become aware of the practice by reading about it in professional publications, seeing it highlighted at conferences, or by word of mouth. Others find themselves contemplating adopting robotics at the request of the school administration, parents, or students themselves. Once teachers find themselves in this position, they realize there's a great deal to know, understand, and sort out. A bit of panic can set in. The purpose of this book is to pare what may seem like a mountain of jumbled information, decisions, and possibilities down to manageable size.

The following aspects of the challenge of getting yourself up to speed on LEGO Robotics are covered in this book:

- The LEGO Robotics materials—what are they and how do they work?
- What do student robotics activities look like?
- What do I need to learn and know?
- How can I begin learning about LEGO Robotics materials and using them with my students?
- How should I set up my classroom and run my class?
- Which path to take: After-school activity group? Competitive robotics team? Or making robotics part of the teaching and learning in a traditional subject area?
- How can I integrate LEGO Robotics into the curriculum and instruction?

- Is robotics compatible with standards-based instruction?
- How can I assess students' robotics work and learning?
- How can we document, share, and celebrate our robotics learning?
- Where can I find support resources, such as tutorials for self preparation, curriculum guides, instructional materials, and communities for collaboration?
- Is colleague-to-colleague advice available?

An important dimension of this book is its colleague-to-colleague advice. Information is presented based on interviews with teachers, professional development and curriculum specialists, and a student—all of whom have deep experience in teaching and learning with LEGO Robotics in American public schools. Their perspectives are useful because LEGO Robotics materials are relatively new; they've been on the market for only a couple of decades. Their use in schools is considerably younger than that, and professional development for their use is even younger. Such professional development tends to be highly specific to narrowly defined programs with clearly defined goals. Reaching out to experienced colleagues for professional advice is something I did as I wrote this book. In the colleague-to-colleague segments, you will find solid advice, based on the hard-won experience of classroom practitioners and those who prepare them. The experience set of these colleagues includes classroom-based instructional use of LEGO Robotics and preparation of student teams to participate in the FIRST LEGO League competition and similar events. In all cases, the first questions voiced were variations on "How would you recommend teachers who are new to LEGO Robotics begin?

For the most part, robotics requires a different type of teaching and learning than the style that forms the dominant paradigm of education in our schools. When students "play" with LEGO Robotics, they are engaging in informed, goal-oriented experimentation. They are using physical science and math knowledge and skills as a support platform from which to carry out their investigations. And in the act of playing, they reinforce and advance that body of knowledge and skills. They also engage in problem solving and social learning, activities we affirm a belief in but have trouble finding good opportunities to make happen in the classroom. Similarly, we also often affirm a belief in hands-on learning, cross-discipline instruction, and project-based learning. Yet, finding the right platform to make sure these types of learning are part of the education we offer students often eludes us. As we'll see in this book, the informed use of LEGO Robotics makes all of this possible.

CHAPTER 1

Robotics Basics

What Is LEGO Robotics?

LEGO Robotics is a body of teaching and learning practice based on LEGO Robotics kits, popular sets of materials that enable individuals without formal training in engineering and computer programming to design, build, and program small-scale, robots.

Students typically design and build a robot in three ways: 1) through imagination and playful exploration, they may create their own robot; 2) they may follow a cookbook-like recipe of directions by someone who has designed and built a robot—and they may modify the directions to create their own versions; or 3) a teacher or a more advanced student may create a "Challenge," a description of a problem that needs to be solved by the creation of a robot, together with a set of parameters the student must work within to create that solution. All of these approaches have value. There is something to be learned from each of them, particularly if teachers view student growth with robots as having a trajectory and understand that one approach may be of more value at a particular time in students' development. A full robotics program may offer several projects in each of the three modes for a balanced whole.

In all three modes, the process is likely to include the following elements:

- Envisioning what the robot will be like and what it will do
- An initial "build"
- An initial attempt to write a program
- Early trial runs of the robot to see if it will do what it has been designed for
- Design modifications and/or program modifications
- Feedback, reflection, and finish

To accomplish the above elements, students will put the robot's body together from construction pieces. This may include programmable "bricks" and/or specialized pieces and connectors, as well as axles, wheels, gears, and other parts. A programmable brick (the robot's central processor) will be incorporated into the design from the beginning; it often serves as a power source and a processor on which the software program runs and as an armature or support that makes the rest of the robot's construction possible and functional. Usually the programmable brick is thoroughly integrated into the structure of the robot.

Shortly after the early form of the robot is constructed, or perhaps in a step-by-step, back-and-forth manner, students will go to the computer to write the program needed to run the robot. Once this has been accomplished, students download the program to the brick or central processor and test the robot to see if it works. The rest of the process is one of back-and-forth, trial-and-error testing, followed by modifications of the robot, the program, or both.

More about LEGO Robotics Kits

LEGO Robotics kits contain the things needed to construct a fully functioning robot: parts needed to construct the robot's body; sensors (small electronic devices that detect and measure things in the robot's environment, such as light, electricity, and temperature); motors to power the robot; gears and other mechanical components; and a small processor, a programmable brick called the "brick." This small computer holds the robot's battery power and program, the commands that the robot will follow to carry out instructions, perform tasks, and solve problems. The processor is typically built into the robot's body as its core. The program is generally created on a conventional computer, using LEGO Robotics software; the program is transferred to the processor, although the newer NXT generation of materials also has a limited capacity to run commands that originate in the processor itself.

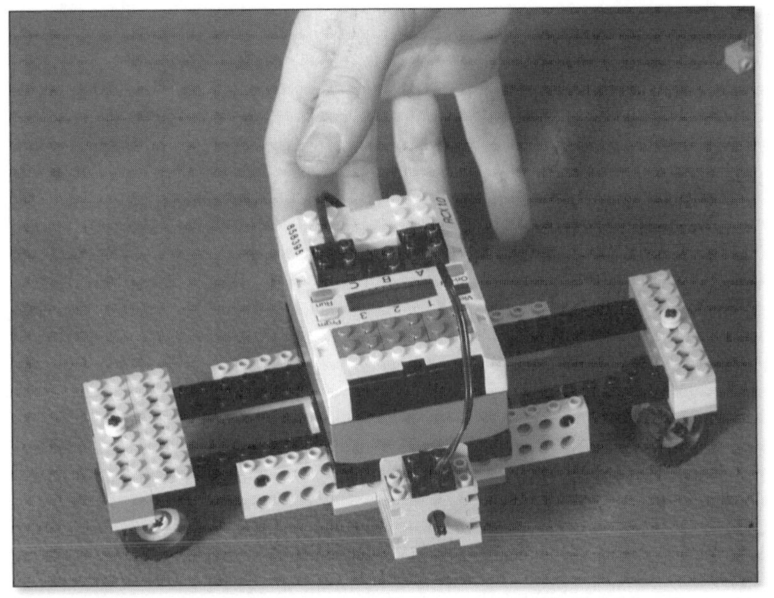

Figure 1.1 A student-created robot contains a programmable "brick," or processor, in the center.

While the range of materials included in a kit is generally complete enough to provide everything needed to construct a wide range of basic robots, purchase of additional components may be required for more advanced or elaborate robots. Generally, after completion of a robotics project, the robot is disassembled so that the parts may be used again for subsequent projects.

While some teachers may use a single LEGO Robots kit to demonstrate or illustrate science, mechanical, or engineering concepts and practices, the far more common practice of using them for hands-on student activities requires numerous kits. Students generally share kits for both instructional reasons (collaborative learning) and practical ones (cost and storage). The ideal ratio of kits to students is from one kit to two students to one kit to three or four students. The kits come in durable plastic bins that are convenient for storage. Over the years, the manufacturer has produced many varieties of kits; some come with software, and others require that additional software be purchased.

What Purposes Might Robotics Serve in the Classroom?

LEGO Robotics materials and practices represent a highly motivating, highly engaging basis for standards-based learning across the curriculum, with particular value in the four STEM subject areas. LEGO Robotics enables and facilitates progressive approaches to instruction, such as project-based learning and problem-based learning, hands-on learning (learning by making things), collaborative learning, authentic learning and assessment, and constructivist learning. The kits and practices are also used as the basis for the very popular FIRST LEGO League extra-curricular and after-school activities and competitions.

While a majority of students will not seek careers in engineering or become information technology (IT) specialists, there is value in giving them solid understandings of how these things work and affect our society. LEGO Robotics is a convenient, practical way to give students a good understanding of programming and how it directly influences our physical environment. This is potentially of great value to schools looking for meaningful ways to make technology-based learning part of the curriculum.

Beyond specific connections to science and math curricula already being implemented and curriculum areas on the radar screen for implementation in the near future (namely, STEM learning), LEGO Robotics offers advantages in the areas of how students learn and in learning unspecified or nonmandated curriculum that will significantly enhance students' success in higher education and the world of work.

LEGO Robotics represents one of the few practical opportunities at this time for schools to implement the following teaching and learning approaches and new curriculum items.

Teaching and Learning Approaches:

- Hands-on activities
- Learning by making things
- Problem-based and project-based learning
- Authentic assessment (products and performances)
- Collaborative learning
- Constructivist learning

New Curriculum Items:

- Collaboration as a reflective body of knowledge
- Learning activities that foster creativity
- Cross-discipline, applied learning

For What Grade Levels Is Robotics Appropriate?

LEGO Robotics may be used with a broad range of ages and ability groups. Robotics activities are flexible and adaptable to the needs of specific student populations. LEGO Robotics has become popular with upper elementary through middle school students, although the activities and concepts may be applied practically and meaningfully in high school level courses. The relatively recently introduced WeDo Robotics kits extend the appropriate applicability of LEGO Robotics to lower elementary grades and into the area of language arts in addition to its STEM connections.

Figure 1.2 Even younger students can participate in LEGO Robotics.
(Photo courtesy Flickr user SpecialKRB.)

Who Can Teach LEGO Robotics?

More and more frequently, teachers are becoming interested in bringing the impact of high motivation, technology-driven relevance, and STEM-enriched content and skills instruction into their classrooms. Though these ideas are appealing, do you ever wonder if you are sufficiently qualified or prepared? Taking the measure of one's abilities is smart and responsible if it is done in reference to an understanding of what's actually needed.

Most primary and secondary teachers wonder about their technical abilities. In reality, the level of technical skills needed to create robots has been pared down by the LEGO Robotics kits, as they are designed to engage and instruct students in ways that they can handle and learn from. You should have a reasonable comfort level with computers, but you don't need to know advanced things like programming. If you can navigate the web, using sites that require a degree of user interaction to fill in information, click buttons, and select "check off" options (common to online shopping or travel sites), if you use email and are comfortable sending and receiving attachments, and if you can use a word processor, perhaps inserting a graphic or other element and manipulating it within the page, then you probably know enough about today's user-friendly computers and software to handle managing your students as they learn with LEGO Robotics.

Robotics involves designing and building machines. Most teachers who are experienced in teaching engineering concepts, such as Simple Machines, or who coach students in building robots to perform tasks, including the experts who are interviewed throughout this book, agree that the optimal skill needed is coaching—prompting and guiding students to experiment on their own to find out what they need to know or to research problems. The web abounds in examples of specific solutions to the myriad little design and construction problems students will encounter. You don't need to be an encyclopedia of experience and knowledge, but rather a learning coach who directs students to the wealth of available materials when they aren't learning from their own trial-and-error experiments and comparisons with their peers' efforts.

LEGO kits are designed so that the robots students are likely to want to build can be constructed by putting well-designed parts together in workable combinations. LEGO Robotics is compatible with a trial-and-error approach, and so the majority of teachers who don't have backgrounds in engineering can guide students through learning experiences that are every bit as valuable as those provided by that small minority of teachers who are specifically teaching engineering-oriented design and build processes.

What may be more challenging for educators new to robotics are the instructional and classroom management dimensions of LEGO Robotics–based activities. With thought, reflection, and the kind of planning teachers typically learn to do on the job, you will be able to master these techniques, especially with the advice given in this book (see Chapter 3: Managing the Robotics Classroom). While LEGO Robotics activities excite and engage students powerfully and provide opportunities to learn science and engineering concepts and skills, as well as a host of subsidiary skills in areas like math and language arts to support these efforts, they tend to be implemented in a way that is far from the traditional lecture-based, teacher-centered, whole group lesson approach that we associate with 19th- and early 20th-century classrooms. For example:

- LEGO Robotics activities tend to have students work independently, although portions of the experience may be done in the traditional whole group setting.

- Students will probably work in teams or small collaborative groups. This is done for practical reasons, to share materials and space, as well as to optimize instructional time and to foster effective learning.
- Out of necessity, the LEGO Robotics classroom gives students a good deal of freedom to move about, interact with peers, and select specific tasks they wish to address at the moment.
- Activities embrace the qualities associated with project- and problem-based learning.
- Designing and building robots is open-ended; to a degree, students will identify what they want to do and work at their own pace, following approaches and processes they feel most comfortable with.
- There is often a social learning, constructivist dimension to LEGO Robotics activities. Students make discoveries about "what to," "why to," and "how to" continually, enjoying and benefiting from sharing their experiences, both successes and failures. Significance, meaning, and practical lessons about how to assimilate what's been learned come from shared, communal aspects of learning to a large degree.

Educators have long sought practical approaches for implementing the aspects of teaching and learning listed above. The good news is that a great many teachers, together with students of varying ages and ability groups and in various subject areas, have made all this happen in their classrooms through LEGO Robotics. This book shares the hard-won advice of those who've already succeeded, offering insights into how classroom organization and management as well as integration into the curriculum can be achieved reasonably easily.

In short, with an open mind, the willingness to try new things and learn from one's initial efforts, a little forethought, and a bit of preparation, LEGO Robotics is something that unspecialized teachers can bring into their classrooms. It does not require long-term, formal study—especially not to get started!

Why Are Robotics Activities Satisfying?

As an example of project-based learning, robotics is, to a significant degree, student self-directed. Students define for themselves the challenges they will tackle, such as: What type of robot will I create? What will I make it do? How will I design and program it to retrieve a ball? LEGO Robots are toy-like; they are made on a scale that is familiar for play objects. And, in many ways, LEGO Robotics activities feel like play. While a great deal of learning is involved, it is informal, experimental, and discovery-oriented. Learning with robotics is risk free. Try something, and if it doesn't work, simply try something else. Above all, LEGO Robotics is learning by making things. Each project involves identifying a challenge to be solved by creating a personal invention. Students start with the creative spark-driven, hatch-an-idea-and-make-it-work design and programming process; move on to the testing and trial phase (and perhaps a modification and re-testing phase); and, finally, present their robots to peers, teachers, and others. A robotics activity has a clearly defined start, middle, and finish; an easy-to-identify "It works!" point of success. Students understand that through their teams' trial-and-error experiments, brainstorming for solutions, and accomplishments they have learned a great deal. As coaches through this creative, scientific process, teachers are drawn into their students' excitement.

What Are the Instructional Goals and Advantages of LEGO Robotics?

The inclusion of a course in robotics, per se, within the overall curriculum is a rare thing as of this writing. But the need to study robotics as an end unto itself is a narrow one—a study for future engineers and roboticists, one from which most students will not derive great benefit.

The application of robotics across the curriculum, in providing practical, hands-on activities in the subject areas of science and math and especially in cross-disciplinary activities considered STEM (science, technology, engineering, and math) is where LEGO Robotics excels. It also has important, effective applications in language arts and other subjects. These curricular connections are fully explored in Chapter 7: Robotics in the Curriculum and in Chapter 8: Connections to Learning Standards.

CHAPTER 2

LEGO Robotics Materials and Software

A History of LEGO

The fifth-largest toy company worldwide in terms of sales, LEGO is arguably one of the most successful lines of play items of all time, racking up accolades for its developmental and educational values. Consequently, the products it has put out over the past half century form a complex history and catalog of items. For the purposes of this book, it is useful to know the history and nature of the basic LEGO materials and the extraordinary innovation that arrived in the late 1980s and early 1990s, LEGO Robotics.

Back in 1932, Ole Kirk Kristiansen founded a small toy company in his hometown of Billund, Denmark, and eventually named the company LEGO. The name LEGO is formed from two Danish words, LEg and GOdt, which translates into English as "play well." To play well describes the philosophy and spirit of the LEGO company and its products perfectly.

While Kristiansen's first efforts were wooden toys, over the years he experimented with numerous designs and materials. In the late 1950s, he became the first in his country to manufacture toys from injection-molded plastic, an approach that has since become a global standard. The core development of the company, the basic LEGO construction brick, has changed little since emerging at that time. In fact, the LEGO company states, "Today's LEGO bricks still fit the bricks from 1958."

LEGO products, particularly LEGO Robotics products, are popular both as in-school instructional materials and as educational play objects used at home and elsewhere. The materials are inexpensive, safe, and durable. Constructing with LEGO pieces is highly intuitive and supportive of learning by experimentation, characteristics that make them very popular with youngsters and the adults who supervise their development.

Students are likely to be familiar with the basic LEGO bricks and the concepts involved in snapping them together to build things. This saves time and assures at least a basic level of knowledge from which to launch any learning activities that involve LEGO Robotics. A related advantage is that LEGO bricks, found in almost every home with children, are often packed away into attics and basements when the children no longer use them. Acquiring additional bricks and supplies, therefore, is easy and cost effective—just solicit donations or visit yard sales for low-cost troves of usable supplies. There are some 2,400 LEGO plastic parts made for various kits and purposes, yet the basic brick shape is part and parcel of all LEGO-based projects and activities. The newer, NXT generation of LEGO Robotics does not provide as many standard LEGO pieces as did its forerunner, the RCX materials. However, the two versions have areas of compatibility, and there are ways to incorporate older LEGO pieces with the new kits.

LEGO Robotics represents a melding of the highly versatile and developmentally sound LEGO construction materials for children with the work of computer scientists, robotics engineers, and educational researchers at a few of the most influential universities in the United States, including Massachusetts Institute of Technology's Media Laboratory and Tufts University. The LEGO Group, with headquarters in Denmark and branches throughout the world, describes its construction bricks:

> ...which are produced with the greatest precision and subjected to constant controls. Each injection mould is permitted a tolerance of no more than one thousandth of a millimetre, so that bricks of every colour and size stay firmly connected, allowing LEGO fans to build entire cities from all kinds of LEGO elements. (http://parents.lego.com/en-gb/LEGOAndSociety/50th%20Birthday.aspx)

Consequently, we can see that this material, originally conceived as a toy, also has the characteristics and nature of a material capable of supporting the robotics activities of adult professionals as well as of children.

On to Robotics

Someone who is beginning with LEGO Robotics in a school in which robotics has been done for a while by others will quite likely encounter legacy RCX materials; these were sold and used very widely until recently. Alternatively, teachers may encounter the newer NXT materials. Whichever vintage the materials may be, they are essentially the same for school or home use, with a few differences in the way they are packaged and marketed. Names associated with LEGO Robotics materials include the name Mindstorms or LEGO Mindstorms for Schools (the educational version), as well as Inventor Kit and Challenge Kit, the latter available for school use.

These are the primary features of the robotics materials that newbie robotics teachers will want to understand:

- LEGO (building) bricks and construction pieces—these are the interlocking pieces from which the body and mechanism of the robot is constructed.
- The programmable "brick" is the onboard processor of the robot (RCX or NXT variations).
- Software (runs on a laptop or desktop computer) to program the robot.

- Program transfer mechanism:
  - IR (infrared transmitter) tower for RCX
  - USB cable or Bluetooth for NXT

  These mechanisms transfer the robot's program from the computer to the programmable brick.
- Motors power and move the robot.
- Sensors detect things like light, pressure, and electric current.

Two Versions of LEGO Robotics Materials, RCX and NXT

Ken Johnson, a LEGO Education sales representative, explains that while the LEGO company has "moved on" to the NXT generation of materials, LEGO Education has acquired quantities of the RCX kits and parts and will continue to support schools and educational users by selling these as long as supplies hold out. This will probably be for a few more years. The message that LEGO Education has been giving, according to Ken, is that eventually the RCX materials will no longer be for sale, and schools should include this understanding in their planning for the future.

As schools transition, one of the issues that they ponder is the compatibility of the old RCX materials with the new NXT materials. Ken points out that they are compatible in several ways: 1) newer versions of the Robolab software can be used with the NXT hardware, 2) the RCX sensors and motors will work with the NXT brick and software, and 3) the older LEGO brick-style RCX pieces can be used in NXT constructions. This is reflected in some of LEGO's curriculum materials, which show how to build a structural framework on the NXT so that it will accept the old parts (K. Johnson, personal communication, April 16, 2010).

The Hardware

The heart of LEGO Robotics materials is a programmable brick—not to be confused with the basic LEGO construction brick. The programmable brick is small and mobile and connects to the construction bricks and other pieces to form the robot. It contains the robot's power source and the computer program the robot will follow.

Robots built with LEGO construction materials are intended to be programmed using software provided by the company. This is done on a computer; both Macintosh- and Windows-compatible versions are available. The student-created program, once written, is then downloaded to a programmable brick, which contains a processor that holds and runs the program. The download can be accomplished in several ways: in the original RCX version, the program is downloaded to the brick through an IR tower (infrared transmitter) supplied with the kit; in the NXT version, the program is downloaded through a USB cable or by using a Bluetooth connection.

WeDo Robotics kits represent a third type of LEGO Robotics for younger students, ages 7–11. WeDo, which has its own age-appropriate software, capitalizes on the snap-together aspect of classic LEGO construction to involve elementary students in real engineering learning and problem solving and in expressing themselves through the language of robotics. Over the next two or three years, WeDo is likely to attract phenomenal attention across the U.S. More information on WeDo is available from the LEGO Education website's "LEGO Education WeDo Concept" page:

www.lego.com/education/school/default.asp?locale=2057&pagename=WD_Con&l2id=3_2&l3id=3_2_6

The Software

While there are many varieties of software that have been developed and adapted for use with LEGO Robotics over the years, newbie robotics teachers are most likely to use the simpler varieties; they are packaged with the basic materials and are intended for those who are new to robotics and computer programming. These user-friendly software programs are Robolab and Mindstorms. Robolab was distributed for use with the RCX before the NXT came along, and Robolab may be used with both the RCX and NXT versions. Mindstorms is sold alongside the NXT materials, but it is not provided in the basic kit and must be purchased separately.

Educators who are beginning to learn about LEGO Robotics do not need to be familiar with the intricacies of the various software versions. What is important is to understand the basic concepts behind the development of the software, how it works, and, most importantly, why this tool provides significant motivation for students' essential learning.

LEGO Robotics materials are not merely toys; they are genuine, fully functional robotics materials. But, they are of interest to educators because they are so practical—relatively inexpensive, easy to use and store, and durable. In addition to elementary, middle school, and high school students, many others are LEGO Robotics users. Professional engineers, roboticists, research scientists, high-level robotics hobbyists, and university students find LEGO Robotics materials to be highly practical and enabling. Many of these users are accomplished in computer science and are comfortable with traditional computer programming. Numerous traditional computer-programming languages have been applied to operate LEGO-based robots.

TIP

"RobotC" is for those confident in their programming abilities and interested in pursuing a more traditional avenue. RobotC is an example of "C" (a computer programming language) that has been adapted for use with LEGO robots. Information about it and a trial download are available at www.robotc.net/download/nxt.

One of the largest and most important groups of LEGO Robotics users is made up of students and teachers in primary and secondary schools. While some students at this level may understand traditional computer programming languages, this is not the norm. The beauty of the software that is intended for use with LEGO Robotics kits (Robolab and Mindstorms) is that it offers the streamlined, user-friendly approach of object-based programming.

In essence, traditional programming language requires the writing of code. This is done with the traditional characters found on a computer keyboard and requires knowing a programming language, a specialized vocabulary, and a system of rules, sequences, and methods. Learning how to write code requires time, effort, and commitment. In contrast, object-based programming is much simpler and more intuitive, allowing the programmer to concentrate on underlying functions and processes without spending the time and effort necessary to master a traditional programming language.

As an example, a bit of programming written in the programming language "C" for a robot would look like this:

```
motor[motorA] = -100;    //motor A is run at a 100 power level
motor[motorB] = -100;    //motor A is run at a 100 power level
wait1Msec(2000);         //the program waits 2000 milliseconds before running further code
```

In the graphic, object-based program, a bit of programming would look like this:

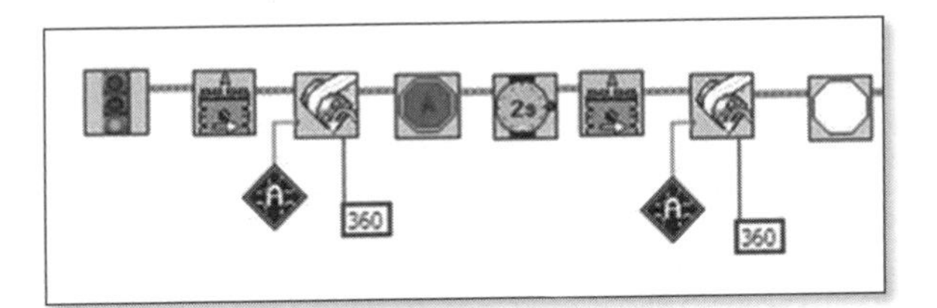

With object-based programming software, the idea is simple. The program is created in a way that is similar to a flow chart. The student drags and drops icons (objects) in the order that the robot will "read" or respond to them. There are icons for start, forward, back, stop, left, right, and so on. By simply stringing these together, students create a program for the robot to follow. Rather than learning an extensive vocabulary of commands and an intricate set of rules by which a program can be composed, students are freed to concentrate on telling the robot what to do. Through this visual, hands-on process, students learn important computer programming concepts that can be transferred to the study of programming using traditional languages, if and when students have the desire or need to pursue it.

More about LEGO's Software: Robolab and Mindstorms

Robolab (RCX *and* NXT)

The LEGO Education website offers the following information about its older common programming software, Robolab:

> **Robolab** software uses an icon-based, diagram-building environment to write programs that control your students' LEGO robotics projects. The latest version of Robolab is designed to support RCX users and ease the transition to the NXT system.
>
> Robolab has progressive programming phases that allow the programming level to match the student's knowledge and skills.
>
> **Pilot** is a basic environment where programs are built using a click-and-choose interface with a limited number of icons.
>
> **Inventor** provides a more open-ended environment with scores of icons and limitless programming options.
>
> **Investigator** uses Pilot and Inventor programming to incorporate data collection into projects.

More information is available for Robolab users through Tufts University's Center for Engineering Educational Outreach, which runs a community website on behalf of LEGO Education providing a range of tools and downloads, technical support, and contacts to other users.

Mindstorms (NXT)

The LEGO Education website offers the following information about Mindstorms NXT, the newer software:

> **LEGO Mindstorms NXT,** the next generation of LEGO Robotics, includes new and exciting software powered by the National Instruments LabVIEW graphical development platform. This icon-based, drag and drop software is intuitive and entertaining for everyone, from children to professional programmers. With its easy-to-use interface, the Mindstorms NXT software empowers kids to quickly program their robotic inventions to do what they want.

In 1986, National Instruments (NI) released the revolutionary software product LabVIEW, which challenged traditional, text-based approaches to programming with its graphical environment. NI LabVIEW empowered engineers and scientists with little or no programming experience to quickly and easily create applications for a wide range of industries from aerospace to zoology. Twenty years later, the award-winning LabVIEW platform is doing the same thing for children worldwide. With Mindstorms NXT software powered by LabVIEW, kids can easily program their own robotics creations to do everything from "sting" their siblings to dance.

Note: *Robolab can be used to program robots constructed with NXT materials as well as with RCX materials.*

More about Programming

The great majority of teachers who use LEGO Robotics kits with their students will use the basic programming software we've just discussed. These pieces of software are more than adequate for the basic robotics designs, builds, and activities that represent robotics for K–12 students. They are widely used for FIRST LEGO League (FLL) team efforts in FLL competitions and other major challenges. In fact, in order to maintain a level playing field, FLL and many other challenges will not allow the use of programming software other than the basic items available to all. The majority of teachers do not venture beyond these programs; perhaps as they amass considerable experience, a few teachers will branch out into more advanced programs.

One of the main advantages of the basic programs is that because they are intended for the great majority of teachers who are not advanced science or technology specialists, they are designed to run on truly typical, off-the-shelf computers that schools normally provide for classroom and lab use. Another advantage is that the basic robotics programs are specifically designed as entry-level, graphic- or object-oriented programming resources. In other words, students can use them to program their robots without getting involved in the difficult and time-consuming learning process of traditional programming including learning programming languages. As a result, students get the big picture of what programming is all about without getting mired in frustrating minutiae.

Furthermore, with the basic software, teachers may successfully play the roles of learning coach, co-learner, or learning manager as they support students in their LEGO Robotics activities. This often is not the case with advanced programming.

Yet, some highly motivated students will want to know "What else is there?" or "Can I go further or off in a different direction?" And some students will eventually perceive the limitations of basic types of software. However, it should be pointed out that programming has creative dimensions. While some may reach instinctively for a new tool when they don't immediately see how the one they already have will get the job at hand done, others will take a fresh look at what they have and attempt to make it work in ways they didn't see previously.

Why use other programming software? Beyond the eternal quest to do things differently or to do more, some teachers want to offer courses in advanced robotics, and others want to teach programming specifically. They may find other, more advanced programs—for example, NXC—to be worthwhile. For those interested in getting a picture of what advanced approaches to LEGO Robotics programming mean, a few resources are listed:

- Comparison charts of programming resources and how they are used:

  www.botmag.com/articles/10-31-07_NXT.shtml

  www.teamhassenplug.org/NXT/NXTSoftware.html

- Forum with discussions about which program to use for specific uses and the relative ease or difficulty of each one:

  http://thenxtstep.com/smf/index.php?topic=50.0

- leJOS—Java for Mindstorms:

  http://lejos.sourceforge.net/rcx/tutorial/getstarted/index.html

- pbLua—for Mac OS:

  www.mastincrosbie.com/Marks_LEGO_projects/pbLua_on_Mac_OS.html

Firmware and More

Something else to note: in addition to software, there is firmware installed in the programmable brick. What's firmware?

> In electronics and computing, *firmware* is a term often used to denote the fixed, usually rather small, programs and/or data structures that internally control various electronic devices. Typical examples of devices containing firmware range from end-user products such as remote controls or calculators, through computer parts and devices like hard disks, keyboards, TFT screens, or memory cards, all the way to scientific instrumentation and industrial robotics. *(Wikipedia)*

From time to time the brick's firmware may need to be updated or maintained.

It is important teachers and students understand two other aspects of the materials and the processes in robotics. The first is the power source, and the second is how students' programs are downloaded into the bricks. Without power, the robot will not run. The RCX generation of materials requires standard AA batteries that fit inside the programmable brick. Also available is a small, portable, battery-loaded power source from which students can draw power for their robots. This merely supplies power and is not programmable. However, in testing and running their constructions, which at various stages and for various purposes may be seen as mechanized models and not full-blown autonomous robots, these power sources (without intelligent directions) are sufficient.

The NXT generation of materials gets power from either AA batteries or a rechargeable battery that fits into the back of the programmable brick. The NXT also comes with some simple preloaded programs that may be used to perform some initial tests on robots.

The second dimension to be aware of is the process by which the program is downloaded into the brick. As we've discussed, students create the programs for their robots using software that runs on a computer; most prefer a laptop that is kept in a spot handy to the rest of the activities of a robotics classroom. Once the program is completed, it must be transferred to the robot. This has been accomplished in a variety of ways during the evolution of the LEGO Robotics materials. The most common methods are through the IR (infrared) tower for the RCX or via a USB cable for the NXT. NXT can also accomplish this with a Bluetooth connection.

Resources for Learning Basic LEGO Programming

The following resource lists provide links to materials specifically about programming LEGO robots with the two most common software varieties developed for this purpose, Robolab and NXT-G. Programming is something that is best understood early on in the process of LEGO Robotics, something to keep in mind as robots are conceived, designed, and constructed. Being mindful of the entire continuum of activities is important, and programming is a key element. The expert colleagues whose opinions are included in this book (see Chapter 10), as well as the author, advise that a great approach for teachers to learn LEGO Robotics is to rely on direct experience without excessive theoretical and technical learning beforehand. Still, before diving in head first, a general understanding and a broad overview of what will be encountered first will help greatly.

When teachers have Robolab or NXT-G software available to them but not both, the impulse to examine materials for just that one would be understandable. However, for most, the best place to begin is not with an understanding of the specific software you will use, but with a general understanding of object-based programming, the approach these two software varieties both employ. For that reason, briefly reviewing resources associated with both varieties of software can be beneficial. Object-based programming is described in this chapter, but reviewing these recommended online resources will give a broader understanding. Furthermore, the body of resources listed includes a variety of approaches to explaining this type of programming as well as a spectrum of voices and methods to demonstrate and illustrate it. Consequently, skimming this body of materials as a prelude to digging deeper for functional understanding and specifics will be useful to those who are new to LEGO Robotics programming.

Robolab (RCX) and Mindstorms (NXT) Tutorial Resources

For each resource, the title, source, URL, and a brief description are provided.

ROBOLAB—RCX

Center for Initiatives in Pre-College Education

Rensselaer Polytechnic Institute

www.cipce.rpi.edu/programs/robotics/robolab

Comprehensive Robolab tutorials

How to Program Robolab

Pittsfield, NH School District:

www.pittsfield.k12.nh.us/HS_Subjects/Science/Robotics/RoboInstructions/Robolab_Instructions.htm

Overview guide to Robolab programming

Introduction to LEGO Mindstorms for Schools

S. Rhodes

www.docstoc.com/docs/20929226/Introduction-to-LEGO-Mindstorms-for-Schools

Handout that includes information on Robolab programming

Introduction to Robolab: Developing Programming and Engineering Skills in the Classroom

Kathleen Crowe, University of Missouri InSITE program

http://engk12.ece.missouri.edu/documents/matl/Robolab%20Lessons.pdf

Comprehensive guide includes programming

LEGO's Quick Start Guide to Computer Control and Robotics Using LEGO Mindstorms for Schools

LEGO Education

http://cache.lego.com/downloads/education/led_quick_start_guide_eng.pdf

A guide intended for all first-time users of LEGO Mindstorms for Schools and the Robolab software (versions 2.0 or higher). It covers software installation and some basic programming principles.

Robolab Programming Notes

Steve Putz/Robotics Learning—Northern California FIRST LEGO League

http://ncafll.home.comcast.net/~ncafll/guides/robolab-notes.pdf

Well-illustrated guide to the components and aspects of programming in Robolab 2.5

Robolab Tutorial

Steve Dakin, Hacienda Robotics

www.qmate.com/robotics/RobolabTutorialSlides.pdf

Sequential overview of major aspects of Robolab programming

Technology Student

V. Ryan

www.technologystudent.com/robo1/robex.htm

A comprehensive course in Robolab for primary students with animated illustrations

MINDSTORMS—NXT

FLL Freak Tutorials

Skye

www.fll-freak.com/nxt/nxt_index.htm

Tutorials on a spectrum of NXT programming issues

LEGO Mindstorms NXT: A Brief Introduction and Tutorial

Chad Cardwell

Part 1—Overview
www.chadcardwell.net *also* www.youtube.com/watch?v=l0vqZQMF0A4

Part 2—Programming
www.chadcardwell.net *also* www.youtube.com/watch?v=AzRRulYvVdY

In two instructional videos, Chad Cardwell explains the basics of NXT. Part 1 presents an overview of the Mindstorms NXT kit and a clear demonstration of how parts work. Part 2 gives detailed programming information.

NXT Tutorial: Essentials

ORTOP—Oregon Robotics Tournament and Outreach Program

www.ortop.org/NXT_Tutorial/

Comprehensive guide to NXT programming features screencast videos

Programming Robots with Ben 1

pittcsc's channel

www.youtube.com/watch?v=olEjOG5qdGk

YouTube video introduction to NXT programming

Now that you are familiar with LEGO Robotics materials and software, here are some considerations: 1) how to present robotics to your students, 2) the kinds of activities you'll guide them through as they use the materials, and 3) how to integrate practices supported by robotics into your your regular daytime or after-school instructional program. The following chapters will guide you through all of this in detail, using step-by-step directions along with recommendations for effective online resources.

Additional Activities

Appendix A and B have additional resources. Be sure to check Appendix B for more tutorial-type activities.

Programming Possibilities

In addition to opening up the world of robotics, LEGO Robotics software demonstrates how the realm of general computer programming can be made accessible for students. There are other varieties of software that work similarly and which are commonly applied to other curriculums and types of instructional activities. A good example is Alice, a software commonly applied to animation, storytelling, and game authoring. Alice is provided free from Carnegie Melon University (www.alice.org).

CHAPTER 3

Managing the Robotics Classroom

While robotics activities are some of the most satisfying learning experiences that take place in a classroom, they can also present significant management challenges. For many teachers, implementing robotics activities may lie beyond their experience and understanding of how this type of instruction is conducted in schools. Robotics activities require a great deal of student independence, which is not typical of the way many classrooms are managed. As students create robots, they experience extraordinary levels of motivation and enthusiasm. Such high levels of energy, activity, conversation, and movement about the classroom can present challenges to teachers who do not thoroughly understand how to plan for and manage it all.

The Physical Setup

The way a teacher arranges a classroom—the placement of seats, desks, tables, computers, and other equipment; the placement of cupboards, lockers, and closets—can influence the success of student robotics instruction significantly. Of course, this is true for all subjects, but a practical classroom layout is absolutely essential for robotics.

When learning takes place as individual or small-group work, arranging the room to allow traffic between single and group work stations to flow smoothly is important. If students need to leave their seats to retrieve work in progress and collect a continuous stream of materials, which may be different for each individual or small group and vary from session to session, the room will have to be laid out to support that. If the students, on completing each phase of their work, need to test or process it away from their desks or if they share resources such as computers, the design must reflect that, too. What about storing projects in progress? Will the classroom need a place to keep them until the following session? When LEGO Robotics is being used, the answer is "yes."

Experienced colleagues advise that robotics is best learned as part of a two-person team or small group of three or four. Providing seating and workspace so that students can work in these configurations is crucial. Students need to sit close to one another to share materials and collaborate, and fairly densely arranged seating will help cut down on noise levels generated by students as they work in teams or small groups.

> **TIP**
>
> The ratio of LEGO kits to students should be at least one kit for every two or three kids—Corbett Beder, Robotics Specialist/Staff Developer

Try to picture what the classroom will look like in action as you plan the physical space. How will you group the students? Will you be able to purchase or acquire 15 robotics sets so that you can have the students share them as teams of two? If so, each team will need a small table or workspace. What about the workspace surface itself? Your students will do well if the desktop or tabletop is flat and smooth, without cracks or gaps on which robot wheels may catch or into which small parts may fall and get lost.

Figure 3.1 A typical robotics classroom arrangement.
(Photo courtesy American School of Bombay.)

Your students will be getting up and down from their seats for a number of reasons during activity sessions. Making sure aisles and walkways are large enough will help avoid traffic problems and help maximize time on task, a serious consideration in robotics classrooms.

The students' robots will run on batteries. Or, they may be using the newer, rechargeable batteries available for the NXT Robotics materials. Either way, ensuring that power is available when it is needed will make things flow more smoothly.

Students will likely use laptops provided by the school to program each robot's instructions and transfer them to the robot's brick. The laptops may be run on batteries or from power cords that need to be plugged into an electrical outlet. Deciding ahead of time which way students will power their laptops when they use them is a smart thing to do. Once you have finalized your classroom's setup, it will be difficult to change it later if you realize that laptops need to be plugged in and there are insufficient outlets. Many teachers will find that it is better to use the laptops' batteries even if outlets are adequate, as running power cords across a classroom can cause safety hazards and damaged equipment. The key factor here, as always when working with laptops, is determining whether there is sufficient time and opportunity to charge batteries before students will use them.

Figure 3.2 Laptops are often used to program robots.

Other features may need to be considered in robotics classrooms. If yours is a class working on preparation for a FIRST LEGO League (FLL) competition, you may find it advantageous to leave a competition play space or "field" set up in the room, so that it is available to students for practice. While it may be advantageous to distribute a class set of laptops only when the class is scheduled to program robots, it might be handy to leave a few computers set up around the room for those students who need access at other times.

Once you and your students advance beyond your first explorations to discover what the LEGO Robotics materials are and how they work, you may decide that pooling parts rather than keeping all the kits separate is far more practical. Over time, most classes will acquire additional parts and supplies. Keeping your class supply of parts in a central area where students can borrow them as they build their robots is a common approach taken by experienced teachers. Setting a parts supply area aside that students may access via a clear path is a time-efficient idea; be sure to include a supply area in your classroom design plans.

Storage

Storage is an important consideration in organizing a classroom to be an effective learning space for robotics activities. Classes involved in robotics need additional storage space. As students involved in robotics may also be using books and other print materials, the classroom may need double the average storage space or more.

Classrooms are often shared among the classes of a single teacher and among several teachers. Considering that robotics materials are highly attractive to all students and are valuable and difficult to replace, secure storage is essential. Locked spaces are a great asset to a robotics classroom. Alternatively, materials may be stored on a cart that is wheeled into a locked closet for security. Managing a large cart, however, may take valuable time from learning activities.

One aspect of the storage issue that may not be immediately apparent is the need to provide a safe way for students to store robot projects that are in progress. Bots (short for robots) at this stage are three-dimensional, bulky, and also delicate. This is especially true of those made with the RCX materials. To keep students enthused and support them in doing their best, keeping the bots protected is necessary. Small plastic leftover tubs, shoe boxes, and other similar containers work well, particularly if a piece of masking tape can be affixed to the outside of the container so that team members' names and class can be written on it. Containers must fit inside a locked cupboard or closet so that only their owners may have access to them.

TIP

A good resource for suggestions on LEGO Robotics storage is "How Do You Store Your LEGO in Class?" Available as a downloadable PDF at www.thenxtclassroom.com/sites/thenxtclassroom.com/files/how_to_store_LEGO.pdf.

This short, illustrated guide points out that "there is no single correct way that suits every classroom," and it offers great ideas as well as suggestions from teachers around the world. Other useful information on building bots, lesson plans, and web resources can be found at www.thenxtclassroom.com.

Room Enhancements

In addition to these basic elements of organizing the classroom for robotics activities, there are a number of ways to enhance it that will greatly add to students' learning experiences.

Cameras

Once a robot has been designed, built, programmed, and run, and the project has been completed, what happens next? In all likelihood, the bot will need to be dismantled and its parts made available for the next project. Apart from fond memories, documentation is all that will remain of the bot to preserve the learning that resulted from the experience of building it. Documentation adds to an important body of class and school robotics knowledge.

Having several digital cameras on hand will make this easy. Documenting a project thoroughly may require both still photos and video recording. Many modestly priced still cameras come with a video function that is more than adequate for this purpose. If you need to add video cameras to your classroom equipment, the user-friendly Flip video cameras—low cost and durable—are a good choice.

Apart from providing the cameras, teachers will need to ensure that students have the space, surface, and light they'll need to produce effective photo documentation. Once the material has been shot, it will have to be transferred to a computer. Thus, camera USB (universal serial bus) cables or SD (secure digital) cards/card readers will be needed. Storing photo documentation will require either storage through the school's network or portable media (like USB flash drives and memory sticks).

Photo-Editing Software

After students have downloaded their photo documentation to a computer, they will need to process and edit the photos. Still photos can be manipulated easily using Google's Picasa resource (for free) or Adobe's Photoshop Elements software (for a modest price). When they are finished, students may want to publish their work online or on a protected school website. Accordingly, teachers will have to assure that the Internet can be accessed in the classroom or that students have access to it in the school's computer lab, library, or other areas.

Viewing Small Things in Big Groups

On occasion a teacher may elect to give a demonstration of how to do something in constructing a robot or designate a student to demonstrate something for the whole class. While demonstrations can be valuable, the logistical problem in doing this with LEGO Robotics is that the bots are quite small, making it hard for the entire class to see them at the same time. The teacher might ask the entire group of 30 or more students to gather around a central table to observe the demo up close. However, a much more effective approach is to use a document camera or video camera to capture the action of the demo and project it in large scale with an LCD projector or interactive white board.

Bulletin Boards

A simple, basic resource for an effective robotics learning environment is a plentiful supply of bulletin boards. Posting examples of handouts, photos of projects, rules, schedules, building instructions, and blueprints will contribute to a smooth-running robotics classroom and enrich the culture of the robotics classroom.

Where to Test the Robots?

Apart from whole class discussions and demos and small groups working to design, construct, and program the robots, students will need to test their bots. While the first parts of the project can easily be done on a tabletop, the bot's program is likely to require it to operate in a larger, more specialized environment. Where practical, creating a dedicated "field" or "mission board" (often a 4 ft x 8 ft sheet of plywood with low retaining walls around the perimeter—something that resembles the field used by FIRST LEGO League) is an ideal solution to this need. Alternatively, a cleared area in the rear of the classroom, a section of hallway, or the school cafeteria can also work well.

A Visit to Phil Firsenbaum's Robotics Club

The author paid a visit to Phil Firsenbaum's after-school robotics club at PS 187 in Manhattan. It was a typical club session at the end of a typical school day.

In attendance were approximately 25 third, fourth, and fifth grade students. The room, a regular classroom used by one the school's classes and its teacher for general academics during the day, is quickly set up by Phil for the after-school robotics club. He moves some desks and tables and sets up a few special support centers in different parts of the room.

At one end of the room, he places two desktop computers for programming RCX and NXT robots on desks. At another desk, he sets up one laptop for programming, using WeDo software (see Chapter 2, sidebar on WeDo Robotics kits). At the other end of the classroom, a school aide sets up and mans an area where students can search through bins of LEGO pieces and parts to use in their projects.

Other than at these centers, students are free to build robots at any unoccupied student desk or on the rug area (this classroom has the classic rug area with a rocking chair).

Students choose their own projects, using LEGO Robotics plans Phil makes available to them from which they build already-designed robots or design, construct, and program their own robots. They are free to go out into a supervised area of the hallway to give their robots more room to run.

Phil is assisted by Maxwell (Max) Shlansky, a high school student from Bronx High School of Science (a transcript of the author's interview of Max is in Chapter 10). Max is a former member of this after-school robotics club. He is thoroughly taken with robots and has deep experience in their construction. Max has elected to assist with this after-school club to earn required community service credits and is available to the students for help, suggestions, support, or simply as someone to whom they can show off their robotics accomplishments.

During the session, some students function as mentors to other students less experienced or less accomplished with robotics. At the conclusion of the session, the students sit on the rug to share. This school has developed a culture of collaborative discussion among students. In this 10-minute sharing period, students are given the floor after raising their hand. Each student briefly describes a robotics accomplishment achieved that day, and many of them give demos of their robots for the group to see and comment on.

Phil laments that only one girl has joined this group. At this school, few girls opt for robotics club as an after-school activity. I spoke to this girl when I visited, and she said she felt girls were insecure about joining the group and would need assurance that other girls would be in the group before they would join.

Classroom Management Factors

Rules, Routines, and Schedules

Establishing a handful of routines, schedules, and rules will make managing the robotics classroom easier. Most of these will have to do with your letting students know how you want them to behave and to assist you in handling the various success factors discussed in this chapter. For instance, it may be wise, especially until students are well acculturated to your classroom, to set a firm "STOP WORK!" time, when all project efforts cease and teams and groups carry out their responsibilities to assure that the classroom is maintained properly. Establish routines to store works in progress in safe, designated storage bins or closets and to make sure that shared materials will be ready for the next class.

Time

Time is a powerful limiting factor in student robotics activities. It is likely you and your students will discover that having enough time to accomplish all the things you want to do on your robotics projects is a challenge. Hold a discussion and ask students to suggest ways to conserve (not waste) time so that as much time as possible can be spent on actually working on their robots. Simply keeping students mindful of time and the need to budget it is important. Keeping a clock visible is helpful. Instead of the teacher being the sole time enforcer, students may take turns assuming this responsibility.

Maximizing what can be accomplished in the time available and not getting bogged down in distractions will be a major part of your challenge. Additionally, distribution of materials and projects in progress, time spent walking around the classroom, and cleanup and returning things to their storage spaces are best handled efficiently so that the maximum time possible is kept free to design, construct, program, and run the bots.

Movement

Keeping the robotics classroom focused and on track requires understanding and planning. One dimension of this is managing how students move around the classroom. The type of work being done requires that students have a large degree of freedom to move around; however, if plans and procedures aren't put into place to ensure that all movement is necessary and that not too many students are away from their workspaces at the same time, the classroom will become, if not outright chaotic, inefficient. Above all, when setting up a learning activity, teachers should envision the flow of students throughout the environment and plan accordingly. As you move from group to group, you'll observe what the students are doing and will notice any students who seem to be walking around unnecessarily. These students may be restless because they cannot understand something or are having difficulty working with the others in their group. Talk to such students to ascertain what is going on and then coach them and/or their groups appropriately.

Groupings

In almost all cases, students will work on robotics projects in pairs or small groups. Careful thought should go into forming these groups. This will be easier in classes in which collaborative group work has been done before. Beyond the obvious decisions of attempting to pair students who work well with one another and avoiding pairing those who do not get along or whose influence on one another is counterproductive, there are other dynamics to take into consideration. Learning styles and interests, for instance, are good things to keep in mind. Creativity in working, ability to follow directions, and capacity to complete tasks are other considerations. Above all, collaborative pairs or groups working on robotics projects are situations in which students' abilities should complement one another. You'll find that robotics students also tend to teach one another; these are opportunities that are difficult to realize in traditional classrooms. You should consider the possibility of letting students choose their own partners, a situation that brings with it the risk that students will make wrong choices, but also one that lets them learn about collaboration, a very important set of skills for 21st-century students.

Distribution of Projects and Materials

After the class has come to order and is focused for the work session, students' projects in progress and additional materials to use in working on them will need to be distributed. This is a simple but crucial step in managing the classroom. Little learning will take place until this is accomplished.

Distribution will take some of the time allocated to the class. Distribution is also an activity that can create problems if not planned for and handled properly. Routines and procedures are essential. How many students do you want to involve in this step? Limiting the number of students up and away from their workspaces is an approach that can help avoid confusion and problems. Limiting this to one student per group work table is a good guideline. Another approach is to designate monitors to handle the initial distribution of projects in progress and additional materials. Once the class has begun to work, students may get up on their own to address their various needs in the course of their work.

Cleanup

Just as the class needs to distribute projects and materials before beginning the work session, it will need to reverse the process before finishing for the day and leaving the classroom. The dynamic here is somewhat different, and the teacher will need a different sort of vigilance to ensure that all runs well. While the students were intent on getting off to a good start earlier, they will now be concerned with getting done and going on to the next thing, a mindset that fosters cutting corners and carelessness. And while it behooves the teacher to support the students in getting on to their next class, assignment, or activity, the way each robotics session is completed will affect the next. This is true both for the class doing the cleanup and for other robotics classes or groups who will need to use the materials or classroom afterward. Care must be taken that materials and resources are put away properly so that the teacher can be assured that nothing of value has been taken without permission and that all will be in readiness for the next session or group. Projects in progress must be put away so that they are undamaged and ready to be picked up again where the team left off. They should be clearly labeled by class and team members' names, so that there is no question as to whose project is sitting safely in a particular storage container.

Structuring the Session

While teachers may have established routines for everything that should happen during the work session, many will find it best to get all students seated and focused on the class that is about to unfold before giving a signal that it is time to begin. Not only will this establish a serious, focused tone to the session that is about to transpire, but it will also cue the students that the robotics class is in the same realm of serious work as other classes and subjects they take.

The start of the session is also a time to introduce new ideas, make suggestions and additions to the assignments, give demonstrations, or call on students to demonstrate a discovery or success they had in the last session. This is also the time to make modifications in the way the class is running, based on experiences of the previous session.

Consider setting aside a few minutes at the very end of each session for students to report to one another on what they learned and accomplished. From the instructional perspective, this is a way to inject some much-needed metacognition into a series of activities that are often primarily experiential. On the practical side, teachers may find that a few minutes are left over after cleanup duties have been performed; rather than sitting and waiting for the bell, the time is well spent in reflection and discussion.

Handouts, Forms, and Journals

Whether they are implemented through reproduced paper sheets or as digital files that run on student laptops, handouts and forms can help impose and maintain structure and order in robotics classes. This is an important dimension of taming the freewheeling spirit of robotics classrooms. While there may be more freedom than in traditional classes, handouts and forms can keep students informed about what's expected of them without endless teacher repetition. They keep students on task and accountable and can facilitate learning in many ways.

A particularly good example of this approach can be observed at the website of the McLean Science Technology Magnet Elementary School. The robotics club's Robotics Resources page (www.smithlearning.com/fifthgrade/robotics.php) provides links to numerous resources, many of which are highlighted elsewhere in this book. It also links to the club's own resources, which will provide good models for newbie robotics teachers. Under the Student Notebook section, there is a Student Expectations checklist that outlines all the things the students should do before, during, and after sessions (e.g., "AT THE END OF CLUB: Come to the debriefing ready to share what you learned and listen to others").

Robotics planning sheets with graphically oriented directions and prompts support students in thinking, planning, and programming. This has both informational/instructional content and a space to support the work. A troubleshooting guide sheet contains helpful information. And a list of challenges—things to try to do with one's robot experiments—may offer your students fun, new ideas. This is a body of useful handouts and forms designed to make activities flow in a smoother, more orderly fashion. Having all these on hand is smart planning on the teacher's part and can help in a pinch when materials and computers are not ready or available.

Ian Chow Miller, of Frontier Junior High School in Graham, Washington, formerly of New York City and Long Island, has created a "My Robotics Journal" form, Figure 3.3. (A transcript of the author's interview of Ian is in Chapter 10).

Name____________
Date____________
Period____________

My Robotics Journal

Learning Target–

1. Today in class I ...

2. Some new pieces I learned today were ...
(use names and tell what they are used for if you can, you can draw as well)

3. I found today was really (difficult/hard/frustrating) because...

4. I found today really (exciting/rewarding/fun) because...

5. I (discovered/learned/read about/saw) a really cool building idea today. It was...

6. I (discovered/learned/read about/saw a new way of programming today. It was ...

7. My partner(s) and I were successful today because ...

8. Tomorrow I hope to ...

Figure 3.3 A journal form used by Ian Chow Miller in his middle school robotics classes.

Classroom Website

A website that functions as a home base "go to" resource for a robotics class will prove helpful. The McLean School robotics club website offers much more than the print handouts mentioned previously. Its offerings include building instructions, sensor information, club paperwork, and more. Establishing a website is something that will support the entire effort of having a LEGO Robotics class, club, or team.

A website is also a great place to post schedules, assignments, news, and photos of students and their robots. An excellent example of a robotics class website is Luke Laurie's "8th Grade Robotics Science Course" site: http://homepage.mac.com/mrlaurie/roboscience.html. Figure 3.4 shows yet another group of robotics students at school with their projects.

Figure 3.4 A screen shot from a school's robotics website.

Assessment

Assessment of robotics activities is different from traditional activities in a number of ways. Like other products and performances that result from project-based learning activities, robotics projects are assessed effectively with rubrics. Rubrics can be created by listing everything students are expected to do throughout a project and learn from the project. This list of actions and learning outcomes become the grade criteria areas of the rubrics. When teachers explain the rubrics to students before the project begins, students will have a greater understanding of what is expected of them and a sense of project ownership.

An essential factor to build into assessment of the project is "accountable talk." Ask individual students to explain the decisions they made in designing, constructing, and programming their bots; this is an important way to stress the problem-solving dimension of robotics projects. When students hear themselves, teammates, and other students describe their decision-making, trial-and-error processes, they internalize what they have learned; the process of organizing thoughts to speak them allows students to comprehend what they have learned more fully and to be accountable for that learning.

It may seem difficult to give students individual grades for group efforts. If this seems inappropriate, one strategy is to give a second grade for the student's performance in his individual role within the group. Thus, one student may be project manager, another head of construction, and another the lead on programming, and each will receive an individual grade for his or her role. As a practical matter, in many groups all members will have had a hand in each aspect of the project. Still, taking the lead or management role for a facet of it can be an important enrichment to the learning process.

For a more in-depth discussion of assessment and further suggestions, see Chapter 5: Assessing Robotics Learning.

Instructional Factors

Robotics projects are multisession activities. Estimating the average number of sessions students will take to finish their projects is important. Straggler groups can be a problem. The teacher should keep tabs on team progress, monitoring for teams that may not be able to finish a project within the allotted time. It's a good idea to build into the schedule a little cushion of an extra session or three by planning a few ancillary and enrichment activities; this will allow straggler groups extra time to catch up with other groups as they work on the extra activities. Enrichment activities can be worthwhile for students who finish ahead of schedule.

Getting returning absentees up to speed on what the class has done during their absence is a challenge in many situations. However, because robotics projects are collaborative, groups can usually help an absentee team member catch up.

Project Culmination

The completion of a robot is the culmination of the extended project for which it was built. Something of a celebration is in order. Of course, if the bots are created for participation in an FLL competition, that is the culminating event. A special session where students show off their completed bots and programmed routines to one another in the class—and perhaps for other groups of students in the school and beyond—is appropriate.

Figure 3.5 An all-girls elementary school robotics team. This team was invited to visit NASA. *(Photo courtesy David Clow Photography.)*

CHAPTER 4

Robotics Activity Ideas

Once the teacher understands how LEGO Robotics materials function, an important next step is to plan activities to guide students in using them. The ideas for activities that follow will illustrate the next dimension of understanding robotics—from the point of view of how to teach it.

In many ways, these activities represent a guide to getting started *by doing*. This idea is supported by a compelling theme that emerged as I interviewed expert practitioners, colleagues who have gone through the process of getting started and have logged significant time and experience in working with students in robotics-based activities. Many of them agree that extensive preparation in robotics skills and theory in anticipation of getting started is often unnecessary and perhaps counterproductive.

> **TIP**
>
> LEGO Robotics is very compatible with learning by doing. Extensive preparation can be unnecessary and even counterproductive.

After a simple effort to get an overview of what the materials are and can do, and armed with an appropriate set of understandings about the types of projects of value for students to do with them, most teachers may begin. They will grow in their role as robotics teachers as their students move ahead alongside them. This is very much in tune with a bit of wisdom that many have heard but rarely seen implemented—that the teacher is the "guide on the side and not the sage on the stage." In providing robotics-based learning experiences, the most effective teachers are usually those who play the role of guide on the side. Reading and reflecting on the advice offered by these expert teachers in Chapter 10's interviews will deepen your understanding of why serving as guide or coach is the ideal role.

Figure 4.1 Some of the best learning takes place through teacher-to-small-group conversations.

If you haven't done so already, it would be wise to set aside a little time to open and analyze a kit and reflect on what is sitting before you. Following that, using either instructions that come with the kit or the extensive catalog of blueprints and directions listed later in this book, try building a couple of simple bots on your own—or perhaps with the help of a motivated student co-learner. Create a simple program for the bot using the programming software and test out how it works. As you work, get a sense of the workspace needed, the time required to locate and assemble parts, the time needed to figure out how to write a program and transfer it to the bot, and the time needed to put materials back and take them out per session. The activities that follow offer solid strategies to help you avoid serious missteps and wrong turns as you begin.

While the bulk of the activities that LEGO Robotics teachers will do with students involve the hands-on, small group work of the students, at times whole class discussions and demonstrations will be very useful. Some of these must be supported with the use of a computer, large screen monitor, smart board, or image projected with an LCD projector. Preparation will include lining up the use of these resources and identifying the media items to present with them.

While the point of robotics is to get the students using the materials directly, teachers should not shy away from a few preparatory and reflective class discussions in the rush to get started putting LEGO pieces together. Also some of the very best learning that will happen will take place through teacher-to-student, one-on-one, or one-to-small group spontaneous conversations about what's happening, why it's happening, and how to solve problems or take advantage of discoveries.

The following activities are offered as flexible suggestions, not a body or continuum of "must do" activities to implement in a certain way and in a certain order. Teachers may read through this set of activities, taking what makes sense to them in view of the goals of their robotics group, the ability levels of the students, and the individuals' capacities to work together. These activities are intended to be tweaked to satisfy the needs and character of individual programs and bodies of students.

ACTIVITY 1

What Are Robots? A Media-Supported Class Discussion

Rationale

The point of using LEGO Robotics is that this body of materials provides simple, hands-on experiences that demonstrate academic and real-world skills in compelling, practical ways. Students will learn engineering principles, like simple machines, gears, and gear ratios, as well as simple computer programming—that is, graphic, object-based programming—through robotics. And they may apply math and other bodies of knowledge and skills. Students will gain a great deal of knowledge and useful experience by an approach that may be described as "robotics for robotics sake." What are robots? Why have people developed robots? How do robots help people get their work done? Which approaches to robotics solutions are best and why? Questions like these frame a study of robotics in context.

Goals

To give students a big-picture context for understanding robots and robotics as they relate to people's work, evolving technology, and mastery over the environment.

Procedure

Ask the students the following focus questions: What are robots? What is robotics? Why have people developed robots? How do robots help people get their work done? What types of robots are there?

Select some or all of these introductory activities: a) show videos of robots in action to the class, b) distribute articles on robots and robotic innovations to the students, or c) assign the students to research an article or other media item about a recent robotic innovation or instance of robots in the news. Ask the students to volunteer answers to the questions and justify and illustrate them by referring to the articles and/or media items. Conduct a class discussion to come to informed consensus. Teachers may assign students to write a short opinion paper recording their individual thoughts. As students continue working with robotics over a period of time, it may be fruitful to revisit these answers for further discussion.

Resources

Classroom Robotics (www.classroomrobotics.blogspot.com) is a blog I maintain; items in this blog are appropriate for Grades 3–12. Other useful websites are Robot World (http://robotworld.com) by Tony Dyson, the man who built R2-D2, and Robots Dreams (www.robots-dreams.com), the blog of robotics expert Lem Fugitt, formerly a software developer and programmer. Articles can be found through a search engine like Google (web search setting) as can videos (Google video search setting). Specialized educational media sharing sites, like SchoolTube and TeacherTube, may prove to be especially fruitful sources of safe and age-appropriate content.

Extension

The basis for a valuable discussion at this point is the distinction between autonomous robots and remote-controlled devices. Both types of machines are highly valuable to people. An understanding of each type and its defining characteristics will add deep understanding about the field of robots and insights into what the students are working on, as they move forward in robotics.

ACTIVITY 2

Be the Robot: Programming Concepts

(Contributed by Dwayne Abuel)

Rationale

This is a very simple beginning activity to do with students as you become familiarized with LEGO Robotics. It introduces them to the concept of programming a robot to follow commands.

Procedure

One participant plays the part of the NXT robot, and one plays the part of the programmer. The goal is for the "robot" student to follow the commands called out by the "programmer." Instructions include pivot turning, moving

Author's Note

While the commands you develop may differ from Abuel's, the basic idea is what's important. By having students give a series of simple commands such as "forward 1 pace," "turn right (45 degrees) once," "back 3 paces," "turn left (45 degrees) twice," forward 2 paces," and so on, and having others follow the commands without reflection or modification, students will begin to understand the nature of programming.

forward, point wheel turn, and moving backward. Each person playing the part of a robot has a left leg and right leg. The robot has a left wheel and right wheel. You will have to assign one leg to be motor A (left leg) and the other to be motor B (right leg).

A pivot turn means one foot pushes one way while the other pushes in the opposite direction. The result is that the person, without moving out of his location, will be able to pivot left, right, or completely around 180 degrees. A point wheel turn means one foot moves in the direction of the turn while the other becomes the pivot and stays stationary. You will notice the turns becoming wider with the point wheel turn.

The programmer can call out a command and a distance (e.g., move forward or backward 5 steps) or a command and the extent of the rotation (e.g., pivot turn right 90 degrees).

ACTIVITY 3

How Do LEGO Materials Work?

Rationale

This session will give the students some basic knowledge about robotics materials as well as how they will be using them in your class, group, club, or team. This is an opportunity to lay some important procedural groundwork, clear students on the materials, establish routines and rules, and clear the path for the many hands-on activities to come.

Classroom Setup

How many students will share a kit? In most cases students will work on robotics in groups of three to four. There are several reasons for this. From an economic standpoint, many schools do not have the funds to purchase enough robotics kits for each student to work on his or her own. Furthermore, having students learn to work collaboratively is valuable, a skill stressed in the emerging 21st-century skills body of practice and philosophy.

Assign students to their work groups—in some cases teachers may allow students to form their own groups or work in groups that have been set up for other purposes. However, teachers will need to be mindful of group dynamics, keeping an eye on how the chemistry among students influences their ability to work well together, and for all individuals in the group to have a worthwhile, profitable experience.

Distribute the materials for this session. As the intention of this activity is not necessarily to build full-blown robots, but to give students the opportunity to discover the basic methods of construction, giving access to all kit materials, including motors and electronic components, may not be necessary.

Procedure

Now that the students are grouped, seated, and equipped with materials, a simple challenge like "What can you create with the parts available today?" paired with the understanding that all will share their discoveries toward the end of the session will suffice for a first experience. Alternatively, teachers may choose to give the class a theme to satisfy, such as vehicles, creatures, or machines, depending on the goal of the group and what else the students are working on in other classes.

While this activity may be done with each student producing an individual product, the amount of materials available and the need to begin working as collaborative groups probably indicates that a group product would be best for this first activity. Before cleanup, ask for volunteers to hold up what they created, describe it as best they can, and share the discoveries they made in the process about how the materials work—problems encountered, problems solved—and thoughts about what more they would like to do.

This class debriefing is at the core of the learning value for this session. In addition to soliciting students' volunteered sharing of experiences, teachers need to encourage students to question their peers, modeling how to probe for responses. Teachers also ask focused questions, often redirecting peers' questions to elicit valuable reflections from each student. Questions such as "Why did you decide to do it that way?" "How else might you have tried it?" "Do you feel this is the best solution?" and others in this vein will establish a thoughtful, reflective environment where students will learn a great deal through robotics, including how to elicit gems of insight when engaged in group debriefings.

Journaling is a natural extension of robotics activities. Teachers may wish to assign students to record the pieces used, note how they were combined, and perhaps draw a simple diagram as a record. Digital photography is a natural extension, too.

Tips

Newbie robotics teachers would be wise to be mindful of the flow of time in robotics activities. This is a delicate balance between students having too much time left over after having completed a challenge, which will foster boredom, and too little time to accomplish something of value and make certain that all materials and projects in progress are put away properly. In most cases, groups should have something on the order of two back-to-back class sessions (85–90 minutes) during the school day or from 90 minutes to 2 hours after school to get their work done. Analyze the task of returning all kits and parts to the state they were in before beginning the session, perhaps add a little extra time to err on the side of caution, and walk the students through your planned cleanup routine, which in essence is the reverse of the materials distribution routine.

If for any reason you decide to store works in progress, to be returned to students so they can carry some aspect of the activity further, another complete set of logistical routines must be worked out ahead of time. Where will the works in progress be kept? How will they be kept secure so that they are returned without damage or tampering from other students? How will they be labeled? All these issues must be worked out beforehand.

Activity Extension

In a class debriefing, discuss "sturdy construction." Ask the students: "What problems have you encountered in making your constructions strong enough? What solutions have you found?"

ACTIVITY 4

Create Your First Robot: A Robotic Vehicle from Plans

Rationale

A vehicle of some sort is a good first robot to assign. The overall goal of this activity is to have the students apply what they know about how the LEGO materials work along with what they understand about robots. The robotic vehicle they build should be able to travel on its own, following a program that student teams will create in a follow-up activity. While this vehicle will be simple, other activities and projects may be built onto it to make the vehicle perform specialized tasks, like climbing up inclines, carrying payloads, or responding to stimuli.

Because this is the first robot the students will build, provide them with plans they can follow to see how it is done. You may, of course, permit them to modify the plans. However, if they do, a teachable moment will be enjoyed as they are challenged to explain the decision they made in making the modifications and in giving a reasonable assessment of whether they improved on the original design or not, as well as the degree of success they experienced.

You will find a large variety of plans for LEGO Robots online, both for the RCX and the NXT generations of materials. Comprehensive listings of some good examples are provided in Appendix A: Classic Robotics Projects, and Appendix B: Robotics Resources. Whether you select a source from the lists or one you identify on your own, the idea is to find a clear, easy-to-follow set of plans to construct a robot using the platform (RCX or NXT) you have available for your students.

Procedure

After distributing kits to groups at tables, direct them to build a robot following the plans you provide. Teachers may opt to allow the students to stray from a completely literal interpretation of the plans if they are prepared to justify their decision to do so. You may want to set limits on the amount of materials they may use in their robots, as well as a limit on the amount of time they may take to complete the task.

In a class debriefing session, call on volunteers to report on their group's experience, success, deviations from the plans and reason why they deviated, and problems encountered and solved. If journaling is to be part of your robotics class's routines, direct the student to enter the day's write-up on the group's laptop. Similarly, direct groups to take a digital photo of the finished bot if photo documentation is part of class routines.

Have the groups clean up by storing their finished robots so they will be undisturbed until the next session. All materials other than the bots can be returned to the materials storage area.

ACTIVITY 5

Basic Programming

Use either Robolab or Mindstorms software for this first experience in programming. Groups will likely need more than one work session to complete this activity.

Goal

Students will understand the concept of programming robots and will learn the basic ideas and skills necessary to create a simple program.

Procedure

Walk the students through a quick, basic demonstration of the object-based programming software that you will be using to program the robots. This may be accomplished in a variety of ways:

- Show the students some videos that illustrate the big ideas of the software and the programming that makes it work. Discuss what they took away from the videos and answer questions they may have as a group.
- Distribute print handouts that illustrate the programming process and discuss it with the students. You will find some of these included in online curricula and examples, a number of which you'll find listed in this book. Alternately, you may choose to produce your own from printouts of programs you create with the software.
- Demonstrate the process directly, using an LCD projector that projects the screen of a laptop or computer for the entire group to see. You may

want to create a whole group lesson around this: students are called up to take turns at programming while peers watch on a large screen, making comments and offering suggestions and feedback.

- Have each team follow the same set of directions on its own laptop to observe the programming process.

After you are satisfied that each group understands the rudiments of programming, direct them to write a program. This should be based on a description of what the robot is expected to do. This may be assigned by you or decided by the students themselves—reflect on the learning outcomes and management involved, though, as you make this decision. A simple routine, something like "forward—then turn left—then back—then turn right" will be sufficient to demonstrate the principles and intricacies of programming.

Once the program has been written, the next step is for it to be tested to see if the students' directions actually tell the robot to do what they believe they told it to do. This involves transferring the program from the computer to the robot's brick and then trying it out.

A group debriefing session will be useful. Have the students volunteer to share the discoveries and aha moments they had in the course of doing the activity. What problems did they encounter and solve?

Extensions

Once the students have written a program and tried it out, they will no doubt have ideas about what else they would like their robots to do. Attempting these may make the basis for another activity. At this point, the groundwork has been laid for each group to come up with its own unique ideas for the behaviors it would like to direct its robot to perform. Sharing their finished routines with one another at the end of the activity can be a rich source of inspiration, satisfaction, and validation.

ACTIVITY 6

Adding Sensors

Rationale

Now that the students understand the basics of the LEGO Robotics materials, there are some more advanced things that the components of the kits can offer. Chief among these is the addition of sensors.

Procedure

Again, starting out with a short demo or video illustration will help paint some of the big picture and give students a conceptual framework to base their experimentation on and for the inferences they will draw from the work. Alternatively, teachers may opt to have students experiment and then share their experiences in a reflective discussion.

A simple challenge like "add a sensor to the robot so that it gathers information that will help it get its job done" is a worthwhile starting place. Later, students may be invited to develop their own challenges to solve.

Once the sensor has been added to the robot, students will want to create a program that involves it. And again, the complete picture is design and build–program–test–modify (either the robot or the program)–and test again. The logistical aspects (what materials and resources are made available to the students at which times together with their management implications) of this activity should be reflected in the above student tasks.

Resources on adding sensors and programming for them are available online. Here are some recommendations for beginners:

- The LEGO Company's own site with descriptions of NXT sensors: http://mindstorms.lego.com/en-us/Products/default.aspx#8547
- LEGO Engineering NXT Sensors describes ports, light and other (touch, sound, and ultrasonic) sensors and gives suggestions for their use: www.legoengineering.com/nxt-sensors-2.html
- Program the light sensor on a LEGO Mindstorms robot: www.wonderhowto.com/how-to-program-light-sensor-lego-mindstorms-robot-79059/view

- The *LEGO Mindstorms NXT 2.0 Discovery Book*'s Chapter 6, "Understanding Sensors," pages 55–87: http://my.safaribooksonline.com/9781593272111/what_are_sensors
- NXT wall follower, video of an "ugly first attempt" that worked: www.youtube.com/watch?v=9-2xJRaeHoo
- Two NXT-Segways, one with a light sensor (and the other with an NXTCam vision sensor): www.youtube.com/watch?v=5fNYDkjgO4M
- Introduction: Motors and Rotational Sensors: www.hanoverhigh.us/departments/science/capps/NSTA/01_Intro_Motors_and_Rotational_sensors.pdf

ACTIVITY 7

Original Design and Programming for a Stationary Robot

Activity 7-1 Rationale

With this type of activity, students move into the fullness of the field of robotics. No longer simply building a robot for the sake of doing so, their efforts will parallel those of professional engineers who design and build robots for specific purposes. Robot construction and programming are part of a bigger picture, one in which problems are identified and solutions created. This activity will give the students some of that bigger picture and begin them on the path of participating in the robotic engineering process with their eyes wide open.

Activity 7-1 Procedure

The field of robotics is rich and comprehensive. People have designed and built robots in every conceivable shape to perform a vast range of tasks. Much of this has been documented online. One worthwhile approach to the activities to come is to have the students do research to inform themselves about the variety of robots. This will give them useful information, as well as inspiration and motivation to participate in this burgeoning field. A simple, web-based research project like "Identify three or more robots that you think are particularly interesting, well designed, and/or useful. Write up your reactions and reflections about each, explaining why each impressed you. Do these robots give you ideas about something you would like to see designed and built? How might you modify or extend the robots you've identified?" These directions and questions will frame the activity properly.

A useful conceptual tool that will support students in this first activity (to design an original robot or to significantly modify a design done before) is the formally conceptualized design process. This is discussed in detail in Chapter 7: Robotics in the Curriculum. The design process framework, a common feature of formal engineering design courses, has many versions. Presenting this framework can be done in a variety of ways, including a formal lesson or discussion about it.

An especially useful resource for teachers that can be adapted for students is a PowerPoint interactive seminar (designed with specific materials for teachers of students in Grades K–5, 6–8, 9–12, 13–16, and informal educators) from the National Science Digital Library's Design Process. For presentations to students, see slides 20–29 (http://learningcenter.nsta.org/products/symposia_seminars/nsdl/NSDL_WS9_Teach_Eng.ppt).

Watching digital videos (from YouTube and other resources), like "Engineering Design Process" by NASA Science, can make learning enjoyable for you and your students (www.youtube.com/watch?v=6PJTlzY0Aak).

There are also a great many print materials to inform teachers on this, as well as information of use in developing instructional materials. Some worthwhile examples are the following:

- Informational sheet for teachers from Teach Engineering Digital Library: www.teachengineering.org/engrdesignprocess.php
- Engineering Design Process from Engineering Is Elementary: www.mos.org/eie/engineering_design.php
- Design Process poster from the PBS Design Squad and MIT InvenTeams: http://pbskids.org/designsquad/pdf/parentseducators/DS_Invent_DesignProcess_Poster_ENG.pdf
- The Works' Engineering Design Process chart, "You Are an Engineer": www.theworks.org/files/docs/EngineeringDesignProcess.pdf

In addition to these above, a particularly useful approach for connecting these design concepts to the hands-on process of designing and building robots is the use of a checklist. After selecting a version of the engineering design process to present to students, teachers can develop a checklist with a bullet for each component of the process and spaces for students to explain how their own work follows the process.

A "challenge" for this activity could be that the robot be stationary, and the students design it to help manufacture a product or help maintain healthy environmental conditions.

Activity 7-2 Rationale

The purpose of Activity 2 is to have students fully realize the original vision behind the creation of their stationary robot. The challenge is for them to program it to perform the functions and solve the problems for which they conceived it.

Activity 7-2 Procedure

Have the students write a series of questions that will guide them in testing their original idea: "What was the robot intended to do before it was built?" "Does it work as expected?" "If not, is this due to a problem in the way it was built or the way it was programmed?" Direct students to write a program for their robot that will enable it to carry out its intended mission. Based on the way their robot behaves, have students answer their own questions.

Have students use their answers to create a "next step" strategy for what to do next with their robot and its program.

About FIRST LEGO League Challenges

A logical progression for student robotics activities is modeled by the activities or "challenges" put to students by the competitive program FIRST LEGO League (FLL). Discussed in greater detail in Chapter 4 of this book, FLL offers a sophisticated approach to student robotics, not only in the standard it sets for professional and academic performance from students and the elegance of engineering design it has elicited from youngsters, but also in the context it has established for the work the students do.

One of the defining student robotics activities is the annual FIRST LEGO League Challenge. Each year the focus of the event is a standard competition challenge, for which all teams globally must prepare themselves and design, construct, and program a robot "that relates to an important real world issue." (See www.firstlegoleague.org/what-is-fll/default.aspx?id=174.) These challenges are designed by a team of engineers and educators and made to be age appropriate (ages 9–14 in the United States and Canada and ages 9–16 in the rest of the world). FLL describes the robot design portion of the challenge as "Build an autonomous robot to carry out predesigned missions in 2 minutes and 30 seconds."

Figure 4.2 A student robotics team. *(Photograph by Luke Laurie.)*

The FLL challenges are available to those who register teams for participation in the program, as well as to those educators who would like to adapt them as instructional activities or modify them or use them as models on which to base their own challenge designs.

FLL challenges move robotics tasks up several notches, from the creation of robots that do things, perform tasks for humans, and solve problems to accomplishing these tasks within an environment that presents goals, parameters, and impediments. In FLL challenges, student robots are expected to achieve a goal; for instance, to collect a certain number or sequence of specific pieces set out on a standardized, large tabletop environment—the "playing field." The robots are preprogrammed by the students to perform and achieve such objectives. As the robots operate on the field, they also must rely on aspects of their programming to navigate toward things that are to their advantage and avoid things that will stand in their way, performing tasks and achieving goals or scoring points that accrue toward achieving those goals. At the FLL event, teams demonstrate how well their robot functions and handles the challenge.

The FLL field usually consists of a course or marked environment printed on a vinyl mat spread over a 4 ft x 8 ft sheet of plywood; the field's perimeter has low borders (often made with 2 in. x 4 in. boards). Moveable plastic pieces set in strategic locations are placed on the mat. The playing field is complex, as are the missions the robots must complete. From the time the annual challenge is revealed, teams of students spend two months wrestling with its problems and complexities. They design a robot solution and program it to perform within the time and operating constraints that are also part of the overall challenge experience. Most teams draw on previous experience and familiarity with LEGO Robotics materials and programming software that they have accrued prior to the release of the challenge.

It may be wiser for newbie robotics teachers to make full-blown participation in a FIRST LEGO League Challenge a future goal, something to do after gaining experience with the materials and guiding and supervising students in using them. There is much students and teachers can learn from participating in FLL Challenges. While the actual FLL Challenge may be beyond the abilities of absolute newcomers, other highly worthwhile challenges—that are simpler and more appropriate for larger groups of students to work on simultaneously—can be modeled on them.

FLL-Style Challenges

More recent FLL Challenges are available for perusal on the FLL website. Access to the complete informational package used by participating teams is available. Here's the overview description of the robot design, build, and program portion, referred to as the "Robot Game," of the 2009 Challenge, titled Smart Move:

> The Smart Move Robot Game gives you first-hand experience in getting a sensor-equipped vehicle (your robot) to *gain access to places and things*, while *avoiding or surviving impacts*, all in a test environment...
>
> Imagine if you could program a vehicle to take you places, or even go by itself...

> Imagine if each vehicle knew where all the other ones were...
>
> Imagine if vehicles could avoid each other and the things around them...
>
> Imagine if vehicles could be programmed to avoid causing or driving into traffic jams...
>
> > Would traffic signals be needed anymore?
>
> If these vehicles did hit each other...
>
> > How might they be built to really keep passengers safe?
> >
> > How might they be built to avoid getting stuck or damaged?
>
> Have you noticed that most vehicles near where you live are only used part of the day?
>
> > How might the number of vehicles in your area be reduced?
>
> What new technologies could sometimes eliminate your need to travel?
>
> Now in addition to imagining and wondering... Try some of this yourself! (www.syraweb.org/Files/2009%20Robot%20Game%20Overview.pdf)

In this description, the challenge designers have established a context that presents a learning game to be played with LEGO Robotics parts but that refers to real-world situations and problems and calls for a real-world solution. The robots students create must function and perform within the reality established by the context, and they must accomplish the mission—to influence that environment in (at least some of) the positive ways mentioned as they operate within it.

The FLL Challenge approach is of particular value to educators who want to create worthwhile robotics activities that go beyond the activities previously described. If we were to analyze the 2009 Challenge to glean the basic types of things the student robots must achieve, we'd list the following items:

- Gaining access to places, the robot must finish its run in a specified place or on a specified spot.

- Gaining access to things, the robot must retrieve items laid out and deliver them to a specified spot—OR—the robot must move or reposition things in its environment according to specifications.
- Avoiding impact with items placed in the environment, the robot must negotiate around obstacles as it works to achieve its goal. The obstacles may be movable or immovable items (i.e., freestanding figures that are easily knocked over or sections of wall that are stationary).
- Avoiding damage to or alteration of pieces the designing team placed on the field, the robot prevents an opposing team from impacting it.

Based on these types of goals and operating parameters, teachers may create similar challenges for their students. There are numerous real-world scenarios that may be interpreted in the scale and with the components of LEGO Robotics that can form the bases for a series of tasks. For example, remove a bomb from a crowded street strewn with wrecked vehicles; rescue a pet from within a burning building; deliver a package to a lunar shelter; rearrange the equipment and furniture in a medical ward for highly contagious disease victims. Enlisting the students to help in creating a challenge can be an exciting activity. A temporary challenge environment can be created by marking off a section of classroom floor or a tabletop with colored tape; erecting barriers made of empty cardboard boxes; and setting up objects to retrieve or avoid, like Ping-Pong balls, dry sponges, spare LEGO pieces, toy figures, and small pieces of furniture. All of these complications lend interest and authenticity to the activity.

For more ideas, see Section F, "Ideas for FIRST LEGO League Challenges" in Appendix B: Robotic Resources.

Culminating Robotics Events

Some sort of culminating event is called for to mark the conclusion of an extended robotics unit or series of related activities. Student robot projects are wonderful combinations of projects and performances and merit the attention and appreciation of peers and partners.

Teachers can cull ideas for such an event from the section on competitions and special events in Chapter 9. Keep in mind that the culminating event's greatest purpose will be to solidify students' learning by establishing an opportunity for them to reflect on the engineering process through sharing. By demonstrating and communicating what they've achieved and learned, students will understand it all more clearly, and the entire experience will be more real. The phenomenon of social learning will be in high gear as students listen, absorb, trade ideas, learn from one another, give feedback, and grow as part of a learning community of peers. Whatever the format, the event should include features such as these:

- An opportunity for students to exhibit, demonstrate, and explain their work
- An opportunity for students to give and receive feedback and to perfect their skills in this area
- Guiding students through the process of documenting and saving their work, so that it has a shelf life much longer than that of the robotics study unit or the culminating event, such as Ambleside school in the U.K. has done: www.amblesideprimary.com/ambleweb/robotzone
- Facilitating performance/project-based alternative assessment of students' work, participation, and learning

Additional Activities

For more activities-related resources, be sure to check Appendix A and B.

The culminating event is an opportunity to exercise a very broad range of skills across many subject areas as students put into practice listening, speaking, writing, and reading skills (English language arts), as well as observation, analysis, and evaluation skills (science), and the 21st-century skills of collaboration and technology skills involved in the use of digital media and student publishing.

CHAPTER 5

Assessing Robotics Learning

As with many aspects of teaching and learning related to student robotics, assessment may take many teachers into new and unfamiliar territory. Involved are project- and problem-based learning, as well as collaborative learning. Many teachers have heard of these approaches but have not experienced them firsthand. In fact, few colleagues in their schools or districts may be intimately familiar with these learning styles.

Furthermore, while teaching and assessing robotics activities involve standards-based learning in traditional areas, both teaching and assessment may highlight or include dimensions that are not often focused on, for example, the interdisciplinary dimensions of traditional content areas. Writing skills and oral skills that support science learning but that are more often associated with language arts classes are good examples of this.

Assessment is an important dimension of robotics-based learning and can add a great deal to the experience.

Assessment as Part of the Whole

Above all, seeing the assessment component of the robotics-based learning experience as an integral part of the whole is wise. In this sense, assessment is not done as an add-on, something that happens solely at the end of the learning experience. It is not an exit requirement, as a final exam typically is in a traditional math class. By keeping the assessment component in mind from the very beginning, teachers can focus on all aspects of teaching and learning. As soon as teachers notice that they are allowing extraneous or habitual practices to creep in and cloud their adoption of this new approach to teaching and learning, they should stop to reflect on what they're doing. Robotics assessment is far less effective when it is tacked on at the end of a course or unit. Students are involved continually, and the quality of this involvement is a dimension of the overall experience that also ought to be assessed continually.

Clarity of Purpose

Be clear about why you are assessing students' work. Is the assessment being included as a formative support, something that will inform both teacher and student about progress and growth in an ongoing process? Or is it being done to keep students accountable for their efforts and behaviors in class? Both are valid and valuable reasons for assessing, but all parties are better off when the purpose is clear. Including a variety of assessment approaches, methods, and instruments will produce a far more balanced result and will make it easier for assessment to contribute to a satisfactory overall experience for students.

Assessments for robotics-based learning should relate to the teaching and learning goals and objectives of the class. What do you hope the students will learn from the class? Assessments should evaluate whether or not students accomplished these objectives as well as how well they learned them. This is more complex than simply asking, "Did the student do a good job?"

Assessment Approaches

In view of the previous points, we will look at some concrete approaches that will make assessment of robotics activities more successful.

Collaborative Learning

Robotics projects frequently are implemented as small group collaborative experiences. This dimension should be reflected in the assessment. Assessment of collaborative learning poses special problems. While the project may be a group effort, it is composed of individual efforts. How to handle this in a way that reinforces the value of collaborative learning without frustrating students who may be more comfortable being graded solely on the basis of their own work is a key issue. The teaching profession will have to devote more time and attention to this as we move further into the 21st century, a period in which collaborative work continues to assume more and more importance. These skills will become increasingly prominent in the aspects of education that prepare students to function effectively in the workplace.

The McREL (Mid-continent Research for Education and Learning) Working With Others web page (www.mcrel.org/compendium/SubjectTopics.asp?SubjectID=22) lists five standards that define the broad areas of collaboration in learning:

1. Contributes to the overall effort of a group
2. Uses conflict-resolution techniques
3. Works well with diverse individuals in diverse situations
4. Displays effective interpersonal communication skills
5. Demonstrates leadership skills

Additionally, descriptions of vital skills, such as "Takes personal responsibility for accomplishing group goals" and "Proposes measures to enhance team effectiveness that affect and define success at collaboration," are on the McREL website. These skills can form the basis for evaluations of student performance in the areas of collaboration. By identifying and defining the elements of student collaboration, we have a lens through which to observe, direct, and assess student performance in this area.

Some students will be more confident as they speak and describe their engineering processes verbally, and others will be better at describing the process in writing. Teachers need to be aware of students' strengths as teams or groups form at the beginning of the school year. Discussing group dynamics at the outset of the school year and urging students to assess their strengths and weaknesses before they form groups would be wise. Each small group will benefit from members with varying sets of skills. Quiet students who observe and write well are as valuable to a team as the creative thinkers and the enthusiastic risk takers.

Portfolios

In the course of a robotics project there are numerous opportunities for students to use planning tools. Some examples are checklists of project stages and components, lists of parts used or requested, descriptions and plans of the robots to be designed and modified, and so on. These all model for students how real projects are planned, implemented, and tested in the real world. These lists can be kept on paper or in a computer file and are to be continually updated by each team or group. Part of the overall assessment can be made on how well students keep these lists complete, timely, well organized, and clear.

Documentation

Quick sketches, drafted drawings, photos, videos, slide shows, and more are a natural extension of robotics projects and may function well as portfolio items that contribute to assessment. As discussed in Chapter 6, robotics projects need to be recorded and archived, and this aspect of the project should be included in the assessment. Teachers may opt to do the assessment directly from students' presentations of their robots and their programmed behavior, from the documentation in whole or in part, or use a combination. Assessing the "live" robot will inject an element of spontaneity in the presentation for assessment, while using documentation will ensure a comfort level afforded by not having to perform "on the spot." Combining the two approaches may be a great way to reward all types of students.

Journals

Some robotics projects are conceived and completed in a day; however, most robotics projects are typically long term. Robotics projects are composed of numerous stages (i.e., envisioning, planning, building, programming, and testing and modifying). They also typically involve multiple sessions in which the work is picked up where it was left off at the end of one session, to be carried forward in the next. As part of this, keeping records of what was done and accomplished and what needs to be done next are as essential in the robotics classroom as they are in the real world. Furthermore, this type of individual journal or sequential recordkeeping creates necessary opportunities for student reflection. Thoughts about the meaning of the work, the connections made, and things to be learned down the road add much to the project's short-term, trial-and-error learning observations and long-term meaning. Journals are also records of learning and effort expended; they can serve as items for assessment. Journals can be kept as traditional spiral notebooks, or in schools where all students have laptops, journals can be kept in a separate file and made accessible to the robotics teacher. (Refer back to Chapter 3, Figure 3.3 for a sample journal page.)

Accountable Talk

At various times during the robotics project, asking students to explain and justify decisions made in the course of their work will reveal the scope and depth of their learning. The ability to follow a justifiable course of action and explain it adequately is an important aspect of learning to solve problems and produce work of value in the world. However, a balance must be struck here. An important dimension of robotics-based learning is pure experimentation. Simply wanting to play with a problem or situation in an open-ended search for possibilities is good student practice. The key is that final, committed decisions should have good reasons behind them. Balancing the two becomes an important part of the lesson to be learned.

Observation Notes

A typical procedure for running a robotics class is for the teacher to speak to the whole group at the beginning of the class period on rules and objectives for the day and then to circulate through the class, visiting each group's work area to observe the work in progress and mentor the students. This is an opportunity to take notes about each short conference. Effort, collegiality, compliance with rules, quality of work, and more can be observed this way, yielding a continual stream of snapshots that form the basis of grading later on.

Artifacts

The production of a functioning robot to satisfy a problem along with a set of design and construction criteria form the core aspects of assessing robotics activities. The robot is the embodiment of the learning and the culmination of much of the work. Students' journals record how they dealt with the programming and construction processes. Assessing robots can be done well with checklists or checklists expanded into rubrics.

Performances

Robots are more than just kinetic machines or digital sculptures. They are designed to have the ability to follow a program, often one that has a specific purpose. Running the robot so that its programming can be evaluated is a principal part of the performance to be assessed. In many cases, the robot and program have been developed to cope with a specific environment or course, and this factors into the performance to be assessed. Additionally, the way the students present the robot to an audience or judges may be considered as part of the assessed performance. An example of this is FIRST LEGO League competition, in which there are guidelines for team behavior and time limits that factor into performance evaluation.

The Culminating Product

The Buck Institute for Education's "Project Based Learning" website, PBL Online (http://pbl-online.org), discusses the role of culminating products in project-based learning:

> A **culminating product** is due at the end of the project and often represents a blend of content knowledge and skills that give students an opportunity to demonstrate learning across a variety of topics and skills. Culminating products are often presented during significant, high-stakes occasions involving audiences beyond the classroom, thus encouraging students to go beyond "show-and-tell" and to demonstrate in-depth learning.

In student robotics projects, the robot and its performance may be seen as the culminating product.

Rubrics

Rubrics are graphic devices that list gradable criteria, which provide the bases for consistent, objective evaluation. Rubrics can be formatted as numbered lists or charts. They describe how students' work will be graded, based on how the object of assessment is evaluated. Rubrics explain how significant levels of success are defined and indicated. Rubrics for robotics may include many of the aspects of the product created and the process through which it was produced. For robotics teachers who are writing their own rubrics, the trick is to know which of many possible criteria are purposeful and practical to include. Going back to the goals and objectives for the class or group will shed light on criteria by which to assess learning and performance.

While a degree of subjectivity is involved in determining which levels a student and his or her group's robot has achieved, to a great extent rubrics take much of the subjectivity out of the assessment equation.

Creating Rubrics

Numerous tools can be found online to help teachers create effective rubrics. RubiStar (http://rubistar.4teachers.org) is one good example. Before creating a rubric from scratch, search through the archives of the many rubrics colleagues have created; some may be used verbatim or used with slight modifications. On the RubiStar site, teachers may add their modified rubrics to the archives for others to use.

A rubric may be created by listing all the things students are expected to do and learn from the project; each thing functions as a rating criterion for the rubric. Each criterion is linked to three or four success levels: "Does little or nothing to satisfy requirements (1)," "Minimally satisfies requirements (2)," "Satisfies requirements thoroughly (3)," and "Satisfies requirements exceptionally (4)." A student's grade is arrived at by evaluating his or her performance for each of the criteria; each criterion is assigned a rating level (number of points). By tabulating all the level values and adding them together, teachers will have a total number of points earned by each student.

Naturally, teachers decide the total number of rating levels/points students need to earn that correspond to the school's grading system. Students in beginning robotics classes may be given a much wider range of points for earning As and Bs than students in more advanced classes.

A significant refinement to add to the rubric methodology is to establish a criterion for the student's contribution to the group effort. Teachers may also want to assign a reflective exercise, such as an essay or oral presentation. The student is asked to report on his or her experiences in working in a collaborative group to tackle a challenge to design, construct, program, and operate a robot. The essay or presentation can become a criterion for assessment and be included in the rubric.

The rubric may also include items that go beyond the robot itself and look at the end-to-end effort and experience of the student; for instance, the research done before beginning the project, sharing problems and solutions in whole class debriefings, and involvement in maintaining the class's workspace.

The criteria shown in Table 5.1 are from rubrics used in actual classroom situations. Links to the sources of these excerpts are given in the resource list that follows Table 5.1.

Table 5.1 Sample Criteria from Rubrics Used in Classrooms and Technology Fairs

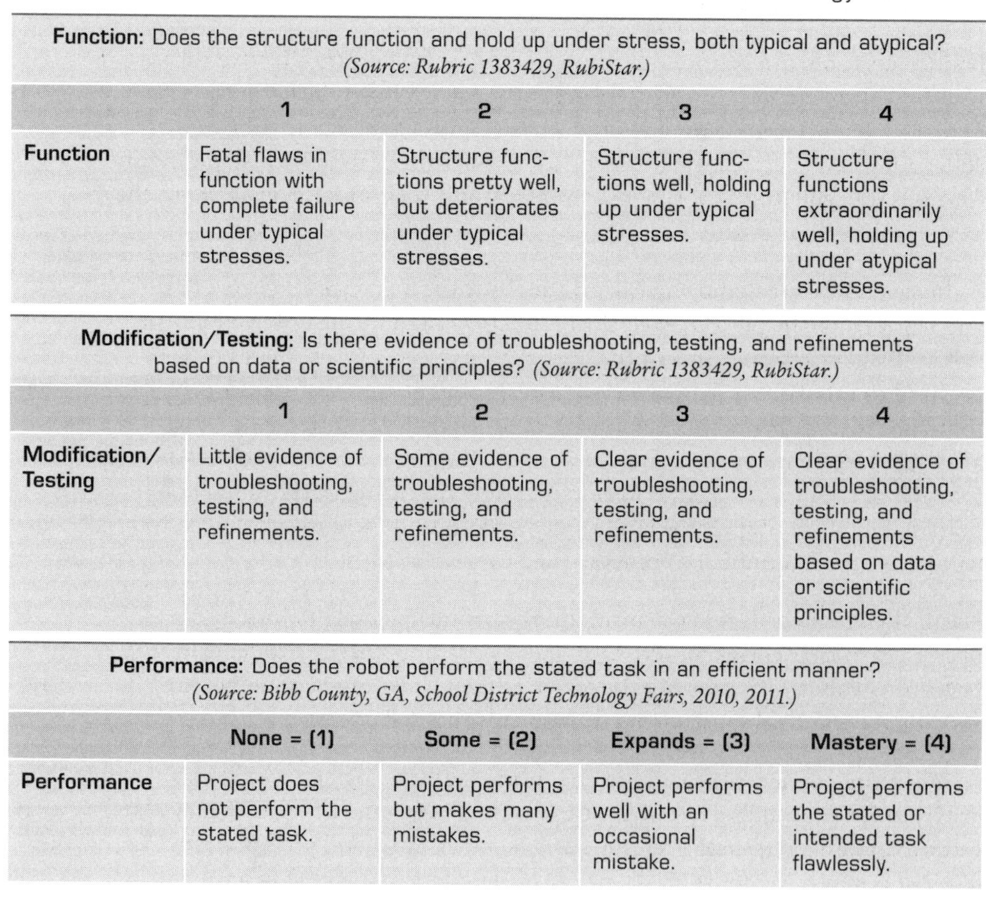

Function: Does the structure function and hold up under stress, both typical and atypical? *(Source: Rubric 1383429, RubiStar.)*

	1	2	3	4
Function	Fatal flaws in function with complete failure under typical stresses.	Structure functions pretty well, but deteriorates under typical stresses.	Structure functions well, holding up under typical stresses.	Structure functions extraordinarily well, holding up under atypical stresses.

Modification/Testing: Is there evidence of troubleshooting, testing, and refinements based on data or scientific principles? *(Source: Rubric 1383429, RubiStar.)*

	1	2	3	4
Modification/ Testing	Little evidence of troubleshooting, testing, and refinements.	Some evidence of troubleshooting, testing, and refinements.	Clear evidence of troubleshooting, testing, and refinements.	Clear evidence of troubleshooting, testing, and refinements based on data or scientific principles.

Performance: Does the robot perform the stated task in an efficient manner? *(Source: Bibb County, GA, School District Technology Fairs, 2010, 2011.)*

	None = (1)	**Some = (2)**	**Expands = (3)**	**Mastery = (4)**
Performance	Project does not perform the stated task.	Project performs but makes many mistakes.	Project performs well with an occasional mistake.	Project performs the stated or intended task flawlessly.

Journal/Log Content: Does the journal provide a record of planning, construction, testing, modifications, and reasons for and/or reflections on modifications? *(Source: Rubric 1383429, RubiStar.)*				
	1	2	3	4
Journal/ Log Content	Journal provides very little detail about of planning, construction, testing, modifications, and reasons for modifications.	Journal provides quite a bit of detail about planning, construction, testing, modifications, and reasons for modifications.	Journal provides a complete record of planning, construction, testing, modifications, and reasons for modifications.	Journal provides a complete record of planning, construction, testing, modifications, reasons for modifications, and some reflection about the strategies used and the results.

Knowledge of Structure and Programming: Has the student evidenced knowledge of robot structure and programming and shown thorough understanding of design, science, and technology behind it? Direct participation in programming the robot? *(Source: DT7 VEX Robot Design Rubric.)*				
	0	1–2	3–4	5–6
Knowledge of Structure and Programming	Little knowledge of why some parts are where on the robot or who put them there. Little or no understanding of what the pieces did. Building/ programming appears to be primarily done by the teacher.	Knowledge of robot structure and programming shows minimal understanding of design, science, and technology behind it. Building/ programming appears to be primarily directed by the teacher.	Knowledge of robot structure and programming shows moderate understanding of design, science, and technology behind it. Building/ programming mostly directed by team members, with help from the teacher.	Knowledge of robot structure and programming shows thorough understanding of design, science, and technology behind it. Building/ programming was done by team members.

Table 5.1 *(Continued)*

Robot Autonomy: Did the robot perform the task(s) without any human intervention? *(Source: Bibb County, GA, School District Technology Fairs, 2010, 2011.)*				
	None = (1)	**Some = (2)**	**Expands = (3)**	**Mastery = (4)**
Autonomous	Human interaction and/or remote control required to operate machine after start.	Some human interaction needed for machine to accomplish stated task.	Little human interaction needed for machine to accomplish stated task.	No human interaction needed for machine to accomplish stated task.

Hardware Design: Were all parts of the robot design focused on solving the stated task in an efficient manner? *(Source: Bibb County, GA, School District Technology Fairs, 2010, 2011.)*				
	None = (1)	**Some = (2)**	**Expands = (3)**	**Mastery = (4)**
Hardware Design	No part of the machine is focused on solving the stated task.	Project has many non-functional parts or parts that have nothing to do with solving the stated task.	Project has some non-functional parts or parts that have nothing to do with solving the stated task.	Entire machine presented a focused and efficient solution for the stated task.

Teamwork: Roles, Responsibilities, and Time Management *(Source: FIRST LEGO League Judges' Handbook.)*				
	Needs Improvement	**Fair**	**Good**	**Excellent**
Teamwork Roles and Responsibilities	No clearly defined roles.	Loosely defined roles.	Defined roles.	Clearly defined roles.
	Not clear who completed which tasks and/or very uneven distribution of work.	Uneven work distribution.	Work is distributed fairly but with individual focus only.	Workload is distributed fairly, and team members understand each other's roles.
	Team members not collaborative.	Team members will help each other if asked.	Team members assist each other without being asked.	Team members fill each other's roles (happily), if needed.
Time Management	Time management is poor or purely directed by the coach.	Time management skills are weak.	Team mentions learning time management.	Team members give concrete examples of learning time management.

The resources in the list below give some good, complete rubric examples.

Rubric Resources: Some Complete Online Robotics Rubrics

Building a Structure: 8th Grade Robotics Rubric

RubiStar: Create Rubrics for Your Project-Based Learning Activities

http://rubistar.4teachers.org/index.php?screen=ShowRubric&rubric_id=1368978&

Building a Structure: LEGO Robotic Challenge, Finding a Light Source

RubiStar: Create Rubrics for Your Project-Based Learning Activities

http://rubistar.4teachers.org/index.php?screen=ShowRubric&rubric_id=1383429&

DT7 VEX Robot Design Rubric

www.cloud9digital.com/moodle/file.php/1/pdf_files/DT7VEXRubric.pdf

Autodesk VEX Robotics Curriculum may be ordered for $200 from www.vexrobotics.com/vex-edu-cad.html: "A comprehensive robotics curriculum created for secondary schools, the Autodesk VEX Robotics Curriculum is designed to help students master the fundamentals of robotics and the engineering design process."

FIRST LEGO League Rubrics for Teamwork, Robot Design, and Robot Project

FIRST LEGO League Judging Criteria

http://edoutreach.wpafb.af.mil/championship/media/fll_judging_rubrics.pdf

http://insciteillinois.org/?download=2009_judging_rubric.pdf

Fluid Power/Robotics

Daniel Muller, High Point Regional High School, High Point, NJ

www.nbps.k12.nj.us/njcccs/Webpage/contents/Other%20activities/Fluid%20Power%20Robotics.htm

Robotics Rubric

10th Annual Student Technology Fair, Howard High School, February 5, 2011
Bibb County School District, Bibb County, GA

http://schools.bibb.k12.ga.us/1551101029155293/lib/1551101029155293/Rubrics%202010/Robotics%20FY10.pdf

http://schools.bibb.k12.ga.us/1551101029155293/site/default.asp

www.bibb.k12.ga.us/technologyfair/Rubrics/Robotics%20Rubric%20-Complete.pdf

From "Tech Fair 2011," go to "Project Judging," then the link to "Robotics" for the FY2010 robotics rubrics used in 2011.

Assessment Advice

In his paper "LEGO Mindstorms 'Can Do Challenge'" (www.sun.com/aboutsun/comm_invest/jgp/docs/cando.pdf), ninth grade teacher Stacey Fornstrom explains:

> The grading focuses on the process and not the results. Students can receive a good grade if they design and follow a complete plan, even if their robot is not able to move any cans from the ring.
>
> The robots make it easy for students to analyze results of their own programs by asking themselves "Is the robot doing what I expected it would?" If the answer is no, "What should I change?" I believe that this is the strength of using the robots. It makes it easy for students to analyze their own results.

Below is an excerpt from an extended conversation with science teacher Luke Laurie about how he does assessment in his eighth grade robotics-based science class:

> **Gura:** What about assessing the students' work? Do you grade the robots? How do you do it?
>
> **Laurie:** The students receive conventional grades that come from homework, quizzes, traditional tests, lab activities, et cetera. Primarily, I look at their time on task and effort. I watch the groups as a whole and their interactions, and I watch the individual students and their contribution to the product. I do look at their products to a degree, but at the same time I have to pull myself back and not say, "Oh, this is the best robot—all of the students in this group get an A!" Instead, I have to look at it from the standpoint of seeing what the kids are bringing to the experience. Some of my students have no computer access outside of school. Some of them come from absolute, destitute

poverty. Some of them have never had any of their own LEGOs to play with and learn how to make structures.

Over time I've developed a series of different rubrics, but I'm not consistent about the use of these. I go about the evaluation in different ways because I don't think any one way of evaluating the students and their robots is perfect.

CHAPTER 6

Documenting, Saving, and Archiving Robotics Projects

Students need to document their work for a variety of good reasons. Firstly, robotics projects by nature evolve—they are not static. Projects change and grow as the focus of the task, challenge, or problem is addressed and satisfied. Each project's evolving learning process should be recorded.

Secondly, LEGO Robotics materials are sturdy but are designed as components of impermanent machines. They are designed to fit together in ways that ensure impermanence. The intention of the manufacturer is for the parts to be used to assemble a robotics project, to be disassembled after the robot has been tested and evaluated, and to be repurposed for subsequent projects. Some parts are better suited to staying in place than others. Some that snap together will unsnap at inopportune times. Gluing or taping pieces together is frowned upon. The impermanence of robots is a given, because successful projects are stepping stones toward learning how to create more complex, sophisticated projects. All this makes keeping records of robot construction important.

Figure 6.1 A completed project, El Camino Middle School.
(Photograph by Luke Laurie.)

Usually, due to economics and storage space issues, schools simply cannot allow finished projects to remain assembled. While most schools will find LEGO Robotics materials to be affordable as a shared, recyclable resource, they cannot afford to give each student a personal kit. Likewise, projects made with the kits are most often collaborative products of the labors of two to four students. Deciding who would take possession of the finished project would present problems. Storage space is always an issue. Where would the school keep the finished projects? Because they are made with electronic components of value, they pose not just a simple storage issue but the more complex one of storing valuable things in quantity so that they are secure from theft.

So, while the shelf life of a given project may be relatively short, a few weeks or months perhaps, its value as a learning experience, as an expression of personal creativity, and as an accomplishment may be preserved through effective, creative documentation with digital media. The web abounds with documentation of student-created robots. There are well-developed websites that present the products of classes of students through text, photos, videos, and other forms of content. One good example is the website of Stephen Paul Linder, research fellow for the Institute for Security Technology Studies and faculty member in computer science at Dartmouth College (www.cs.dartmouth.edu/~spl/Academic/Robots/), which presents a number of the robots his students have produced, some with LEGO Robotics materials. Other good examples are the gallery and robots pages of the Zeus school robotics team's website (www.sdarobotics.org/robots.htm). A search on YouTube will turn up plenty of singleton efforts at publishing documentation of a particular robotics project.

Photos and Video

Preserving student robotics projects through Web 2.0 publishing is a handy solution to the aforementioned problems (their evolving nature, impermanence of parts, economic constraints, insufficient storage space, and shared ownership). Documentation adds much to the overall continuum of learning opportunities afforded by robotics projects. Furthermore, by easy distribution through email or resources like blogs, documentation of projects can be preserved, archived into searchable repositories of similar projects, and disseminated easily and without significant cost.

A robotics project produces a finished robot and usually a performance. The performance is the behaviors a robot has been built and programmed for that may be demonstrated within a specified environment, representing a challenge or problem. Each robot's performance cannot be effectively preserved other than through digital media documentation, such as an uploaded video. While it might be possible to keep a robot in a state ready to deliver such a performance, the performance itself, dependent on the robot's presence in a specific environment (like the FIRST LEGO League's challenge field) makes the likelihood of observing the full performance again doubtful. Adding other factors to the equation, like the presence of competing teams or judges or referees, and the likelihood of repeated performances is further lessened.

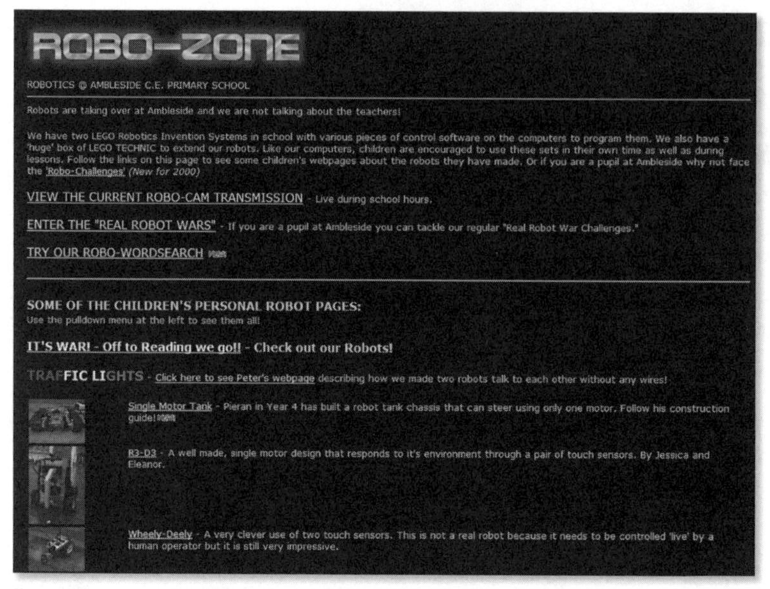

Figure 6.2 The website of Ambleside Primary School.

An even more compelling reason for including digital media documentation in the overall student robotics program is the preservation and dissemination of the culminating event. The production of student robots involves a great deal of work, perseverance, and personal discipline. The completion of these projects is a milestone event calling for acknowledgment, reflection, and celebration. Furthermore, these events represent the work and learning of entire groups who are focused on a shared set of goals, interests, and concerns. Celebratory culminating events are a fine addition to a program, something that offers its own brand of learning. These events provide reflections on what has been learned and accomplished, acknowledgments of mistakes made and overcome, accounts of good luck in making discoveries, sharing the value of collegial help offered and accepted, and ideas about next steps to take for creating more complex robots.

To do justice to such an event, documentation might include photos of participants, including images of finished projects and projects in stages as they evolved. It might include videos of the robots in action and reflections by their builders on experiences, including advice to peers who may work on the same challenge. Throughout the planning, building, and testing processes, students need to create audio recordings, video footage, stills, and scans of student drawings. Students can also scan selections from plans, journals, blogs, and other process documents—all of these can be used as documentation of the entire project, and highlights of this mass of data are selected to use in the culminating event. The final items of a project's documentation are videos and stills of the robot's performance and teamwork during the culminating event. Once compiled, the materials may be organized and finished in a word processing program and distributed to students, parents, and members of the school community as a static file. However, with today's user-friendly, open-ended, free web publishing resources like blogs and Google Sites (www.google.com/sites), the possibilities are vast. Photos may be uploaded to photo-sharing sites like Picasa (http://picasa.google.com), in which albums, slide shows, and videos may be produced, along with accompanying text in the form of captions, and then embedded in a blog. Likewise, YouTube or school-friendly equivalents, such as TeacherTube or SchoolTube, will allow video to be uploaded and then embedded in a free website, Facebook page, or blog.

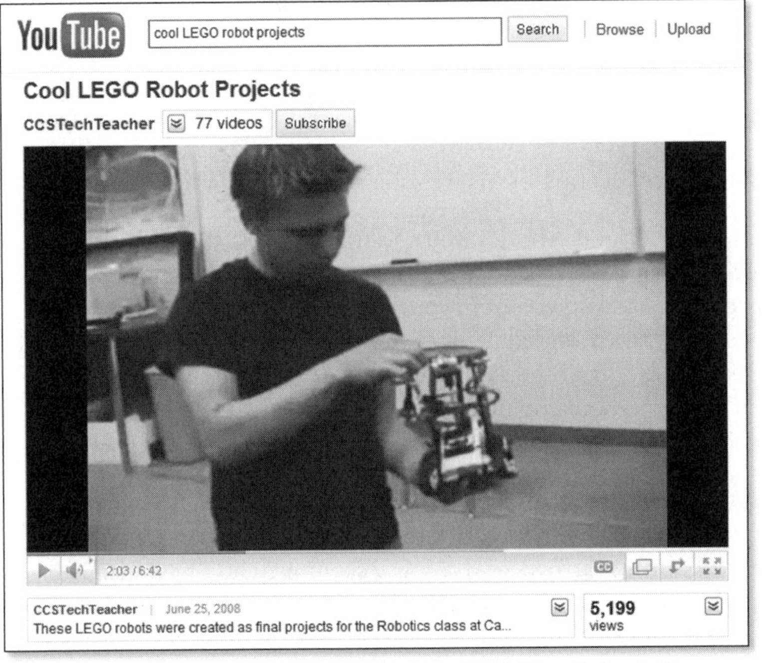

Figure 6.3 A YouTube video is used as a showcase for K–12 student robotics projects.

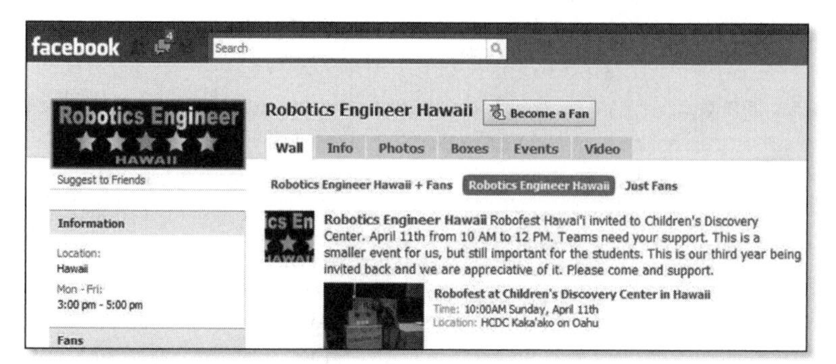

Figure 6.4 Facebook page for student robotics culminating event.

Documentation is an aspect of robotics projects that needs to be made part of the overall learning far in advance of culminating events, though. While there is a need for documentation of culminating events, documentation efforts beginning at the start of projects are useful learning tools.

Journals

In the Class Resources section of his website, Luke Laurie writes:

> Every time you work on robotics, you should be taking down a few notes during your work, and a few notes at the end to help you remember what you worked on. In your journal, you can describe the things you learned, the challenges you faced, and your plans for future work. The journal should be kept in a single place in the science section of your notebook. (http://homepage.mac.com/mrlaurie/roboscience.html)

Journaling can be a natural complement to robotics activities. Students use journals to keep a running narrative of what they did, problems encountered, solutions devised, things learned, and things accomplished. The journals help teachers with assessment. Students also find that journals help them to keep up their projects' continuity and momentum, as robotics projects are slowly evolving in multisession efforts. Beyond being the site for record keeping, journals encourage students to reflect on why things went the way they did with their projects and help them understand the significance of their experiences.

Thus, journals do much to deepen learning. When used for assessment, the journal will contain a record of design tests, changes to the robot's design or program, and the reasoning behind these. It may also include reflections on the application of scientific principles demonstrated by the project.

A blog variation that will serve students well is to have them keep an illustrated record of the progress of their robots that includes an entry for each work session. The illustrations may vary from quick but accurate sketches that make clear which LEGO pieces were used and how they have been fit together, to digital photos quickly taken at the end of the work session to record the robot as it looked when students left off.

These practices offer the instructional bonus of fostering learning in the area of language arts. In her paper "Robotics and the Language Arts Connection," technology specialist Linda Reynolds explains the following:

> Language arts plays an important part in the design cycle. Keeping accurate records of what was done and how it was done is very important in the evaluation process. If part of the robot doesn't work, but you can't quite remember how you put it together, redesigning it will be difficult. If students keep a daily journal of their work they will be able to refer to it during the redesigning phase of the project. The journal needs to be specific and not just today I worked on my robot. An example: One of our team's robot chassis wouldn't turn properly. Something was wrong with the back wheel base structure. The student who had designed that part decided to take it apart and fix it, but after it was in pieces on the table, he didn't have a clue as to how it went together. He didn't have any drawings or journal entries that talked about how the back wheels were designed. The only recourse was to just start all over again. Keeping an accurate journal of the building process or even just taking pictures of the process would have saved a lot of extra work. (www.botball.org/_files/Paper_Reynolds_Language.pdf)

Blogging lends itself well to journaling; see Figure 6.5 for a great example.

Figure 6.5 A student robotics club blog.

CHAPTER 7

Robotics in the Curriculum

Will a school choose to implement LEGO Robotics? And if so, where and how will it fit under the general umbrella of a school's instructional program? The answer is contingent on at least three factors. First, an understanding of the significance and advantages of including this body of practice is needed. Does the teaching staff "get" the vision of how a robotics program can work to achieve worthwhile instructional goals? Second, can robotics fit practically into a segment of what's already being taught? Third, if integrating robotics into a traditional class becomes the goal, assuming that a series of entry points in the chosen subject are found, will activities and materials (LEGO Robotics and others) be available to support it?

In many cases, robotics will first become part of a school's offerings to students as an extracurricular, after-school activity or as a special interest or club activity. Educators who become aware of LEGO Robotics, perhaps by observing the activities of other schools or classes, will be attracted by its extraordinary capacity for motivating young people. As soon as teachers and administrators begin to wrap their minds around what this body of practice involves, they will soon see the promise of deep learning in a variety of subject areas. Robotics embodies a compelling combination of high motivation and high learning value. And while it may be enough in the beginning to offer robotics as an after-school club activity, some teachers will inevitably wonder where and how it might fit into the regular, daytime instructional program.

As we'll see, robotics can fit nicely with a variety of traditional subjects already being taught. In many ways, robotics will powerfully enhance standard subject matter. And in countless other ways, if teachers are inspired by adding robotics, finding ways to make it part of the regular program is a legitimate objective to ensure that the school's overall instructional program is relevant and vital.

A number of approaches can be considered. The most direct is simply to offer a robotics class. The class might fit into the place formerly held by industrial arts classes no longer being offered. In some districts, technology classes supplanted some or all industrial arts courses. A robotics class could make a worthwhile version of or addition to a technology class with only a little retooling and some professional development.

However, many schools may not have the capacity, available time, or inclination to offer students a dedicated robotics class. A worthwhile approach to take then would be to integrate robotics into existing courses periodically, without revamping the traditional curriculum. By including a robotics-based unit here and there, across subject areas, students would receive an education enriched by robotics as part of a greater whole.

Schools that have an after-school robotics club or a team that participates in competitive robotics events already have class sets of materials and a staff member or two able to support the rest of the staff in their periodic integration of robotics into the curriculum. This can make for an easier, holistic approach to robotics integration.

Methods, practices, and curriculum are intertwined when it comes to using LEGO Robotics in the classroom. The curriculum connection chosen must be related to an instructional approach the teacher is comfortable with or one that, while significantly different, is something the teacher would like to try. LEGO Robotics is very much oriented toward "playing" in the sense of experimentation (and reflection on and drawing inferences from it), social learning, and trial and error. Those who are primarily comfortable with teaching through teacher-led discussions, whole group learning, and a textbook as platforms for content delivery will find most applications of LEGO Robotics to be extremely different from what they are used to. Making the shift to take advantage of this body of resources will involve a shift in style and approach, including giving up some control over the students and the shape and flow of activities that traditional approaches afford.

One of the many pluses, though, is that for teachers and school communities willing to make such a shift in style and approach, LEGO Robotics offers a framework around which efforts can be focused and coordinated. It is forgiving of shaky initial steps. Teachers will have to give students some background information on the big ideas underlying LEGO Robotics, such as: What are the materials and how do they work? How does the programming software work? What are the sorts of things that people do with these materials and software? However, these questions can be answered by showing students introductory videos and/or facilitating student exploration and reflection. Introducing robotics concepts and operations does not require teachers to be experts; instead, teachers become focused co-learners. And, of course, teachers will have to set up their classrooms to support the logistics of running a class smoothly using these new materials and resources (topics that are discussed at length in Chapter 3).

Some of the dynamics of exploring this new teaching approach are described well by Ian Maud, a secondary teacher in Australia, in his paper "Learning by Stealthrobotics in the Classroom" (http://findarticles.com/p/articles/mi_6957/is_4_54/ai_n31161076/):

> Firstly, if a teacher takes a traditional approach to presenting robotics where they deliver some theory, then a short bit of prac[tice] time, restrict the pace of the class to the learning pace of the mid-fielders and take a very step-by-step approach ... you'll probably end up with traditional outcomes. The beauty of robotics is that it liberates the individual learner: students need no longer be tied to the "You can't learn this until I've taught you!" approach. It lends itself particularly well to a situation where a goal or outcome is explained, but the

> means is left open-ended. Students will take their own approach, progress at their own pace, try unique, weird and wonderful strategies, and set limits to their work that may in some cases be far beyond what their teacher would have thought them capable of. A truly wonderful robotics classroom allows for achievement by all students, determined by their own planning and ability level. And arguably the best part of the process is that much of the learning occurs "by stealth."

Despite the changes and challenges that robotics may present to teachers, its important advantages far outweigh any initial challenges. Robotics offers a solid body of practice for adding variety to traditional, book-driven, whole group instruction. Robotics' hands-on and minds-on activities center on small group collaborative work, an approach that is often glossed over because an appropriate practice related to it may be hard to identify. When real-world applications are desired to enhance particular subject matter, robotics is an opportunity to involve students in activities that clearly demonstrate the connections between concepts and reality. For teachers who are interested in embracing some often-discussed progressive approaches to instruction, such as project- and problem-based learning, authentic activities and assessment, and self-directed learning, robotics reflects all of this in addition to being rich in connections to essential curriculum. Additionally, robotics offers opportunities for wonderful capstone activities. The presentation of finished projects is an event suitable to command the attention of a school community. Students' learning over an extended period of time and across a variety of subjects while they have created robots is showcased, giving them approbation for academic achievement.

Robotics has great promise for integration into various subject areas. However, identifying areas of alignment, those in which the content to be taught has commonalities with robotics, is not a prescription for integration or the assurance that integration is practical.

Science and Robotics

Science is the core curriculum area most often associated with student robotics. In a broad sense, robotics expresses approaches to learning that should underlie all science activities, unifying concepts like systems, order and organization, and form and function, as well as inquiry processes like observation, inference, and experimentation. Furthermore, robotics has potential as a method to demonstrate and teach specific portions of the physical science curriculum, such as Newton's Laws and simple machines. Robotics serves in some schools as a hands-on, problem-solving extension for physical science classes.

Robotics has also become an important tool used by scientists across science's many sub-disciplines. Robotic devices are built to traverse and navigate a wide variety of environments where humans cannot go. For instance, a volcanologist may send a robot into a caldera to monitor the movement of lava, or oceanographers may send robots to the floor of the ocean to gather information and relay it back to them. LEGO Robotics materials include a variety of data sensors that can gather information to be processed after collection. Part of the study of science involves learning "science as human endeavor" (National Science Content Standard #8), which explores how scientists go about the business of doing science, something that includes the development of tools and methods. Robotics is one of the most important of these.

The PBS science series *Dragonfly TV* produced an episode titled "GEMS (Girls in Engineering, Math, and Science)," in which middle school girls explain the value of robots in helping scientists do work in dangerous and remote environments, like Mars. They then go on to build their own LEGO robot, capable of performing specified tasks, making the important connection between robotics and scientific exploration and research. The video shows them developing concepts, designing robots, testing them, and then modifying the robots so that they will perform the tasks required. The girls understand that this process is similar to that followed by scientists crafting a research robot. The episode is still available on the Internet at http://pbskids.org/dragonflytv/show/gems.html. The website includes a narrative, titled "GEMS by Sasha, Makeisha, Claire, Hannah, Annice and Emily," from the girls featured in the episode:

> We're members of our school's GEMS team. GEMS stands for Girls in Engineering, Math and Science. Our team prepared to participate in a robotics competition, building a robot that completes two tasks. Our question: How do we design a robot that moves quickly and turns in a tight circle?
>
> **What did we do?**
>
> We compared two basic designs: a four-wheeled robot and a three-wheeled robot. The robot had a programmable brain that received the commands the girls wrote on a computer. We wrote a simple program

to make the robot travel in a straight line at top speed, and then turn in as sharp a circle as possible. Once we settled on a design, we added a robotic arm that could pull a latch and place a foam ball into a bin. Then it was off to the competition to put our designs into action!

What did we find out?
We discovered that we got the fastest speed and the tightest turns using a three-wheeled design. We also learned that engineering often involves lots of failures before you succeed. At the robot competition, we had to modify the robot's software to successfully complete the first task, pulling a latch. Once we made the proper software changes, we had to work on the second task, dropping the ball into a bin. We were running out of time and our first design wasn't working, but we made a last-minute change, and our robot worked perfectly.

It is important to show students that robotics has become an important subject in its own right, a new branch of science that is often tapped to serve the other sciences. Another example of robotics taught from this perspective is the former "Robots on the Road" program by NASA; some of the materials are still available on the web. This website (http://aesp.psu.edu/robots.cfm) explains the program, and on the site a link (http://aesp.psu.edu/files/ROTR%20Standards.pdf) discusses the program's applicability to National Science Standards Alignment:

> Robots on the Road [ROTR] is designed to introduce students in Grades 5 through 8 to the field of robotics. Traveling Specialists from NASA's Aerospace Education Services Project (AESP) are currently visiting schools across the country to engage students in exciting, hands-on robotics activities. Specialists use LEGO Mindstorms robotics kits to challenge students to use problem solving, team building, and critical thinking skills as they investigate one of eight different robots. The ROTR activities are designed to promote process skills that are necessary for students to be successful not only in the classroom, but in any discipline they wish to pursue later in life...
>
> **Robots on the Road: National Science Standards Alignment**
> *Overview:* The Robots on the Road classroom activity for middle school can last from 45 minutes to an hour and a half in length, depending on the schedule restraints at individual schools. During this activity, an education specialist will introduce NASA's future exploration goals as well as basic robotic principles. The students will

then be divided into small groups and assigned a LEGO robot. Using a hands-on, inquiry-based approach, the students will determine the purpose of the robot, what sensors it uses, and how those sensors work. After the students have explored their robot, the groups will report to the rest of the class what they have learned. The specialist will then lead a discussion on past, present, and future NASA robots and how the LEGO robots, particularly the sensors, relate to NASA technology.

Data Collection and Robotics

As part of the movement to make "real" science part of today's curriculum, science teachers often engage students in activities that involve the collection and interpretation of data. Because much data in the real world is collected digitally, it is natural for data collection to be supported by technology in the classroom as well. Over the years two main approaches have been developed that add much to the classroom experience: traditional or indirect data collection and direct data collection. Using the traditional method, students may go online to access data indirectly; that is, the data is presented by others who collect or report it. Weather data, tide data, and figures that show population trends—like numbers of wildlife involved in migration—are common examples of this sort of data collection activity. Alternatively, students may make direct observations and measurements and enter their own data into spreadsheets or other software designed to store sets of data. Then they manipulate data sets to analyze and interpret them. They may use rulers and tape measures, thermometers, anemometers and barometers, pressure gauges, and other tools to collect information. Many of these common measuring devices have evolved into more accurate, low-cost, durable, miniaturized digital devices.

An interesting extension of traditional data collection activities for students, allowing students to participate in ways that mirror what's done in the world beyond school, is to integrate data collection with robotics. Robots carry the data collection devices and operate them to collect data and store it, using their onboard processors and memory. Later the data will be downloaded to a more robust computer for processing, analysis, and representation graphically or by other means. LEGO Robotics kits come with sensors, digital data devices that measure phenomena like pressure, voltage, temperature, and more. Beyond the basic sensors that come with the kits, others are available, some from third-party manufacturers that are compatible with the LEGO materials.

In LEGO Robotics data collection activities, students design robots to carry sensors that they select in order to solve challenges. Students can explore this dimension of robotics once they have sufficiently learned the basics of designing, building, programming, and troubleshooting robots.

For more information on LEGO Robotics data collection, the following websites are useful:

Robot Science Featuring Data Logging:
www.education.rec.ri.cmu.edu/previews/nxt_products/science_data_logging/preview/inquiry/inquiry.html

Older project movies, like "Acidity Tester":
www.vernier.com/nxt/projects.html

Wired Science Video Illustrating Remote Data Collection via Robots:
www.pbs.org/kcet/wiredscience/education/2008/03/in-your-classroom-the-quiet-zo.html

71 Things to Do with LEGO Mindstorms and Data:
www.marshall.edu/LEGO/Tufts/71ThingsToDoWithDataLogging.html

Remote Sensing and Tele-robotics for Elementary and Middle School via the Internet:
www.ni.com/pdf/academic/us/journals/Remote_sensing_and_tele.pdf

Robotic Science and Data Logging:
www.legoeducation.us/about/newsletter/item.aspx?ap=1&nli=42&art=2520&bhcp=1

Building a LEGO ROV Using the Mindstorms Robotics Kit:
www.mbari.org/education/internship/01interns/01papers/winter.pdf

Developing Conceptual Understanding of Mechanical Advantage through the Use of LEGO Robotic Technology:
www.ascilite.org.au/ajet/ajet24/chambers.pdf

Math and Robotics

Math abounds across the spectrum of robotics activities. Math is used in the planning and construction of robots, as well as in their programming. Common robotics activities involve such perennial dimensions of math learning as counting (pieces required to build a robot); measuring (the sizes of pieces, the distance a bot will travel); estimation; ratios (such as gear ratios);

geometry of pieces (structures made of collections' pieces, paths for the robot to navigate).

The web page titled "SDMS Grade 6 Math Curriculum" (www.weirdrichard.com/sdms.htm) gives a long list of items commonly included as part of required math curricula that can be taught through the use of "LEGO constructives." The examples are not of full-blown, motorized robots but of LEGO parts or stable collections of parts incorporated into full or partial architectural constructions or simple machines. The list includes math subjects like converting metric measurements to equivalents, powers and exponents, and measuring angles. The LEGO pieces are used in a variety of ways, sometimes as manipulatives, sometimes as physical representations of things like bar graphs that aid in visualization of math concepts, and sometimes with a more direct relationship to building and programming robots. The page gives six photo-illustrated sample lessons, all of which include pictures of standard LEGO pieces functioning as materials to support math learning.

One example of a strong math connection to a robotics project involves figuring the distance a robot will travel by calculating the circumference of its wheels. By measuring the radius or diameter of the wheel and applying the correct pi-based formula ($c = \pi \times d$ or $c = \pi \times 2r$), the distance of one full wheel rotation, the circumference, is arrived at. By extension, multiplying the circumference by the number of rotations the wheel will make (or be programmed to make), the total distance traveled can be calculated. Or, depending on what is to be achieved and how the work is to flow, the reverse might be calculated, dividing a given distance by the circumference to arrive at the number of wheel rotations.

However, while the connections between math and robotics are clear, how to use robotics to teach math may be less obvious. In their article "Designing Technology Activities that Teach Mathematics," Silk, Higashi, Shoop, and Schunn astutely state:

> Research conducted by our team suggests that just because math is present in an activity, it doesn't mean that students will learn math. ... Subtle changes in the design and setup of the lesson make a substantive difference in what students learn. (*The Technology Teacher*, December/January 2010, p. 21)

While robotics activities may naturally reinforce skills and knowledge and offer opportunities for students to observe and/or discover the application of skills and knowledge, using robotics to introduce new content and foster its initial learning requires a focused, hands-on effort on the part of the teacher to ensure that the targeted learning actually happens.

Many teachers will find it difficult to use robotics as a way to introduce concepts, although in reflecting on a robotics activity, discussing it, and attempting to comprehend what was observed, new concepts may be covered. Above all, if structured properly, robotics activities will model and demonstrate for students the actual, important roles that numbers play in constructing machines that work. When students have to log carefully and explain the process of designing and building their bots, they may count and record the numbers and types of pieces used, describe the relationship of 8-tooth gears to 24-tooth gears when they are paired in a drive train (ratio of 1:3), or program a robot to travel three units of distance and make a 60-degree turn three times to describe an equilateral triangle.

An example of an activity that uses robotics to demonstrate the application of math is found on the web page titled "Robotics in the Classroom: Using Robotics and Congruent Triangles" (www.education.wichita.edu/m3/models/prek-12/mhoward.htm). In this geometry lesson for ninth–twelfth graders, students plot a specified path on the classroom floor and then program a robot to follow it. Actually, two variations are given—one is a whole group exercise supported by an interactive white board, and the other is a small group activity supported by student laptops. The project web page gives a link to a downloadable PDF student worksheet, photos of the activity in progress, as well as text description and teacher reflection on the activity.

One crucial issue in math instruction is that huge amounts of content, ideas, and skills are contained within a single year's math curriculum; covering it all within the given time can result in students' superficial understanding and sense of the overwhelming scope of mathematics. Furthermore, math, as it is commonly presented to students in our schools, comes off as highly abstract, with little connection to the real-world applications for which and from which most of it is derived. Much has been said and done about creating "real-world math" curricula, but often in implementation, this only results in written references and allusions to real-world situations incorporated into textbooks and print materials. All of this seems divorced from the real world to students. Robotics, as part of the context of engineering-based learning, provides an alternative. Robotics offers a series of highly motivating activities that require students to use many bodies of factual knowledge and skills to participate in and complete the bots to their own satisfaction.

As an example, the robotics section of the Highlands Middle School (Pearl City, Hawaii) website (www.highlands.k12.hi.us/~dabuel/ussmo_teachers/Robotics_and_Math.html) offers a suggested connection to math learning. Included is an illustrated description of an activity designed for students to learn the Pythagorean theorem through robotics construction. The idea is to create a teachable moment in geometry by designing a hands-on activity, in the first example, designing and building a frame for a ship. Students will need to be certain about measurements they take as part of the project. The site's explanation adds, "The math concepts were covered through hands-on experiences but without making the students aware of the concepts and terms." In other words, students can learn important math concepts and apply them by recontextualizing them as they enjoy a highly engaging, playful activity.

Technology and Robotics

Many schools offer a technology class, sometimes called computer lab class. What is offered in such classes varies greatly from district to district and school to school, contingent upon the hardware, software, and other resources available, as well as the expertise, interests, and inclinations of the teachers. While in some states educating students to be technologically literate is mandated, for the most part this literacy isn't assessed formally through a high-stakes test. Consequently, computer labs and their programs are often viewed as something beyond the core of what is most important.

Educational technologists have long expressed the opinion that technology is best taught within the context of its supportive role for teaching and learning in the content areas. In this sense, technology classes are something of a contradiction, as they have frequently taught bodies of applications, like PowerPoint, as ends unto themselves. Consequently, robotics offers an opportunity to revitalize technology as a subject area—to give it renewed focus and to infuse it with an important and exciting body of content and skills. In the course of doing a robotics project, students typically do research involving the use of web-based search engines; review digital media-based materials for building instructions and blueprinted plans of robots; keep records using applications like word processors, digital imaging, and photo processors; share ideas and feedback using online bulletin boards, wikis, and blogs; create reports and publish them using desktop and e-publishing applications; and capture final products and performances and upload them to media-sharing sites like YouTube. By requiring the above high-level activities, robotics provides a more meaningful basis for teaching and learning many of the technologies that are being taught in technology classes. Additionally, robotics offers opportunities to learn programming skills, which have largely been eliminated from technology courses in favor of simpler technologies and applications more commonly encountered in higher education and the world of work. LEGO Robotics, however, uses object or icon-based programming. Elementary through high school students quickly learn this graphic form of programming and comprehend the basic ideas that underlie how humans communicate with computers and robots.

A major advantage of including robotics as part of technology courses is that it offers a highly effective feedback mechanism. Once a robot has been conceived, constructed, and programmed, whether or not it works is easy to evaluate. Modifications of constructions and programs can be accomplished quickly and tested quickly, offering a highly effective platform for learning. While a course in computer science may be beyond the reach of many schools or be beyond the needs of most populations of students, high-value subject matter may be quickly injected into marginal technology classes by the inclusion of LEGO Robotics.

Engineering—the Missing "E" in the STEM Curriculum

While STEM education calls for engineering to be offered as one of the key components of the curriculum and instructional program, it is often either missing or glossed over. This is particularly true of elementary and middle school STEM instruction.

Because there is no tradition in our public schools of offering engineering as a subject (other than in some specialized high school programs), few curricula or teaching practices exist—an obstacle for those who would like to teach it. Our schools have always offered math and science as subjects. University-level programs prepare teachers in these areas, licenses are issued by state departments of education to certify math and science teachers, and many fine textbooks are available. While a number of engineering content items and related activities are integrated within traditional math, science, and other courses, they are not always labeled as such and not always covered or taught in ways that truly support their understanding as engineering. These engineering activities are seen through the lens of the "parent" discipline.

Even for those schools and educators who understand the short shrift engineering has been given and those who see the need to change this and make engineering an important part of the instructional program, new bodies of practice and materials can be challenging to adopt. LEGO Robotics is one of the few exceptions to this. A great deal of what educators need to make engineering a prominent part of the instructional program is already available through LEGO Robotics. This is a body of resources and practices, as well as a global community of educator enthusiasts, that is already more than a decade old!

Whether you plan to offer a full-blown engineering class, an after-school club, or simply want to introduce an engineering thread into an existing course, there are a couple of big ideas and frameworks that will help. One of these is the engineering and design process framework that is widely used. This framework breaks the end-to-end process of engineering design down into distinct, recognizable stages or phases. One typical version of this is an eight-stage process that comprises the following components:

1. Identify the problem to be addressed. Clearly define the problem for which your design will be a solution. This clarity will provide impetus and focus for the work to come. It may be useful to revisit this starting phase from time to time, especially when encountering problems or overwhelmed with possible approaches.
2. Research. Get information about the problem that will help focus and inform thinking and next steps. This may be seen as having two stages of its own:
    a. Investigate the current situation. How are people experiencing the problem, and how are they addressing it?
    b. Look at the thinking and work of others, like yourself, who are attempting to go beyond step a (above). What other solutions, or out-of-the-box ways of dealing with it are being worked on and discussed?
3. List possible approaches and solutions. List every way to solve the problem that comes to mind. It is helpful to describe these in several ways, such as written descriptions, diagrams in 2-D and 3-D, or brief

notes on a whiteboard. It may also be useful to describe *next step work* that would be done for each solution.

4. Select the best solution from this list. Choose the solution that seems as if it will be the most likely to succeed and explain why. The explanation will give greater clarity and focus for the work to come and will help down the road when the success or failure of the solution is evaluated.

5. Prototype or model the solution. Come up with a fully defined "test" version of the solution. This is done before fully committing and investing in a final solution. It may save time, money, and resources by revealing flaws in the design before it's too late to change directions.

6. Test and evaluate the solution. Using your prototype, evaluate the success of your solution. Does it do what it is supposed to do? Does it solve the problem without creating others? How close does it come to satisfying the need identified at the beginning of the process?

7. Report your solution. As you prepare a presentation to explain the solution, you'll achieve greater clarity and focus. In the report explain why the solution was needed—how it works—how it solves the problem. Also, present your thinking on how the solution will affect the world (take this as far as practical), the project's costs, how will it affect people, and any other expected outcomes.

8. Refine your solution. Based on all of the above, what next steps would you engage in to carry the design process further? What did you discover by testing and evaluating and reporting on your solution?

There are other frameworks for the engineering design process that list similar steps. Some of these include things like narrowing the research and analyzing the criteria for a solution. Whatever list of stages you use, though, the important thing is for students ultimately to understand the process and see it as a natural approach to analyzing the world and addressing the problems they encounter in it. It would be wise to present this as an extension of other problem-solving constructs presented to students.

In its Lunar Plant Growth learning challenge, which it offered as appropriate for students in Grades K–12 (three separate grade/age level sets of implementation plans were provided), NASA for Educators offered an engineering/design process framework with the following steps:

1. Identify the Problem
2. Identify Criteria and Constraints
3. Brainstorm Possible Solutions
4. Generate Ideas
5. Explore Possibilities
6. Select an Approach
7. Build a Model or Prototype
8. Refine the Design

For further details on each of the eight steps, see the website (www.nasa.gov/audience/foreducators/plantgrowth/reference/Eng_Design_5-12.html).

Robotics Challenges as STEM Subject Integration Catalyst

STEM education comprises the related content areas of science, technology, engineering, and math. However, most students experience these subjects as unrelated, due to long-term traditions in school organization and classroom pedagogy. These subjects are frequently taught in classrooms situated side by side, yet isolated from one another. Teachers follow curricula and practices that make each subject an exclusive or primary focus with scant effort to relate each area to a greater whole, to a meta-subject called STEM.

In the course of science instruction, some attention is paid to math as an enabling body of knowledge, and in math classes mention is made of science's need for mathematics. Both areas make some use of technology, perhaps by using websites, interactive whiteboards, data probes, calculators, and the like. However, broad reflection on the role of technology in the application of math and science in the real world is not often part of what is taught. A natural remedy for these disconnects and isolated approaches can be found in robotics, as it is the platform on which activities that feature all STEM disciplines may be staged. Robotics activities are presented as problems or challenges for which the design, construction, and programming of a robot is the solution—effectively integrating STEM subjects to make the whole effort function.

Robotics is a body of materials and practices that involves science, technology, engineering, and math. As students create robots to solve problems, they use these disciplines synergistically in an authentic manner, experiencing more real-world learning value from the aggregate than as the sum of individual results. In this sense, robotics becomes a "STEM catalyst," fostering connections and demonstrating how each part contributes to the whole. Teachers interested in making robotics part of their teaching are wise to look for models of challenges that are of high value.

Of course, open-ended exploration of robotics materials and the wonderful ways they can be made to work spontaneously will happen as students familiarize themselves with the idiom in which they will be working. This value is fully realized when it is applied to real-world problems that require real-world, engineered solutions, namely, robotics challenges.

The FIRST LEGO League (FLL) organization has concentrated on student robotics challenges. Each year FLL engages teams of students, coached by adults who generally are their teachers, in formal challenges that solve problems related to a central theme. These challenges offer a problem, a clearly and appropriately defined set of criteria, one of which is the standardized set of LEGO Robotics materials that students may apply to creating a solution. The solution must be a programmed, self-directing robot. Furthermore, FLL challenges are specifically designed for students in Grades 4–8 and are vetted for real-world and standards-based curricular relevance. They are intended to be challenging yet eminently "do-able" for the participants. While formal participation in FLL may not be practical for all school groups, drawing on the challenges may provide curricular support that can make the inclusion of student robotics in the instructional

An FLL Example

In 2009, the FLL theme was Smart Move, and the FLL Challenge was to create efficient transportation. Teams had to solve a particular problem with the mode of transportation they selected. The robot game included activating access markers, collecting loops, toggling a lever to move a truck, avoiding warning beacons, parking at one of two specified locations, and so on.

program worthwhile. FLL challenges may be used, adapted, or serve as models for teachers' own efforts in identifying or creating challenges to drive this sort of instruction.

A complete list of FLL challenges may be found at http://en.wikipedia.org/wiki/FIRST_Lego_League. The first three challenges (2006–2008) can be downloaded from the web in their original, complete forms as PDFs. The fourth challenge (2009) can be found on its original website.

Nano Quest (2006): www.usfirst.org/uploadedFiles/Who/FIRST_History/2006_FLL_Challenge.pdf

Power Puzzle (2007): www.usfirst.org/uploadedFiles/Who/FIRST_History/2007_FLL_Challenge.pdf

Climate Connections (2008): www.usfirst.org/uploadedFiles/Who/FIRST_History/2008%20Climate%20Connections%20Challenge.pdf

Smart Move (2009): www.usfirst.org/roboticsprograms/fll/smartmove1.aspx

Robotics in the Humanities

We tend to view robotics through such thick science, technology, engineering, and math lenses that connections to other disciplines and school subjects may not be immediately apparent. However, solid connections to non-STEM areas do exist.

Social Studies and Robotics

Robotics can provide motivation, focus, and powerfully relevant connections to themes studied in social studies. For example, an important theme in social studies is exploration. As humankind has reached farther in its explorations, robotics has become an essential branch of technology. Lunar and extraterrestrial exploration are very much reliant on robotics. Studying the robots used by NASA, why they are needed, and building their own similar bots can be meaningful activities for students, especially as they reflect on the whys and hows of human exploration.

A particularly good example of an extended unit of study that involved a classic social studies theme was featured in *Converge Magazine* (Spring 2008; http://media.centerdigitaled.com/Converge_Mag/pdfs/issues/ConvergeSpring.pdf). I wrote the article, titled "Domo Arigato Mr. Roboto," highlighting a multidisciplinary unit of study on the theme Industrial Revolution: Past, Present, and Future Inventions. This unit used LEGO Robotics as a hands-on resource to support student engagement, focus, and hands-on involvement. This was an initiative that involved fourth graders in numerous schools throughout the borough of Brooklyn in New York City's public schools. The article explains that although the program (Industrial Revolution: Past, Present, and Future Inventions) is multidisciplinary, involving other areas like science, its major thrust is to tie robotics to the required study of the Industrial Revolution, teaching it in a way that makes immediate sense by not just studying the social effects of the adoption of machines, but by grappling with and studying the design of the machines themselves. Simple machines, by the way, is a standard component of the New York State learning standards in science. However, while much science was learned in this project, and for that matter math and language arts were involved as well, its primary curricular entry point of social studies was well served.

What's most impressive about the Brooklyn program is that it is a sterling example of careful curriculum planning allowing for the use of robotics, an activity type that absolutely galvanizes students, to be used in regularly scheduled classes to teach mandated curriculum for which the teaching staff is held accountable. Furthermore, this project involved every school that offers fourth grade within a very crowded Brooklyn district that has a great many schools. The school's technology coordinator, Nancy Velez-Crespo, points out:

> This program will help our students with their state science test in May by helping them refine their relationship with their physical science lessons into new, creative, and innovative ways of learning.

English Language Arts and Robotics

Numerous areas of learning within English language arts (ELA) instruction can be coordinated with robotics activities.

Many teachers who have integrated robotics into their programs have found that journaling is a natural connection between ELA and science. While keeping a journal has been a common ELA practice for years, it can easily lose sparkle and effectiveness if authentic foci aren't identified. Keeping a journal can become strained, chore-like, and contrived. Students often find there is little that they have to write about that seems worthy of the effort. In contrast, when journaling is made part of an exciting robotics activity, seeing its purpose does not require much of a stretch. Not only does the journal have a function for documenting the work and effort students have put into the activity (in terms of receiving credit toward a grade or evaluation), but it also has a solid function toward achieving the goal or end product of the activity, the finished robot. As part of a detail-oriented, experimental, trial-and-error, grounded effort that is ongoing and is necessarily accomplished over the course of numerous separate work sessions, keeping a record of what was attempted, what was accomplished, and what failed is useful and essential. Writing reflections in their journals about robotics projects helps students organize and focus their thinking about how to solve problems and what steps to take next.

In her essay and letter to her school community titled "Robotics and the Language Arts Connection" (www.botball.org/_files/Paper_Reynolds_Language.pdf), technology specialist Linda Reynolds describes her take on robotics' connection to language arts: "To promote the robotics club at John Glenn, I always emphasize how much of the process involves writing—critical thinking and problem solving." In describing the robotics program at John Glenn Middle School of International Studies, she states "Robotics is a perfect example of the design cycle, something which is closely associated with the need for clear and accurate writing."

One perennial ELA activity that is clearly aligned with workforce success is procedural narrative. This is an item that appears in a significant percentage of high-stakes tests and other accountability measures. Procedural narrative, like a recipe or a "how to" set of instructions, requires students to write the process or procedure by which something is created or accomplished. Writing procedural narratives clearly and concisely is crucial to success in fields such as technology, science, engineering, medicine, manufacturing, and construction. In addition to being widely applicable to real-life needs, this skill embodies a good deal of what is essential to nonfiction writing: a clear sense of constituent parts, logical sequencing, a concise descriptive style, clarity, and a practical voice. The ability to explain to a reader how a team designs, builds, and tests a robot will serve students well in higher education and in their professional lives.

One of the most promising types of language arts activities to have evolved over the past two decades is storytelling. It focuses on oral skills and involves listening, reading, and writing. Interestingly, technology has given this body of practice a big boost. The emergence of digital (technology-supported) storytelling has facilitated the practice greatly. Communications technologies, such as web-based search engines, facilitate research for storytelling projects. Applications, such as Inspiration (graphic organizer software), PowerPoint (slide show presentation software), and word processors, support pre-writing activities by helping students organize their thinking and early drafts. Digital audio software enables easy recording of oral performances and allows these recordings to be integrated into presentation applications (PowerPoint or VoiceThread). Additionally, Web 2.0 online publishing and media-sharing resources (blogs, YouTube, and others) allow for the global dissemination of students' storytelling projects.

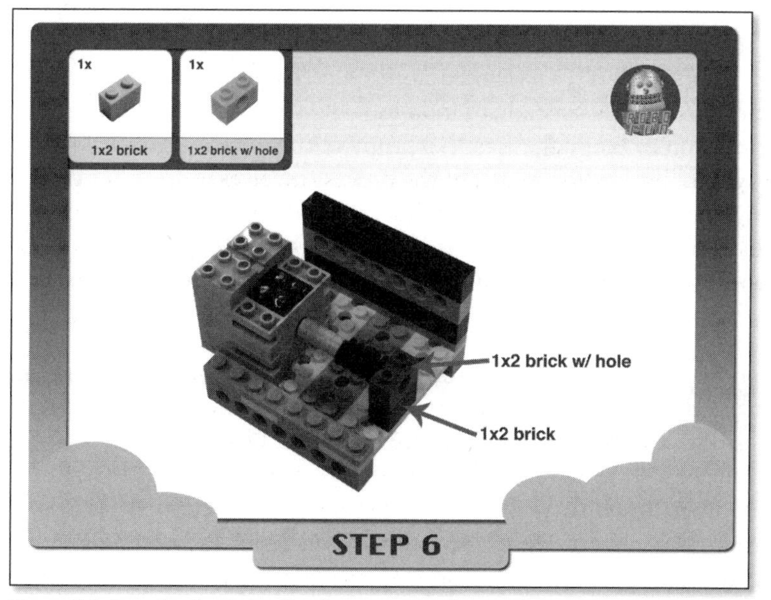

Figure 7.1 Robotics lends itself well to procedural narrative and storytelling.

Tapping robots to support storytelling activities makes good sense, as robots are usually designed as human stand-ins. They can take much of the performance anxiety out of storytelling and provide other positive advantages. For example, in their paper titled "Robotics in Child Storytelling," C. R. Ribeiro, M. F. M. Costa, and C. Pereira-Coutinho of the Instituto de Educação e Psicologia and Departamento de Física, Campus de Gualtar, Universidade do Minho, Braga, Portugal, describe a project:

> [It] involved the use of LEGO Mindstorms robotics kits by students with ages between 9 and 12 years old. It involved the construction and

> programming of robots, addressing the dramatization of the popular tales *Little Red Riding Hood* and *The Three Little Pigs* as the final goal. Also, other groups of students implemented fashion and dancing shows ... with robots.
>
> Each of the robots performed as one of the characters of the story/show, following a set of steps according to the script that was programmed by the students. The work involved also a previous step where the robots were built and "dressed" according to its role.
>
> The final results show the applicability of ER [educational robotics] to this level of learning/teaching. The students were able to successfully complete the project, achieving the proposed aims and also showing high levels of motivation and enthusiasm through its whole duration. The work culminated with public shows that served as a way to involve the community.

As LEGO Robotics becomes more well-known and highly regarded for integration into instructional programs, practices such as using robots to help students communicate verbally gain momentum. As an example, The LEGO Group has released the WeDo line of LEGO Robotics materials. The company specifically speaks about application for language arts instruction: "WeDo sample topics include Language and Literacy: narrative and journalistic writing, storytelling, interviewing and interpreting."

Now that we've seen several ways LEGO Robotics can be incorporated into the traditional curriculum, let's take a look at how it connects to learning standards.

CHAPTER 8

Robotics Connections to Learning Standards

Take a look at almost any set of educational standards, and there's a good chance you'll begin to see connections to robotics. And the longer you teach robotics, the more connections you'll find.

Robotics and Science Standards

When educators think about where in the curriculum robotics activities fit, science is often considered the most likely. Robotics, per se, is not usually part of the mandated science curriculum that has been created to address national and state learning standards. Robotics in the classroom is simply newer than the traditional bodies of practice those documents are based on. Nonetheless, as robotics expresses many dimensions and applications of science, it can be tapped for standards-based science instructional activities. An examination of science standards documents will show many possible points of connection for teachers willing to locate, adapt, or develop curriculum that explores the connections.

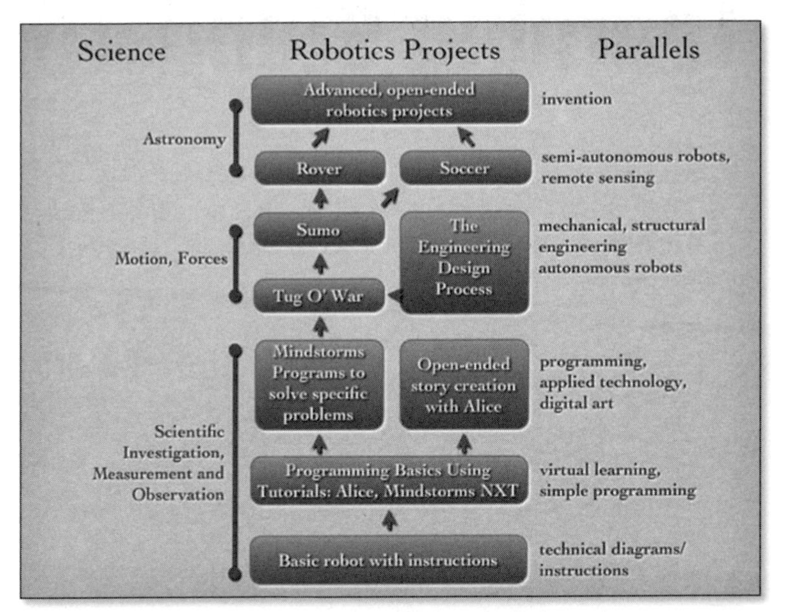

Figure 8.1 Parallels between science standards and robotics projects.
(Standards developed by Luke Laurie; http://homepage.mac.com/mrlaurie/roboscience.html)

Figure 8.1 is taken from the website of Luke Laurie, science teacher at El Camino Junior High School. In this chart, Laurie plots the standards addressed through the use of LEGO Robotics (NXT and Mindstorms) in robotics projects designed to cover the required California eighth grade science curriculum.

The U.S. National Science Education Standards (established by the National Committee on Science Education Standards and Assessment and the National Research Council) have eight categories of content standards for science learning. Content standards A–G are subsumed by the first standard: Unifying concepts and processes in science.

Unifying concepts and processes in science

A. Science as inquiry

B. **Physical science**

C. Life science

D. Earth and space science

E. **Science and technology**

F. **Science in personal and social perspectives**

G. History and nature of science

There is strong potential for connections between student robotics—which embraces the study of robotics materials, methods, and approaches and the use of robotics to achieve goals and to solve problems across many other disciplines and traditional parts of the curriculum—and all of the eight major categories presented in the standards document. However, the connections are most obvious in the uppermost category, unifying concepts and processes in science, and in standards B, E, and F:

- Science content standard B—Physical science
- Science content standard E—Science and technology
- Science content standard F—Science in personal and social perspectives

Furthermore, in the first content standard (unifying concepts and processes in science), clear connections exist between robotics activities and applications to the five conceptual and procedural schemes within this category:

Science content standard—
Unifying concepts and processes in science

- Systems, order, and organization
- Evidence, models, and explanation

- Change, constancy, and measurement
- Evolution and equilibrium
- Form and function

In the following tables, aspects that are clearly related to robotics appear in **boldface**. Table 8.1 illustrates the physical science standards (content standard B) that relate best to robotics by various grade levels.

Table 8.1 National Science Education Standards/Physical Science Standards

K–4

- **Properties of objects and materials**
- **Position and motion of objects**
- **Light, heat, electricity, and magnetism**

5–8

- **Properties and changes of properties in matter**
- **Motions and forces**
- **Transfer of energy**

9–12

- Structure of atoms
- Structure and properties of matter
- Chemical reactions
- **Motions and forces**
- **Conservation of energy and increase in disorder**
- **Interactions of energy and matter**

Source: www.nap.edu/openbook.php?record_id=4962&page=106 (Reprinted with permission from National Science Education Standards, 1996 by the National Academy of Sciences, Courtesy of the National Academies Press, Washington, DC)

Physical Science: New York State Science Standard for Physical Setting

A further example of clear connections between robotics activities and mandated learning standards are the "Key Ideas" found in the New York State Science Learning Standard for Physical Setting, which could easily be used to form the basis for science content-rich robotics activities. A good example is the following key idea for Physical Setting (PS) from Standard 4—Science.

Key Idea 5

Energy and matter interact through forces that result in changes in motion.

For the Elementary Level

- Describe the effects of common forces (pushes and pulls) on objects, such as those caused by gravity, magnetism, and mechanical forces
- Describe how forces can operate across distances

For the Intermediate Level

- Describe different patterns of motion of objects
- Observe, describe, and compare effects of forces (gravity, electric current, and magnetism) on the motion of objects

Source: From the New York State Education Department. Science Learning Standards for Physical Science Internet. Available from www.p12.nysed.gov/ciai/mst/sci/sciencestand/physical_setting.html; accessed 03/30/2011.

The science and technology category (content standard E; Table 8.2) presented in the National Science Education Standards (U.S.) provides clear connections to robotics activities. Technological design is an apt description of robotics and the ways robots are used to further scientific investigation. The robotic extraterrestrial rovers, for instance, often the basis for student robotics activities, illustrate a clear connection between science and technology.

Table 8.2 National Science Education Standards/ Science and Technology Standards

K–4

- **Abilities to distinguish between natural objects and objects made by humans**
- **Abilities of technological design**
- **Understanding about science and technology**

5–8, 9–12

- **Abilities of technological design**
- **Understanding about science and technology**

Source: www.nap.edu/openbook.php?record_id=4962&page=107 (Reprinted with permission from National Science Education Standards, 1996 by the National Academy of Sciences, Courtesy of the National Academies Press, Washington, DC)

The category of science in personal and social perspectives (content standard F; Table 8.3) presented in the National Science Education Standards (U.S.) provides many areas of connection with robotics. Robotics applications have proliferated in medicine and in meeting natural and manmade environmental challenges. These real-world examples can form the basis for student robotics activities.

Table 8.3 National Science Education Standards/
Science in Personal and Social Perspectives

K–4

- Personal health
- Characteristics and changes in populations
- Types of resources
- Changes in environments
- **Science and technology in local challenges**

5–8

- **Personal health**
- **Populations, resources, and environments**
- **Natural hazards**
- **Risks and benefits**
- **Science and technology in society**

9–12

- **Personal and community health**
- Population growth
- Natural resources
- **Environmental quality**
- **Natural and human-induced hazards**
- **Science and technology in local, national, and global challenges**

Source: www.nap.edu/openbook.php?record_id=4962&page=108 (Reprinted with permission from National Science Education Standards, 1996 by the National Academy of Sciences, Courtesy of the National Academies Press, Washington, DC)

Robotics and Math Standards

To carry through robotics activities, students visualize many aspects of math and use math in a real-world context. Above all, in robotics activities, students apply math they've already learned, reinforcing that learning, and learn new math content in "just in time" ways. They may take detours from working on a project to acquire some needed knowledge or understanding on the spot. The math learning and practice afforded by robotics is powerful in its authenticity, as students access and apply math learning from many different parts of the curriculum. While math curriculums are usually organized in sequences of concepts and skills unrelated to anything other than the focus required to teach them, robotics connects them naturally—as students solve problems and accomplish building and programming tasks. The following 10 standards are available from the National Council of Teachers of Mathematics (NCTM):

Content Standards

- Number and Operations
- Algebra
- Geometry
- Measurement
- Data Analysis and Probability

Process Standards

- Problem Solving
- Reasoning and Proof
- Communication
- Connections
- Representation

Mandated math curricula tend to be lengthy and complex, and many teachers opt to teach from texts and other materials designed to cover the requirements so that students score well on standardized tests. However, an examination of math standards and common elements in robotics-based activities shows many areas of connection.

The more salient connections between robotics and four of the NCTM content standards and the more obvious connections between robotics and four of the NCTM process standards are described below. These standards for teaching, reinforcing, or applying mathematics learning have been endorsed by the National Council of Teachers of Mathematics. The complete list is available from www.nctm.org.

NCTM Content Standards Addressed

Number and Operations

- Understand numbers, ways of representing numbers, relationships among numbers, and number systems
- Understand meanings of operations and how they relate to one another; compute fluently and make reasonable estimates

In building robots, students will rely on math to count, recording quantities of and computing specifications of parts and collections of parts. Similarly, in using programming software, students will need to quantify, compute, and modify commands numerically. Students also will need to estimate, calculate, compute, and predict the behaviors of robots in environments using numbers.

Geometry

- Analyze characteristics and properties of two- and three-dimensional geometric shapes and develop mathematical arguments about geometric relationships
- Specify locations and describe spatial relationships using coordinate geometry and other representational systems
- Use visualization, spatial reasoning, and geometric modeling to solve problems

Geometry is a defining characteristic of robot parts, aspects of robot programs, and the environments where robots are expected to perform tasks.

Measurement

- Understand measurable attributes of objects and the units, systems, and processes of measurement.
- Apply appropriate techniques, tools, and formulas to determine measurements.

Measurement figures prominently in building robots, programming them, and refining their behaviors within the environments established for them to perform their tasks.

Data Analysis and Probability

- Formulate questions that can be addressed with data and collect, organize, and display relevant data to answer them

Using sensors and onboard processors to collect data is the focus of data collection activities, an important subset of student robotics activities.

NCTM Process Standards Addressed

Problem Solving

- Build new mathematical knowledge through problem solving
- Solve problems that arise in mathematics and in other contexts
- Apply and adapt a variety of appropriate strategies to solve problems
- Monitor and reflect on the process of mathematical problem solving

Robotics projects necessitate problem solving at the individual and small group level.

Communication

- Communicate their mathematical thinking coherently and clearly to peers, teachers, and others

Robotics projects are most frequently assigned as collaborative group work. Within this context, group members must effectively communicate their mathematical thinking in order to complete challenges and solve problems successfully.

Connections

- Recognize and use connections among mathematical ideas
- Understand how mathematical ideas interconnect and build on one another to produce a coherent whole
- Recognize and apply mathematics in contexts outside mathematics

Though robotics is a branch of technology considered to be separate from or outside mathematics, it requires many mathematics applications. Students working on a robotics project will use numerous mathematical concepts. Math concepts that are taught and learned in isolation are connected to the projects and applied by students as they carry out robotics projects.

Representation

- Use representations to model and interpret physical, social, and mathematical phenomena

In several ways, a robot is a model that interprets and expresses physical and mathematical phenomena.

Robotics and National Educational Technology Standards (NETS)

Student robotics activities present learning opportunities that realize a great many of ISTE's National Educational Technology Standards (NETS) for Students (2007). The descriptions below give a good idea of how this plays out in actual classroom implementation:

NETS for Students are fulfilled by robotics.

1. Creativity and Innovation

Students demonstrate creative thinking, construct knowledge, and develop innovative products and processes using technology. Students:

a. apply existing knowledge to generate new ideas, products, or processes

b. create original works as a means of personal or group expression

c. use models and simulations to explore complex systems and issues

d. identify trends and forecast possibilities

In many student robotics projects, students are called on to create a robot that will solve a problem(s) and/or function in specific ways within an environment that has specific parameters or characteristics. The FIRST LEGO League challenges are good examples of this. Students draw on previous knowledge, researching the problem and various robotics solutions to it before creating their own robot. Robots are very much an expression of the knowledge, sensibilities, and values of the students who create them. In a real sense, the robot is a model or a simulated life form tasked to explore specific systems and issues. Planning, designing, and programming involve predicting outcomes and possibilities.

2. Communication and Collaboration

Students use digital media and environments to communicate and work collaboratively, including at a distance, to support individual learning and contribute to the learning of others. Students:

- a. interact, collaborate, and publish with peers, experts, or others employing a variety of digital environments and media
- b. communicate information and ideas effectively to multiple audiences using a variety of media and formats
- c. develop cultural understanding and global awareness by engaging with learners of other cultures
- d. contribute to project teams to produce original works or solve problems

Student robotics takes advantage of the proliferation of media-sharing resources to videotape and upload completed robots in action. Student roboticists, individuals, groups, and whole classes compose a worldwide, cross-cultural online community that shares many aspects of its learning and work through a body of blogs, bulletin boards, wikis, and other Web 2.0 publishing resources.

3. Research and Information Fluency

Students apply digital tools to gather, evaluate, and use information. Students:

- a. plan strategies to guide inquiry
- b. locate, organize, analyze, evaluate, synthesize, and ethically use information from a variety of sources and media
- c. evaluate and select information sources and digital tools based on the appropriateness to specific tasks
- d. Process data and report results

Following the engineering design process, students research and evaluate robots created by others before they begin to work on their own projects. Doing web-based research, they have access to a wide variety of documentation, analysis, and reflection on robots. Approaches, techniques, and tips are all available. To complete the cycle, students may follow suit and archive their own experiences, thereby contributing to a growing body of knowledge and practice shared by an audience ready to embrace their contributions.

4. Critical Thinking, Problem Solving, and Decision Making

Students use critical thinking skills to plan and conduct research, manage projects, solve problems, and make informed decisions using appropriate digital tools and resources. Students:

a. identify and define authentic problems and significant questions for investigation

b. plan and manage activities to develop a solution or complete a project

c. collect and analyze data to identify solutions and/or make informed decisions

d. use multiple processes and diverse perspectives to explore alternative solutions

Student robotics projects involve open-ended solutions to challenges or problems. Students are tasked with finding an approach to solve these with robotics materials provided. This involves researching robotics solutions developed by others, analyzing and evaluating methods and approaches, and selecting a strategy. Robotics solutions must function within clearly defined parameters. Failure of a robot to perform within these is an anticipated developmental stage of a solution that results in an informed quest for alternative approaches and solutions.

5. Digital Citizenship

Students understand human, cultural, and societal issues related to technology and practice legal and ethical behavior. Students:

a. advocate and practice safe, legal, and responsible use of information and technology

b. exhibit a positive attitude toward using technology that supports collaboration, learning, and productivity

c. demonstrate personal responsibility for lifelong learning

d. exhibit leadership for digital citizenship

Student robotics activities depend upon collaborative group work; team members conduct online research, cooperatively evaluating various websites' adherence to science and engineering protocols. Success involves learning to function within a group; offering and accepting feedback and assistance from team members, mentors, and others outside the group; and taking a leadership role when appropriate to carry the group's work forward.

6. Technology Operations and Concepts

Students demonstrate a sound understanding of technology concepts, systems, and operations. Students:

a. understand and use technology systems

b. select and use applications effectively and productively

c. troubleshoot systems and applications

d. transfer current knowledge to learning of new technologies

Student robotics activities involve many different aspects of digital technology: online research to support a project, digital record keeping of work in progress, and writing and publishing documentation of completed projects. The core of robotics involves the design of machines conceived to follow directions created on programming software, giving students a powerful understanding of the real-world presence of software-created content. Robots give quick and clear feedback about whether or not the use of software and mechanical devices is effective and productive. Troubleshooting is an integral part of the design, construction, and programming of robots. In robotics, new experiments continually build on the experience gained through previous successes.

Robotics and 21st Century Skills

The Partnership for 21st Century Skills has developed skills maps for core subjects such as English, geography, mathematics, science, and social studies. Most of the skill outcomes from the Partnership for 21st Century

Skills' 21st Century Skills Map (www.p21.org/documents/21st_century_skills_english_map.pdf) are shown in column two of Table 8.4. These categories correspond to the skill areas that comprise the outer arch of the 21st Century Skills Student Outcomes Rainbow (www.p21.org/index.php?option=com_content&task=view&id=254&Itemid=120), for instance, the 4Cs (Critical thinking, Communication, Collaboration, and Creativity) are part of the Learning and Innovative Skills portion of the rainbow's arch. The rainbow is the centerpiece of the Partnership's Mile Guide to 21st Century Skills (www.p21.org/documents/MILE_Guide_091101.pdf). The author created Table 8.4 for the purpose of visual simplification. Some of the most common, clear connections between student robotics and 21st Century Skills are indicated in this table.

Table 8.4 Pertinent Areas of the 21st Century Skills Map from the Partnership for 21st Century Skills (English)

21st Century Skills	Descriptions/Outcomes (K–12)	Robotics Connections
	Learning and Innovation Skills	
Creativity and Innovation	• Demonstrate originality and inventiveness in work • Develop, implement, and communicate new ideas to others effectively • Be open and responsive to new and diverse perspectives • Act on creative ideas to make a tangible and useful contribution to the domain in which the innovation occurs	Robotics activities, apart from those designed to teach students robotics basics by having them follow plans and blueprints created by others, are focused on creativity as students envision, build, program, test, and modify an original robot to solve a problem. Robotics is open-ended, with no prescribed approach required for development of a robot. Posting documentation of attempts and successes with robotics through the use of digital media and online media sharing are common practices of student robotics.
Critical Thinking and Problem Solving	• Exercise sound reasoning in understanding • Make complex choices and decisions • Identify and ask significant questions that clarify various points of view • Frame, analyze, and synthesize information in order to solve problems and answer questions	Robotics activities are classically presented as challenges or problems to solve. The evolution of a robot involves making choices and decisions on approaches to take to ensure functionality that will satisfy or solve the problem. Such choices and decisions are high stakes, as there is little flexibility in what works and what doesn't in the design and construction of a robot.

Table 8.4 *(Continued)*

21st Century Skills	Descriptions/Outcomes (K–12)	Robotics Connections
	Learning and Innovation Skills	
Communication	• Articulate thoughts clearly and effectively through speaking and writing (and visuals/multimedia)	Student robotics projects are often assigned and organized as small group collaborative learning. Consequently, communications among group members are frequent, essential elements of the work. Keeping records of progress and reflections on discoveries in writing and with illustrations (drawings, photography, and video) are typical, vital elements of such projects.
Collaboration	• Demonstrate the ability to work effectively with diverse teams • Exercise flexibility and willingness to be helpful in making necessary compromises to accomplish a common goal • Assume shared responsibility for collaborative work	Robotics activities are generally implemented as small group, collaborative instruction. To succeed at the robotics challenge, students must function as cooperating group members in a variety of ways.
	Information, Media, and Technology Skills	
Information Literacy	• Access information efficiently and effectively, evaluate information critically and competently and use information accurately and creatively for the issue or problem at hand • Possess (and share) a fundamental understanding of the ethical/legal issues surrounding the access and use of information	Robotics projects are presented as challenges or problems to be solved. Researching similar solutions that have been developed and reflected on previously is an important approach for students. Analyzing, evaluating, and applying such content to the problem at hand are key aspects of robotics-based learning.

21st Century Skills	Descriptions/Outcomes (K–12)	Robotics Connections
	Information, Media, and Technology Skills	
ICT Literacy	• Use digital technology, communication tools and/or networks appropriately to access, manage, integrate, evaluate, and create information in order to function in a knowledge economy • Use technology as a tool to research, organize, evaluate, and communicate information, and the possession of a fundamental understanding of the ethical/legal issues surrounding the access and use of information	Research on robotics solutions to problems that were developed by others, as well as the problems themselves, is a basic element of student robotics projects. Sharing ideas and issues with a community of peers working on similar projects is a prominent feature of the field of student robotics. Both involve sophistication in the use of web-based research and authoring and publishing resources.
	Life and Career Skills	
Flexibility and Adaptability	• Adapt to varied roles and responsibilities • Work effectively in a climate of ambiguity and changing priorities	Robotics activities are often presented as open-ended challenges or problems to solve. Experimentation, following constructs like the engineering design process, is an underlying assumption and organizing principle of instruction. There is no assured, prescribed solution to achieve. Rather, successful responses in the form of finished robots are responses to shifting conditions and requirements.
Productivity and Accountability	• Set and meet high standards and goals for delivering quality work on time • Demonstrate diligence and a positive work ethic (e.g., being punctual and reliable)	Robotics activities involve the evolution of multisession projects marked by clearly defined deliverables that often involve completion benchmarks and due dates.
Leadership and Responsibility	• Leverage strengths of others to accomplish a common goal • Demonstrate integrity and ethical behavior • Act responsibly with the interests of the larger community in mind	Collaborative group work is at the core of robotics activities and offers opportunities to learn and practice leadership, as do robotics competitions for teams.

Source for first two columns: www.p21.org/documents/21st_century_skills_english_map.pdf

Robotics and English Language Arts Standards

While robotics may not immediately call to mind learning in the area of English language arts, on consideration and reflection, numerous connections emerge. Robotics activities are commonly organized as collaborative group learning. Furthermore, the finished robotics projects are involved in students' presentation of a product and performance for an audience. These long-term projects evolve over many work sessions and require much reflection and improvement as they evolve. Consequently, keeping records for many purposes is essential. All of these dimensions require the use of language; as a result, robotics projects offer opportunities to learn and apply language arts skills.

Because robotics fits well with cross-disciplinary teaching and can be applied for many purposes within disciplines, connections to virtually any learning activity can be made.

In 1996 the National Council of Teachers of English (NCTE) and the International Reading Association (IRA) jointly published Standards for the English Language Arts (U.S.). The 12 standards cover the following skills:

1. Reading for perspective
2. Understanding the human experience
3. Evaluation strategies
4. Communication skills
5. Communication strategies
6. Applying knowledge
7. Evaluating data
8. Developing research skills
9. Multicultural understanding
10. Applying non-English perspectives
11. Participating in society
12. Applying language skills

Some of the closest connections between robotics and the NCTE/IRA standards are listed below. Seven of the 12 standards have been selected. The most relevant text is **boldfaced**. The full standards are available from NCTE/IRA (www.ncte.org/library/NCTEFiles/Resources/Books/Sample/StandardsDoc.pdf).

Standard 1: Reading for Perspective

> **Students read a wide range of print and non-print texts** to build an understanding of texts, of themselves, and of the cultures of the United States and the world; **to acquire new information; to respond to the needs and demands of society and the workplace; and for personal fulfillment.** Among these texts are fiction and nonfiction, classic and contemporary works.

Reading and interpreting technical directions and descriptions in the form of text and illustrations is a key area of activity in student robotics projects.

Standard 3: Evaluation Strategies

> **Students apply a wide range of strategies to comprehend, interpret, evaluate, and appreciate texts. They draw on their prior experience, their interactions with other readers and writers, their knowledge of word meaning and of other texts, their word identification strategies, and their understanding of textual features.**

Robot blueprints and other technical texts used in student robotics activities require effort and focus. They also provide motivation and built-in feedback about success in following them. Because robotics activities are collaborative, discussing the meaning of texts, collaboratively interpreting them, and reflecting and commenting on them with peers are common aspects of the student robotics experience.

Standard 4: Communication Skills

> **Students adjust their use of spoken, written, and visual language (e.g., conventions, style, vocabulary) to communicate effectively with a variety of audiences and for different purposes.**

Within the course of completing a robotics project, students must communicate with peer learners, teachers and mentors, and audiences who will observe the performance of their completed robot. This stream of ongoing, focused communication includes oral language and written records as notes, plans, and reports.

Standard 5: Evaluating Data

> **Students employ a wide range of strategies as they write and use different writing process elements appropriately to communicate with different audiences for a variety of purposes.**

Common writing elements of student robotics projects include journaling to record progress, problems, and solutions; reflections on discoveries and the process of developing a robot; documenting finished projects or project elements in text (and other media) reports; and uploading documentation of the final robot performance to media-sharing web-based resources.

Standard 7: Evaluating Data

> **Students conduct research on issues and interests by generating ideas and questions, and by posing problems.** They gather, evaluate, and synthesize data from a variety of sources (e.g., print and non-print texts, artifacts, people) to communicate their discoveries in ways that suit their purpose and audience.

Student research of background information on the problem for which they are developing a robot, as well as other approaches and solutions to robots previously produced for the same or similar purposes is a common, preparatory exercise for student robotics activities.

Standard 8: Developing Research Skills

> **Students use a variety of technological and information resources (e.g., libraries, databases, computer networks, video) to gather and synthesize information and to create and communicate knowledge.**

Students frequently research or gather information used to develop their robotics solution through web library research, use of student robotics community bulletin boards, and online media-sharing sites. Analysis, planning, and the exchange of ideas based on information gathered is frequently processed by collaborative groups through the use of blogs, wikis, and shared document resources, like Google docs.

Standard 12: Applying Language Skills

> **Students use spoken, written, and visual language to accomplish their own purposes (e.g., for learning, enjoyment, persuasion, and the exchange of information).**

Student robotics is a language-rich field of study. Writing, speaking, and listening, as well as the use of digital media (photography, video, audio, and others) are all commonly employed to facilitate robot design, building, and programming. Students employ these language dimensions for their own success or as part of collaborative work.

Source: Standards for the English Language Arts, by the International Reading Association and the National Council of Teachers of English, © 1996 by the International Reading Association and the National Council of Teachers of English. Reprinted with Permission. www.ncte.org/standards

Standards Are Invaluable Tools

Often teachers identify content and themes to implement with students that they think are important or interesting. Knowing that a strong connection can be drawn to standards helps verify that these are indeed worth the students' effort and valuable class time. This is particularly important when a teacher is contemplating introducing new material into the instructional program. Similarly, in writing plans or assessing what's been presented to students with a supervisor, standards are common points of understanding, a sharp lens through which the value of activities may be agreed on.

Standards also represent a tool to help plot the overall course of study and its many constituent activities; the total program in which students will be engaged over the course of a school year. It may be advantageous to deviate from standard curriculum because certain alternative activities are particularly worthwhile or desirable. However, when that is the case, educators must verify that a year's course of study is complete, providing all the learning that states require of their schools. Standards documents make this possible. Importantly, not only do they help define what must be learned, they also delineate how well it must be learned.

As the world becomes more complex and more education becomes the goal for each student, tracking all of what's required of and all of what's provided to students becomes a complex affair. Understanding that some dimensions of learning–like the application of technology, for instance–really must be accomplished through varieties of curriculum integration and cross-disciplinary learning, we can see that standards become increasingly valuable as tools by which it all can be plotted.

While standards aren't a curriculum, they are a compass by which a creative, responsive, and conscientious teacher can verify that the curriculum, whatever the sources from which it is assembled, is the correct one; one that will bring students to the learning and knowledge that is required in their grade level; one that will achieve this through activities that satisfy the needs of the learners.

In all these senses, standards are invaluable tools guiding educators to work beyond the traditional, but do so with the certainty that they are on very firm ground–assured that their students are getting what they need while the instructional program is kept fresh and relevant. This is an ongoing process, a moving target, and a variety of professionalism we should all embrace further as we strive to keep teaching vital.

CHAPTER 9

Robotics Events and Competitions

Many teachers who attend a robotics competition for the first time report how impressed they are by how similar in format and in spirit the competitions are to traditional school sporting events. Seen in this light, we can understand how robotics events fit in with long-standing traditional approaches to extracurricular activities, long acknowledged as offering true educational value to students who participate at any level. Values such as character building and social development, important for the formation of solid citizens, are frequently mentioned as key aspects of these activities. The beauty of robotics events is that they are also spoken of in terms of science, technology, engineering, and math instruction, the components of STEM learning. Fun, exhilarating robotics events foster learning through an alternative approach. Robotics clubs and competitions offer social development, character building, and STEM education—all in one! What could be better?

Schools may create their own robotics events or, as is often the case, schools may join national organizations that promote events and initiatives and offer deep support, relieving schools of much of the work. Of these organizations, the largest and most popular is FIRST, which runs the annual FIRST LEGO League series of events, as well as the Junior FIRST LEGO League events.

Figure 9.1 Excitement and crowds at a student robotics competition.

What Is FIRST LEGO League?

FIRST LEGO League, also referred to by its acronym FLL, is an international educational initiative for students ages 9–14. FIRST stands for "For Inspiration and Recognition of Science and Technology." A newer initiative, Junior FIRST LEGO League, has been organized for younger children ages 6–9.

Creating FIRST LEGO League robots requires only the standard LEGO materials found in the Mindstorms kits. The FLL program is principally a competition based on a challenge, a formalized problem to be solved by the application of robot design and programming. A fresh FLL Challenge is created each year, an event that is highly anticipated by FLL teams and enthusiasts around the world. The challenges present problems that relate to real-world situations, often items that are in the news or public awareness. In addition to the creation of the robot, there is a research component of participation. FLL teams compete first in local tournaments as they work their way toward the top level, a final competition held in a single location. While the format is one of friendly competition, the intention and effect is largely of "coopertition" or cooperating to share experiences and knowledge gained through the mutual experience of working on robots.

FIRST LEGO League

For
Inspiration and
Recognition of
Science and
Technology

The official website of FLL (www.firstlegoleague.org) describes its program as follows:

> FIRST LEGO League (FLL) is a global program created to get children excited about science and technology. A hands-on program for ages 9 to 16 (9 to 14 in the U.S. and Canada), FLL uses Challenges based on real world scientific problems to engage children in research, problem solving, and engineering. The cornerstone of the program is its Core Values, which emphasize friendly sportsmanship, learning, and community involvement.
>
> Each yearly Challenge has two parts, the Project and the Robot Game. Working in teams of three to ten children and guided by at least one adult coach, teams have 8 weeks to:
>
> - Build an autonomous robot to carry out pre-designed missions in 2 minutes and 30 seconds
> - Analyze, research, and invent a solution to a real world problem
>
> The culmination of all that hard work for many teams is the participation in an FLL event—much like a high energy sporting event. Referees monitor and score the Robot Game. Judges review team presentations. An FLL event is a pumped-up environment with music and excitement that celebrates the work the children have done throughout the season.

As an example, the 2009 Challenge was titled "Smart Move" and offered deep involvement in the design process of transforming transportation to develop better ways to move people and goods. The details of the challenge are available from the FLL website (http://usfirst.org/roboticsprograms/fll/smartmove1.aspx).

The FLL website also provides a history of all the challenges, going back to the beginning in 1998 with the challenge "Race against Time"; robots raced through mazes for the best time. No further details about the pilot year's challenge are available on the web page as of this writing. However, some of the full challenge documents can be found on other unofficial sites.

> **TIP**
>
> **Robotics Team Practice**
>
> www.youtube.com/watch?v=ZQFjrddSf5g
>
> This YouTube video of a medium-sized robotics team at practice gives good insights into many aspects of what goes on with a team and what to expect if you start one.

FLL presents new challenges on its website for all to see. While the challenges provide guidance for teams that intend to participate directly, they also offer value for groups and classes that simply need a good set of problems to sink their intellectual teeth into. Teachers will find much in them worthy of adoption and adaptation. Above all, they can be models for challenges teachers create to fit the needs of their classes and students. Teachers who don't have sufficient experience, assistance, funds, materials, or time to coach a team that will directly participate in the official FLL events may borrow from the challenges. As they gradually bring their school's program up to speed in the use of LEGO Robotics, these teachers and their students will eventually be ready for FLL participation.

What Is Junior FIRST LEGO League?

FIRST LEGO League, the global student robotics competition and education program, serves students aged 9–14 (outside the U.S. and Canada, 9–16). But what about younger kids? Can they get in on the learning and fun? Yes! Junior FIRST LEGO League (Jr.FLL), the newest member of the FIRST family of programs, is geared for children as young as 6. FIRST LEGO League (U.S.) started Junior FLL in 2004. It started with several hundred teams, and interest has grown steadily with roughly 2,000 Jr.FLL teams registered for the 2010 competitions in the United States and Canada.

The Experience of Keith Wynne

Junior FIRST LEGO League Is Big Learning

Keith Wynne, an elementary school teacher in Brooklyn is the New York City area planning committee chairman of Jr.FLL. An elementary grades science specialist, Wynne grew up in Westchester, New York, immersed in science and engineering. His father, an IBM research physicist, afforded him a front-row observation post on these exciting fields. This lifelong passion combined with a desire to work with kids resulted in his career choice.

"Our job is to prepare our students to be technologically literate world citizens," Wynne asserts. Trained in early childhood education, he believes the "principle behind good science teaching is to honor and foster inquiry-based learning. Children need to learn by doing. They need to interact with the world and explore." Junior FIRST LEGO League provides opportunities for children to become inquiry-based learners.

Wynne's path to heading up Jr.FLL efforts in New York City, its largest area of activity, was an interesting and circuitous one. After graduating with a bachelor of science degree in early childhood development and education from the University of Delaware, he taught English in Japan for two years. After that he put in stints as a fifth grade teacher in the Bronx, a universal pre-K teacher in a Harlem charter school, and taught first and third grades along the way. His experiences in Japan led him to pursue a master's degree in international educational development from Columbia University's Teachers College. Currently in his sixth year of teaching science, he is the science specialist at PS 58 in Brooklyn's Cobble Hill neighborhood, working with students in kindergarten through fifth grade. Among his activities there, he coaches two Junior FIRST LEGO League teams.

Chairing the Jr.FLL Planning Committee is an outgrowth of his coaching a Jr.FLL team at PS 58. A few years back, he made Jr.FLL the yearlong focus for the science activities he presented to the school's second graders. He involved three classes in the effort, spending one period a week making Power Puzzle, the year's FLL challenge, the class's science enrichment theme.

The Experience of Keith Wynne *(Continued)*

What's the Difference between What FLL Kids and Their Younger Jr.FLL Counterparts Do?

"The K-3 set work on the same theme or challenge, but Jr.FLL does not require any computer-based programming for their projects. Jr.FLL participants are asked to prepare a model or a device, but it doesn't have to be a full-blown robot, an autonomous device that follows a program. The point of the Jr.FLL program is to introduce younger students to the principles of FIRST and FLL. Like the older kids, they enter their projects in an event, one that's graded by judges who use a similar rubric. But this is not a competition; it's an exhibition.

"Jr.FLL teams may use LEGO Robotics, though if they wish, they can use the RCX or NXT or the new WeDo materials, but it is not a requirement. This program for younger students shadows the regular FLL program, and the youngest participants are even included in the massive New York City FLL competitive finals event, currently held at the city's Javits Center. There were 17 Jr.FLL teams involved there this year. These Jr.FLL participants have their own exhibition within the day's proceedings and receive their own awards at the end of the day ceremony. The youngest participants bring their awards back to their home schools, committed to a lifelong journey following their interest in robotics. They are ready to participate in the regular FLL program and then the FIRST Robotics program, as they work their way through middle and high school."

At What Age Could Kids Start Making and Learning from Making Robots?

"As early as possible! Eight-year-olds certainly can handle designing, building, and programming robots with the NXT materials, and with the new WeDo sets, they can begin even younger. It really depends on the support they get from adults. They do need to be taught programming and get suggestions from adults, but they learn a good deal on their own, too." In explaining robots and programming to his students, Wynne likes to tell them, "Robots don't know if you are a boy or a girl, don't know the color of your skin or the language you speak at home. They only know what you tell them to do and whether the program you gave them works!

"As a science teacher and having grown up around research and meeting and observing famous scientists with my dad, I can tell you that the teamwork and the problem solving that the children do in FLL is an exact replica of real-world engineering work. It's exactly the same as what professionals experience in NASA or any other top-level project. There's no difference in the experience the children have. They argue their ideas; they figure out what works, what doesn't, and how to make it all work out in the end. They do real research and programming and share in success together. It's great!"

FIRST LEGO League Specifics

FLL Challenges

At the core of the educational value of FLL activities are the challenges, a blend of engineering expertise and educational insights. These challenges require students to draw on science learning and research and on engineering skills and technology to produce a functioning, competitive robotics solution to a problem. FLL challenges also offer fun, excitement, and opportunities to gain confidence and to learn how to work well with others in a scenario that in many ways resembles the world of work more than that of school.

FLL Teams

The heart of participation in the FLL challenge is the team. Teams can be formed by any group of students under the guidance of an adult coach. Teams do not necessarily have to be school groups, although many teams originate in schools, extending or taking on new work and relationships between students and teachers. The FLL website states:

> A FIRST LEGO League (FLL) team has up to ten children ages 9 to 16 (9 to 14 in U.S. and Canada) and at least one adult coach. In addition, most teams have one or more technical, scientific or engineering mentors. Teams solve the annual Challenge with guidance from their coaches and mentors.
>
> Team registration varies by country; teams can only register in areas with an existing FLL Operational Partner. Please contact the Operational Partner in your country or region for details on how to establish and register a team.

FLL Core Values

No discussion of FLL would be complete without emphasizing its core values, something FLL puts front and center. FLL's educational goals go far beyond teaching about robotics:

> The FLL Core Values are the cornerstones of the FLL program. They are among the fundamental elements that distinguish FLL from other programs of its kind. By embracing the Core Values, participants learn that friendly competition and mutual gain are not separate goals, and that helping one another is the foundation of teamwork.
>
> - We are a team.
> - We do the work to find solutions with guidance from our coaches and mentors.
> - We honor the spirit of friendly competition.
> - What we discover is more important than what we win.
> - We share our experiences with others.
> - We display Gracious Professionalism in everything we do.
> - We have fun.

TIP

A list of operational partners is available at www.firstlegoleague.org/where-is-fll/globalcontacts.aspx?id=56.

FLL Models an Extended, Technology-Supported Community

FLL maintains a series of forums online through its website. Operating in a bulletin board style, the forums are a resource for learning and sharing between participants and enthusiasts. The forums model well how individuals separated by great distances can work together by applying simple communications technology. Participation in the forums addresses technology standards that involve global citizenship. Links for FLL and Junior FIRST LEGO League forums can be found at http://forums.usfirst.org/forumdisplay.php?f=50.

Other Events and Programs

While FIRST LEGO League may be the most popular of the organized initiatives involving student robotics, it is far from the only offering. Robots Net's Listing of robotics competitions (http://robots.net/rcfaq.html#LNK015) shows many dozens of different offerings around the world. While many are intended for students younger than those who participate in FLL or involve more sophisticated robotics equipment than LEGO Robotics, opportunities for our target groups of students abound.

Teachers or schools that cannot participate in FLL may organize their own events. Many schools and youth organizations do this. A great deal of information is available on how to plan your own challenges. I organized Bots in the Bronx for two consecutive years in affiliation with Fordham University's Regional Educational Technology Center. It filled a need for an accessible event for what was, in 2005 and 2006, an emerging school robotics community in the Bronx and served several hundred youngsters each year. As the community grew, Bots in the Bronx was subsumed by the NYC FLL organization. Similarly, schools may opt to create specific events to satisfy their own needs.

Western Kansas LEGO Robotics Competition

Some of the programs created to satisfy more local needs include the Western Kansas LEGO Robotics Competition, produced by Fort Hayes State University (www.fhsu.edu/smei/Lego-Robotics; see the link for "brochure"):

> This year there will be a total of 5 different Robotics events (registrants may participate in as many events as they want to):
>
> **There & Back**
>
> This event is a line-following race. The goal is to follow a black track (0.75″ wide black electrical tape placed on a white board) as rapidly as possible. Robots must leave the start area, traverse the line course, turn around at the halfway mark, and follow the line back to finish at the start area. Robots must follow the line; lost/wandering robots will be disqualified.

Maze Solver

The goal of this event is to traverse a maze (with wooden walls) as quickly as possible. The overall size of the maze will fit within a 4′ x 4′ area. The event will be timed; each robot will be given a total of 3 minutes to solve the maze. The team which completes the maze in the least amount of time will win.

Speed Limit

This event requires that the robots race—while obeying a speed limit. There will be lines on the race track. Students will be given the target speed limit at the start of the competition in terms of # of lines / # of seconds (the maximum speed the robots will be required to achieve will be less than 0.2 m/s). Students will NOT be allowed to measure the length of the track or the distance between lines! ...

Search & Destroy

The NXT 2.0 kit is required for this event (the ball launcher attachment is necessary). The goal is to shoot at the enemy team's robot and score (7 balls can be loaded into the launcher at startup). The robots will be placed in an arena formed by black tape on a white board. ... Elimination rounds will be held till the winner is determined. Each round will be allowed to go for 2 minutes. The team with the most hits (in the shortest amount of time) will win the round.

Mystery Event

The details of this event will only be disclosed at the competition.

Sonoma County Robotics Challenge

Another example of a home-brewed robotics program and event is the 2010 Sonoma County Robotics Challenge, promoted by the Sonoma County Office of Education (www.scoe.org/pub/htdocs/robotics-challenge2010.html). This is another event with a focus less ambitious than that of FLL that offers students different activities.

Robofest NYC and RoboChallenge

Robofest NYC (http://visionedinc.org/robofest) was a remarkable event produced by Vision Education & Media in New York City (VEMNY) in 2008. The event satisfied a specific set of needs for the local educational robotics community. While New York has very heavy participation in FLL activities, many felt the need for alternative activities and challenges and an opportunity for youngsters to participate in a less competitive environment. Robofest NYC, a celebration of student robotics, offered an exhibition of student robots and a "dance with the robots" activity, among others. The day offered student robotics activities for the several hundred people in April, after the FLL competition cycle had concluded.

Figure 9.2 Mark Gura interviews young LEGO roboticists at the Robofest NYC event.

RoboChallenge is an event specifically directed at promoting "engineering for K–12 students on the Central California Coast," directed by Luke Laurie. Its website (http://homepage.mac.com/mrlaurie/robo/robochallenge.html) gives the following description:

> **What is RoboChallenge?**
>
> RoboChallenge is a program designed to reach students from underserved communities surrounding The University of California at Santa Barbara with the highly motivating and richly educational

field of robotics. Students in RoboChallenge build LEGO robots for a variety of challenges, such as Sumo, Tug O' War, and Line Following.

Why RoboChallenge?

RoboChallenge was created to encourage students in underserved communities in the Santa Barbara area to pursue careers in Math, Science, and Engineering. There are other robotics programs out there, but we felt that we needed to develop a program that was extremely cost efficient, using LEGO Mindstorms materials. The program was modeled after the concept of the LEGO robotics classes offered at UCSB for graduate and undergraduate engineering students.

Programs such as FIRST can provide amazing experiences for those involved, but are cost prohibitive and offer robotics opportunities to only a handful of students at a school site. We wanted schools to be able to build multiple robots, be able to work in groups of three or four students maximum, and enable as many students to be involved as possible. The schools we targeted were schools that lack many of the financial resources available in wealthier communities.

An effective engineering outreach program needs to do more than work with students who are already college bound. Highly ambitious and talented students do need encouragement, but an effective outreach program brings in students who might not have any STEM motivation. In designing RoboChallenge, we emphasized the fun of engineering design and programming and the inclusion of all ages and ability levels across a demographic region traditionally underserved by higher education.

To get as many students involved across a broad geographic region, we developed a model that uses the skills of ambitious teachers, provides them with sufficient low cost LEGO robotics materials, and allows them to involve as many students as they want. Some schools have had as many as 50 students in a year. On average, approximately 200 students have participated annually from 10 schools, building as many as 50 robots.

International Programs

Besides FLL, several other LEGO Robotics-based programs and events are international in scope. While not quite as well-known as FIRST LEGO League, they are popular, worthwhile events. The Botball Educational Robotics Program engages middle and high school aged students in a team-oriented robotics competition based on national science education standards. By designing, building, programming, and documenting robots, students use science, engineering, technology, math, and writing skills in a hands-on project that reinforces their learning (www.botball.org/about). Additionally, RoboCup is a very popular international program (www.robocup.org/about-robocup) that uses robot soccer as the focus of learning and activities. Of particular interest for students through age 19 is RoboCup Junior, which is more closely aligned with the use of off-the-shelf LEGO Robotics materials.

CHAPTER 10

Interviews with LEGO Robotics Experts

LEGO Robotics is an area of instruction guaranteed to take teachers into new territory. While adopting it is something almost all teachers can aspire to, it is complex. Adopters will have to understand and embrace new materials, new approaches to instruction, and new ways of interacting with students, as well as different ways of organizing and managing their classrooms.

While LEGO Robotics has been growing in popularity since the early 1990s, for most of that time it was something of a curiosity, a bit of futuristic education squeezed into school organizations as an add-on, something that few within the schools fully understood or appreciated.

Consequently, most schools have, at best, one or two teachers on staff who can offer advice and insights to newcomers. Often, districts can offer very little in terms of professional development, mentoring, or solid advice. Still, advice from teachers who have made LEGO Robotics work in their classrooms is one of the best touchstones for those undertaking the task on their own.

To address this need, 11 LEGO Robotics experts were interviewed.

Interview	Interviewee
A	**Dwayne Abuel** Technology Coordinator, Highlands Intermediate School, Pearl City, Hawaii
B	**Maxwell (Max) Shlansky** High School Student/Assistant Robotics Teacher, New York City
C	**Ian Chow Miller** Teacher, Frontier Junior High School, Graham, Washington
D	**Evan Weinberg** High School Science Educator, New York City Public Schools
E	**Phil Firsenbaum** Educational Consultant/Student Robotics Specialist, New York City Area
F	**Corbett Beder** Student Robotics Specialist/Staff Developer, New York City Area
G	**Laura Allen** CEO/President, Vision Education & Media, New York City (VEMNY)
H	**Luke Laurie** Middle School Science Teacher, El Camino Junior High School, Santa Maria, California; Director, RoboChallenge
I	**Mike Koumoullos** Teacher, Aviation High School, New York City
J	**Chris Dudin** Robotics Teacher, New York City
K	**Mark Sharfshteyn** Chairperson, New York City FIRST LEGO League Planning Committee

All these experts have used LEGO Robotics for many years. Most of these experts have been classroom teachers; others have worked with students in after-school or club activities. In the aggregate, these interviews represent many years of hard-won experience in preparing teachers to make LEGO Robotics a successful part of their teaching. As you work your way through the different types of materials in this book, it will be highly useful to embrace the advice of these experts as part of the understanding you take away.

The experts interviewed in this chapter range from teachers with extensive personal experience teaching with LEGO Robotics or coaching FIRST LEGO League (FLL) teams, to teachers who have provided mentoring and professional development to many others. Some are LEGO Robotics professional development specialists, spending all or the majority of their time at this. A number of the experts have experience in all of these areas. One, who is still a student, learned LEGO Robotics in a school program years ago, has remained a learner and enthusiast ever since, and teaches younger students in an after-school program.

INTERVIEW A

Dwayne Abuel

Technology Coordinator, Highlands Intermediate School, Pearl City, Hawaii

Dwayne Abuel has been with the Pearl City Department of Education for more than 10 years. He holds a degree and license in secondary music education for Grades K–12. Abuel is the author and webmaster of a site that focuses on the LEGO Robotics NXT system (https://sites.google.com/site/roboticsengineerhawaii).

Mark Gura: Can you explain a little of your own background—what in your personal development led you to become a student robotics advocate and expert?

Dwayne Abuel: As a kid I especially loved playing with building blocks, Lincoln Logs, and LEGO. I remember tinkering with all kinds of electronics. Most intriguing to me were the mechanics of things. Playing with my friend's Pong game on his little TV was the start of me playing with technology. My interest with robots started with the show "Kikaida" [Japanese superhero] in the early 1970s.

I studied at the University of Hawaii at Manoa. Writing symphonic music didn't look like a lucrative job, but I still wanted to do something in music. I decided that teaching music was something I would enjoy. Later I began using computers with sound in my band and music teaching.

A friend of mine allowed me to play with his old IBM 8086 computer, which was tethered to a robotic arm. This interested me. Eventually, after teaching for a while, I bought my first LEGO Mindstorms Robotic Invention System 1.0.

Eventually I got an opportunity to teach the Punahou Schools Robolab Summer course, which used the LEGO Mindstorms Robotic Invention System. Not too long after that, my principal offered me an opportunity to teach LEGO Robotics in a classroom setting.

After the first year of teaching the LEGO Robotics System, I began seeing basic math skills and concepts during building and programming. I could see that they were teachable moments. As I taught, it became more and more apparent that when I pointed out the math, the students could make sense of how the math applied to what they were doing. This led me to build a website of ideas about how to integrate LEGO Robotics—or any robotics—into teaching. Creating this helped me realize what skills are involved in doing LEGO Robotics. The site, a work still in progress, gives a picture of what integrated robotics learning would be like.

After meeting the president of isisHawaii, Lynn Fujioka, I partnered with isisHawaii [an organization that brings STEM resources to eSchools] to provide my robotics learning materials and teaching methods to train teams for FIRST LEGO League. This became the base training for Robofest.

My own teachers treated me like I was "dumb," and this motivated me to prove them wrong. Many felt I would not be one to go to college; one said I would end up working at McDonald's. To this day, this drives me to want to figure out how to bring about more teachable moments that foster learning through one of my interests, robotics. Much of my work in this area is on my "Robotics Engineer Hawaii" website.

Gura: What colleague-to-colleague advice on how to integrate LEGO Robotics into regularly scheduled academic classes can you share?

Abuel: First, robotics is a tool that engages students. Students want to play with this resource. It's a lot more interesting than paper and pencil. Second, LEGO Robotics is a low-cost resource that can help students realize important ideas, just the sort of classroom tool we need. Third, the LEGO Mindstorms robotics—NXT to be more specific—is technology that is being used in today's industry. The sensors, NXT brick [brain of the system], its coordinated use with computers, NXT-G programming software, and actuators [motors/servos] that come with the set have real-world ties. Industry uses the same kinds of technologies to achieve its own goals.

In my opinion, robotics can be tied to any academic subject just by using it as a tool. You will have to find a good purpose in teaching robotics in the first place, though. It would be rather irresponsible to have students do robotics per se and call it STEM education. Working with colleagues in different areas of expertise, I was able to put together a meaningful and purposeful robotics curriculum that gives students an opportunity not only to learn robotics, but to make real-world connections as well. The real learning happens when robotics is tied in to specific concepts of other subjects. As a robotics curriculum specialist, what I create for teachers I work with are teachable moments, points from which robotics and their subjects can be related and skills and concepts can be taught, making important connections.

Teachers should work at getting engineers, researchers, and similar professionals to come in and assist with lessons. These professionals will make the tie-in for you. This will make the math feel real and not just academic, this will give science another dimension, and pretty soon robotics will not feel like a toy; rather, it will feel like a real-world tool—as it should be.

Robotics, however, is a multi-discipline subject. This makes it difficult for educators and administrators alike to bring it into a classroom setting as a required course. Rather, robotics often becomes an elective or an after-school program. Amy Martinson, principal of Highlands Intermediate School, is an innovator. She had given me the chance, before I was hired for my current job, to teach robotics as an industrial arts course. It was taught as a regular subject at our school, and a great many students and parents wanted this course to continue. But the school needed my help in running and maintaining the technology instead, and so we now do robotics after school.

Last, be realistic about goals and expectations! Make sure you tackle objectives one by one. Don't overwhelm students with a task to build full-blown, autonomous, walking robots and expect this to be done in two class sessions. Know how long a task takes by doing it yourself first. It is often smart to "dumb down" the tasks and objectives one by one. Part of the learning that takes place involves understanding the functionality and limitations of sensors, the

NXT, the NXT-G [programming software], and actuators [motors]. Breaking things down to help students understand each thing one step at a time and giving them time to explore will make them that much better at it all. Time is needed. When you observe what is going on with each build that's happening in class, you will identify those "teachable moments," and you can then insert your little math and science lessons. On the other hand, if you rush through, it will be difficult for students to solidify their learning.

Gura: Can you comment on the way teachers use or might use LEGO Robotics in math instruction?

Abuel: From my personal experience, I offer the following observations: 1) Know your grade level, 2) know your math standards, 3) know your robotics set, 4) find all your teachable moments by making your own connections to standards, and 5) test it. Here is my caveat, though: teach in digestible chunks, use the multilevel classroom concept, and always ask this question to the students, "Are you sure?" This will make them wonder whether their solution is really correct or not. Have them test, test, and re-test their robots, and if everything is correctly in place, the math concepts will be drilled into them.

In robotics-based learning, as you would do with science projects, you present a problem to solve. You use robotics as a tool to foster understanding, to help students solidify learning in certain areas of math. I've had many conversations with math teachers and observed many test score results that demonstrated the students' lack of understanding in basic math fundamentals. Robotics can help students learn particular concepts because it offers a form of learning they can understand. Their regular math teacher would tie in the math concept with the robotics activity and through that "teachable moment" produce an "aha moment" for the student. I try to bring in online games that help make that connection for them, too. The idea is to make sure both sides, robotics and math—with a little side order of science, complement each other well.

A good example is measurement. There are so many opportunities for measurement learning. The NXT robotics set is easily measured in centimeters versus inches. Here we can really emphasize "cm" and do conversion to inches later. Some day these students may encounter "cm" measurement in the workplace. One activity that you can do is to premeasure out a course that you create. First, you'll have to know that if you use the regular NXT wheel, it has a diameter of 5.5 cm. If you multiply 5.5 cm by "pi" (3.14) you get 17.27 cm, which is the measurement of distance of one rotation of that wheel. If you measure out a straight-line course and measure it to be 35.54 cm, this is two rotations of the wheel. Create a 90-degree turn, which is about 270 degrees of a wheel's rotation on a pivot turn. Then you can add more from there on. The idea is that you teach the students how to figure this out and then they go to the mission board and plan their mission. They will start measuring immediately and programming more accurately. The nice part about the system is that it is not always accurate. This may be due to the physical imperfections of a mission board or condition of the battery power or junk on the robot's wheels that collected during a test. Generally though, the students troubleshoot it all, the robot will comply with what it was programmed to do, and the mission is successful.

Here's another example I've found using the NXT set that has to do with building with triangles. Students wouldn't ordinarily build a bunch of triangles and put them together to observe the stability of this approach. However, in the course of constructing robots, the instructor can point out how triangles can be used to build a sturdy structure, something student robot builders care about. Being that there are so many right angles, the Pythagorean theorem fits perfectly. Another math concept you can teach during this process is scale factor/transformation. There are opportunities to build large triangles and then smaller triangles, and scaling up or down for a particular build provides opportunities to practice and learn from the many calculations involved in this.

One more example involves studying sensors. Although this may be more science than math, it does require math skills. When a student studies trigonometry, at some point sine and cosine are introduced. The students then begin their journey in understanding more complex plotting, more complex linear connections, figuring out how triangles fit into the calculation, and eventually leading into waves and frequencies. A great YouTube video (http://youtube.com/watch?v=FUMpGuLIQ5M) demonstrates this.

So which robot sensors deal with waves and frequencies? The ultrasonic sensor or sonic sensor, sound sensor, light sensor, temperature sensor, magnetic sensor, just to name a few. Each sensor has its own specialty and its own way of approaching how it senses things in the environment that makes each unique from the other.

The bottom line is to make your connections and be sure you test your approach to see if the students are learning the math you are focusing on.

INTERVIEW B

Maxwell (Max) Shlansky

High School Student/Assistant Robotics Teacher, New York City

Max Shlansky was a student participant in Phil Firsenbaum's robotics class as an elementary school student. Now, continuing the cycle of learning and teaching, he assists Phil in teaching a very similar group in the same school. Max, a junior at the Bronx High School of Science, was 16 years old at the time of this interview.

Mark Gura: You are at Bronx High School of Science now, but what do you intend to study after you graduate and go to college?

Max Shlansky: I'm looking for an engineering focus in my choice of a college major.

Gura: As a much younger kid you were involved in an after-school robotics class. Did you get robotics experience any other way?

Shlansky: When I was in elementary school, fifth grade I think, robotics was actually part of the curriculum. My teacher taught it in class. After I got into LEGO Robotics this way, I took the after-school class with Phil Firsenbaum.

Gura: Were LEGOs part of your life as a little kid?

Shlansky: Yes, they definitely were. But I didn't get into LEGO Robotics until I got it in school, Phil's class in particular. But I have memories of being a little kid and going to store with my grandparents and finding the newest LEGO set to build. The interesting thing, though, is that before I was involved in Phil's class, the LEGOs I would use were all instructional. You might go to Toys "R" Us and buy a boxed set that would teach you how to make a spaceship or something like that by following step-by-step instructions. When I was introduced to LEGO Robotics, it was the next step, building without instructions. What could you do on your own? I had never really done that with LEGO before I came to the robotics materials.

Gura: But you actually got into robotics because of your fifth grade teacher? What was your impression when this showed up in class? Was this something you and the other kids were very much taken with? Was there a "coolness factor"?

Shlansky: There definitely was a coolness factor to it, especially because our teacher entered our class into the FIRST LEGO League competition. And even though teams are much smaller than a full class of students, our teacher got the entire class involved. There wasn't just a select small group of students within the class included. Not everyone was involved with the robotics part of it; there was a T-shirt committee and a cheerleading group, for instance, but everyone did something. I was one of five or six students involved in the group that actually designed, built, and programmed the robot.

The whole idea that the class was doing half a year's work building up to the huge FLL competition contributed to our interest in robotics.

Gura: So how is it that you were in the group that did the robotics? Was it OK with the other kids that not all were hands-on with the robots?

Shlansky: My classmates were definitely OK with playing other roles. There wasn't a class-wide interest in doing the robots instead of other things. As I remember it, the kids chose what roles they would play. We had a voting system to choose. How did I get to be in the robotics group? I think the teacher had observed my interest in robotics before we did the FLL stuff, and so it was clear that this was something I would want to do, and I was chosen.

Gura: So how did your class FLL team do?

Shlansky: Actually, of 200 schools participating, we were one of just six elementary schools. The rest were all middle schools and high schools. We did very well; we came in seventh place, and were given a team spirit award.

Gura: And what about the after-school class?

Shlansky: Phil was teaching an after-school robotics class at the same school, and I joined it.

Gura: And after elementary school, did you say goodbye to LEGO Robotics when you went on to middle school?

Shlansky: No, I definitely did not leave robotics behind. I never continued it at school past fifth grade other than the teaching I'm helping with now. But in the fifth or sixth grade, I asked my grandparents for a LEGO Mindstorms kit for Christmas.

Gura: Was there robotics at your new middle school? Were there other kids you met there that you worked on robotics with?

Shlansky: There was no robotics at my middle school. I didn't share any robotics with friends there. I continued pursuing robotics on my own at home.

Gura: Some educators seem to think that LEGO Robotics is educational. Do you agree?

Shlansky: I agree 150 percent. I would say, honestly, if there was one thing I would even remotely remember learning in the fifth grade, it was things I learned with LEGO Robotics—things like how gears work and how they affect each other. LEGO Robotics sparks a different type of educational process in the learner's mind. It's more of a creative thinking. In dealing with LEGO Robotics, you have to think outside of the box. You face a problem, and you are forced to work your way around it. I don't think that's something commonly taught in schools.

Gura: But do you feel you picked up some traditional things like math skills?

Shlansky: Yes, to some extent. In school nowadays I can always relate things back to LEGO Robotics. My science fair project in seventh grade, for instance, was about how gears affect riding a bike. For this, I constructed something out of LEGO Robotics to show how the gears affected the speed and power and the relationship between the two in a motor and its output of energy. It really relates back to that kind of creative thought process that I think you should be exposed to at a young age.

Gura: Has your involvement with LEGO Robotics influenced you in your desire to study computer science and engineering?

Shlansky: Yes, I don't know much about advanced engineering. LEGO is a simplified form of what engineering might be. But my overall experience has sparked my interest, and through it I learned to enjoy that type of experience—having a problem you are faced with and you have to figure out how to work around it and build something for it. I would definitely like to learn more about engineering because of my experience with LEGO Robotics.

Gura: What more do kids learn from LEGO Robotics-based learning? Do they learn things like self-discipline, responsibility, working with others, conflict resolution in group work, reflective learning?

Shlansky: I'd say it definitely helps kids learn those types of things. I have distinct memories of working with other people in my class back in fifth grade on our design for the final robot to use in the competition. We were constantly collaborating on our ideas. If someone had an idea, an addition to the robot, nobody would ridicule him. We'd definitely take it into consideration. It was definitely not "an every man for himself"-type situation. We didn't have six different people building robots. We definitely had just one robot that all six worked on. In that regard, it definitely teaches group work and how to get along with others.

Gura: So now you're a robotics teacher. How does that feel?

Shlansky: I've had a passion for working with kids. I enjoy it.

Gura: How would you describe what you do with the kids?

Shlansky: It's really not formal demonstrations. If anything, I try bringing myself to their level and just working along with them. I'll pick one student for one class and spend half the class helping him build his robot. I won't build it for him. I will just simply help by giving little hints on how to make things better and work with him. And I'll spend the second half of the class helping someone else. Once in a while, a student will come to me with a problem, not knowing how gears work or something like that, and then I'll teach that. There's only been a few instances where I've held a class discussion and given an overall tutorial. But generally my goal is simply to work with the students and help them.

Gura: And how does that work out?

Shlansky: It works out great! I would definitely say yes, I see a dramatic increase in their knowledge and understanding of robotics from the start of the class to the end of the class. At the start, they're trying to make something like a simple robotic backscratcher. They would just stick a couple of pieces onto a motor to create something and would be amazed by that. But by the end of the class, they build a more sophisticated item like a car with gears and a chain-driven belt. Even I'm impressed with it.

Gura: What do you think kids who are just starting with this don't understand about working and learning with LEGO Robotics?

Shlansky: When they're first starting, they don't really know what to expect. Maybe they've worked with simple LEGOs before, and now just slapping on a couple of motors—they think that's amazing enough. They don't really understand the full potential of what they can accomplish with the materials. Maybe it would help if you gave them obstacles. Maybe you'd say, "I'm going to give you a steep incline, and I want you to build a robot that can climb up a 45-degree angle." I remember doing that in fifth grade with Phil. He'd give us an angle and tell us to build a robot that could climb it. We'd have to figure out: Should we use wheels? Should we use treads? How should we configure the gears? Lately, it's more of a free for all, just build what you want kind of thing. But the obstacles or challenges and deadlines give students incentives. I also remember my other teacher would give us races. You'd build a robot and race it down the hallway, and the winners got M&Ms as prizes.

Gura: So what do kids who are new to working with LEGO robotics not understand about how to learn in the robotics class?

Shlansky: Well, that relates back to the creative thought process that can develop out of working with LEGO Robotics. You can always follow instructions and make simple robots out of the book. But once you ditch the book, it's all up to you. I'm not sure if that can be taught, or perhaps it just develops over a period of time.

Gura: What can you do when you see that a kid gets stuck on a problem?

Shlansky: In that situation there definitely should be a teacher who can help out, or perhaps group collaboration can help. I've noticed that really striving to be the best helps. It's a personal incentive for me. When we were doing those M&M races in the fifth grade, I was always trying to make my robot the fastest, and, yes, I ran into some problems and worked around them. In our class I'm there to help, and I've given the students permission to call on me for help.

Gura: Anything else you'd like teachers to know about LEGO Robotics?

Shlansky: I think, 100 percent, this should be taught in schools. Like I said, it's really the only thing I remember from fifth grade. If there's one skill I took from that entire year, it's robotics. It hasn't given me just a sense of what engineering is, but also it's shown me a sense of creativity, something that's hard to teach. This is definitely one way of getting it done. Students that go into it definitely need someone there to help them out. If you are just starting to teach it, I would definitely start by building from instruction books so the students can see what the robots can do and then slowly take away the instruction books and give them challenges. The students really need a goal. You can't just say "build whatever!" because students often won't know where to start, what they want to do. If a student comes to me with a robot and says, "Hey Max, can you program this for me?" I'll say, "First of all, I'm not going to program this for you; you're going to program it, but I can help you." And then I ask, "Well, what do you want your robot to do?" That's what the programming is all about; you have to figure out what you want your robot to do. But 90 percent of the time they don't know. Knowing what you want the robot to do should definitely be established from the very beginning of the project. This is not a *working out of a book* thing. You should encourage them to think about what they want, and that will push them past a creative block.

"...if there was one thing I would even remotely remember learning in the fifth grade, it was things I learned with LEGO Robotics—things like how gears work and how they affect each other."

INTERVIEW C

Ian Chow Miller

Teacher, Frontier Junior High School, Graham, Washington

Ian Chow Miller has taught for 12 years and is now teaching for the second year at his current school, Frontier Junior High School in Washington. He was a teacher in New York City for eight years and before that taught on Long Island for three years. He has been teaching regularly scheduled robotics classes for five years. In graduate school he took a course in educational technology and was introduced to the constructivist work of Seymour Papert, who developed some of the software that runs LEGO Robotics. Ian was very impressed with robotics' ability to support student creativity and learning by discovery.

Mark Gura: How did you come to LEGO robotics?

Ian Chow Miller: I was requested to become involved with it by my principal at I.S. X318 [a New York City middle school specializing in math, science, and technology through arts], Maria Lopez, who allowed me to attend Vision

Education's LEGO Robotics retreat for teachers in the Poconos. I was just blown away by what I saw and learned. When I went back to the graduate education class I was taking, I couldn't stop talking about LEGO Robotics to my peers. I was hooked. My principal asked me to start an FLL (FIRST LEGO League) Club after school, and I was happy to do it.

Gura: What would you recommend to teachers who are considering using LEGO Robotics, those who are requested to teach it or are interested in doing it on their own?

Miller: I think that if you sit down for half an hour with some kids and some LEGO robotics materials, you'd be amazed at what they can do. They take to it intuitively. I think that's because most software and hardware is designed for a younger age group who've grown up with technology.

I'll give them the bare minimum of building instructions, and they'll produce a moving car and program it with the onboard programming that the NXT has; they'd do it without any directions. And if they can do that without any directions, you can imagine what they'll do with just a little bit of help and a little bit of background. Your job as a teacher is to assume the facilitator's role that educators talk about, but that often is not seen in teaching traditional subjects. Kids might say to me, "How do I do this or that?" and I often say, "You look like you're stuck there. So, why don't you go to this website (or that book), and you may find some diagrams or some help." I'll come back 5 minutes later and ask them if I can help, and they tell me, "Oh, no, we already figured it out!"

Students rarely do something because they personally want to produce the product or result. They want to get a good grade, or they want to please their parents. Nobody really wants to do a complete body of arithmetic practice examples for its own sake. But with robotics, students really want to see their end products. So, any teacher who has trepidation about doing this with students needs to know that you just need to spend a little bit of time with them—you don't have to teach them directly. If you do that, they're just copying what you show them. What you really want them to learn, more than anything, is that they can work out their own ideas through trial and error. You build something and try it out. If it doesn't work, you go back, you change the build, and you change the programming, over and over. This is so hard to do through the traditional process of gradually improving rough drafts in science or social studies, but in robotics they're eager to do it!

A great example of this level of engagement is my first period class. We teach a tutorial class after first period in my school. My first period class, which I have for tutorial afterward, simply keeps working on its robots after first period. The students just don't want to stop. In Danish "LEGO" means *play well*; they're learning, they're working, but they look at it as playing with the robots. They want to make the robots go faster, climb up a hill better, or shoot something farther; there's great learning embedded in all that play.

To me, it's almost impossible not to learn from LEGO. For instance, if I give it to my 2½-year-old son, and two pieces don't click one way, they'll click another way. He'll learn this without being told that that's the way the two pieces go together. It becomes a very natural learning process. You don't have to teach them what to do; you just have to facilitate their learning.

Gura: So you are not advising that teachers necessarily need to learn the materials well or become experts?

Miller: As a teacher, you've got to let go and not be afraid to learn with the kids. Be a learning facilitator. That's really what you need to be. Show them how to get the information. I have all sorts of information on my class website and links to all sorts of things. The information is out there—we just have to let the kids know how to find it. This stuff is very intuitive and requires very little in the way of teacher training.

Gura: So if you were a teacher who finds out before summer vacation that she's expected to do LEGO Robotics with students in the fall, the typical response of locking oneself away with a kit and not surfacing until you "get it down" is really unnecessary?

Miller: Actually, I'd say it's the wrong approach. You don't need to hide yourself away. You'd want to play with the kit for sure but with another person. You don't want to do it in isolation. I would follow the build instructions that come with the kits or that are to be found online and then start modifying and changing things and learning what things do. There's more information online or in books than you could possibly learn in 10 summers. I would just start building and modifying as I went along; for example, "How could I make this different, better, make it look more like a racing car than a truck?

Also—I like the LEGO robotics WeDo kits. I was introduced to this at the Tufts Engineering conference last spring. I got a chance to play with it. I found it to be really neat. I think kids will like it. They've put fail-safes into it. You can't undo the program—it automatically saves—there are no batteries to worry about.

This year as a final project, I've given an advanced group an assignment to build something and make up a story about it. Next I'm going to get some younger, elementary grade kids in and have my students tell the story to them. Then my students will ask the younger kids to think of ways to change the story. We'll see if my students can build or change the robots to fit the way the audience changes the story. I think one of the big ideas from the LEGO group in putting this kit out was to have it be part of the storytelling process, not just robotics, but have it be integrated into the language arts program.

Gura: In your program you teach robotics classes, and you also have an after-school robotics FLL team. Can you comment on the learning value in the regularly scheduled robotics class?

Miller: I shy away from calling my robotics class a math or science class. What I used to do with gear ratios the first couple of years I taught LEGO Robotics was create charts and give them these ratios, maybe give a little demonstration first. I'd really have the kids understand gear ratios as a mathematical concept and how to calculate and reduce fractions so you could find your gear ratio, and so on.

But this year I reversed it and challenged the students to design the slowest vehicle, the fastest vehicle, or the vehicle that goes up the steepest incline. But they have to use two or more meshed gears of different sizes to create the speed or the power. I let them experiment with that, and then at the end, I have them calculate the gear ratios once they had their cars performing the way they wanted. There was no need to have them do all the calculations and prototype first. With LEGO Robotics, you don't have to do that. I just wanted them to dive into it, get the experience, and ultimately learn the concepts. What they are really doing is learning the design process, which, of course, involves math and science, and I don't want to bog them down with an incredible amount of numerical calculation for a process that is so organic. I think I am improving their math aptitude and skills. It's my intuition that if I make it too computational or too much of a hard science class, I'll lose some of the kids. This is not an elective. Every eighth grader in the school has to take robotics with me.

Interestingly, it is the Career and Technical Education (CTE) department of Washington state and our district that provided guidance, push, and funds to get this program going in our school. In fact, I went along with one of my students and the state director of CTE down to testify in front of the state Congress about funding student robotics statewide. We realize that if you want to catch more than just the hardcore "geek" group, you need to catch the students earlier. If you wait until the ninth grade, you'll only have 10 percent of the kids who will even be willing to really give it a try. But if you give some basic engineering to younger kids, you can capture their attention and keep them engaged in this type of learning.

INTERVIEW D

Evan Weinberg

High School Science Educator, New York City Public Schools

Evan Weinberg is now in his seventh year of teaching. He teaches biology classes at KIPP (Knowledge Is Power Program) New York City College Prep High School. Previously an advanced placement (AP) physics and mathematics teacher, he is a FIRST Tech Challenge coach at KIPP, something he describes as "teaching an energetic group of ninth graders how to put together gears and motors to create robots."

Mark Gura: When did you first encounter LEGO Robotics?

Evan Weinberg: As a university student at Tufts. I took a required course that included use of the RCX to do some basic programming; I used Robolab, and I learned to build robots. But really I wasn't very good at it. I put stuff together, and it would fall apart. I got through all the challenges, but I wouldn't say my designs were very good. I had to learn, and I had to get some experience building. The only way to do that is to build stuff that doesn't stay together and then see how to keep it from falling apart. Based on my excitement at the possibilities of that course, I got a Mindstorms kit and used it through college. But I really didn't get all that much experience with it until I arrived at the high school, and I saw that the students were involved in a FIRST team. It was with the LEGO robotics RCX that I actually learned programming. I was recruited to help out with the FLL beginner workshops for other teachers. Robotics is so much fun. I love seeing the kids go through the frustration of getting something wrong and then working to figure out how to get it right.

I taught the kids what I knew in mechanics, and we learned to build, looked at some designs that had already been done and how to put gears together. What I was especially proud of was that I had students who were using the materials to solve problems that I had been given in my second year of engineering studies at Tufts. I figured if I can get them to be motivated enough to do that, this had to be something very special. I became at that point a LEGO Robotics believer for life.

Really the inspiration for all of it was my work with Chris Rogers at Tufts University. He's largely responsible for getting many of us to see the value of LEGO Robotics as a great tool for teaching engineering and problem-solving skills. So a lot of what I did was modeled off his work and philosophy and what he tried to instill in us. This included some healthy competition, challenges, points for innovation, and points for exciting and catastrophic failures of design. Building on this and starting the engineering class got me to really think about how I would teach kids to build with LEGO elements and experiment. I found that it really reinforced my educational philosophy deep down—which is that you need some basic information, some basic skills to get your foot in the door and start building robots.

Gura: So, playing and tinkering is good, but not exclusively. The idea is to first get some basic concepts down and then the playing and tinkering is more valuable?

Weinberg: Exactly. It's unlikely that a student is going to discover why a differential gear is so amazing. But if you see it and you learn to build it, then you might get ideas later on about how to implement it in your design. There is a lot of brilliance that's already been established in mechanical design. There's a lot out there, and we don't have to reinvent the wheel. There are certain things that we can start with and then using that tool set, be creative and come up with designs that use those tools.

Gura: You are a lifelong science student, you're adept at mathematics, and you're comfortable teaching high school-level physics. However, there are probably many teachers who may have fewer capabilities than you have but still want to bring LEGO Robotics into the lives of the students at their schools. How hard is it? Does one have to have the same experience and abilities as you to become a robotics-using teacher?

Weinberg: No, of course not. But my feeling is that in order to be able to help your kids "play," you have to play, too. You need to go home, open up a new robotics kit, find all the pieces, and see how they go together—not because you need to be one step ahead of the students but because you need to experience the same sorts of frustration that they are going to have. As an adult, you can step back and think about what is going on in front of you. It's important that you do your own homework. As soon as you get one of these kits, try as best you can to put stuff together and see what happens. It was like that for me, too. I didn't start out as a good LEGO Robotics builder. I started by getting things wrong, over and over and over again, until I found a design that worked. And maybe it only worked a little, but that was a start, and then I learned how to build on top of that and, over time, figured out how to do things effectively.

My understanding is that people don't start at the same spot, but everyone can work and play and practice and get to a level where one can achieve things. At first as a newbie, you're looking at this gigantic box of parts and won't know what to do. You can't just hope you'll be struck by some bolt of inspiration that's going to turn you into a LEGO expert. You have to play; you have to have your own growth curve because ultimately the kids are going to do the same thing. You have to be the voice of organization, the voice of patience, and voice the message to the kids, "It's OK, you're going to get it wrong until you get it right!"

Gura: I keep hearing you use the word "play."

Weinberg: Yes, I mean experimenting and learning without with any specific goal in mind. That's the way play works. You need to figure out how things go together. Sometimes I "play," too; adults play! There's not necessarily any reason why a guy changes the carburetor in his car. He could pay someone else to do it, but he just wants to see what happens when he tries different things. It's the same with LEGO robotics.

Gura: So you have to make space in your mind for play as a way of knowing and learning and doing. That really is a shift. But you make it sound likes it's one that's doable for anyone.

Weinberg: Yes, absolutely, AND there's nothing wrong with trying to build something that someone else has designed. It wasn't until I saw someone using a certain piece in a particular way that I really understood this concept. I had no idea what the differential was until I saw someone use it, for instance. It's a combination of playing, experimenting until you hit a wall, and saying, "All right, let's try building something where I don't have to use my imagination and I can see what other people have done."

Gura: How about using LEGO Robotics not for an after-school club or team but in the context of teaching real curriculum?

> "... I had students who were using the materials to solve problems that I had been given in my second year of engineering studies at Tufts. I figured if I can get them to be motivated enough to do that, this had to be something very special."

Weinberg: It can be difficult to come up with a direct application. For instance, the teacher can say, "We've been graphing lines, and now you are going to build and program a robot to graph lines, a really good tool for application of the use of data." Students can use the robot to gather a body of data, how far the robot has traveled, for instance. Then, if they download that data into software that lets them see it as a table, all of a sudden data isn't just bunch of numbers that the teacher threw up on a chalkboard. There's something special about seeing real data being generated on the spot. Also, there's definitely a "wow factor" to bringing a robot into the classroom to capture the students' attention, especially for parts of the curriculum that are not exciting on their own, like exponent rules in algebraic expressions, for instance. Using robots can bring that to life.

Gura: What's the magic, what is it about a robot that galvanizes kids, engages them, creates the "ooh and ah" factors?

Weinberg: When you have a robot that drives to the edge of a table and then suddenly turns around to avoid falling, you're seeing that device interact with the real world the way you would. It's a very a cool realization, the autonomous aspect of it. The robot doesn't need anybody to control it, and it's the kids who design and program it. Kids love that!

INTERVIEW E

Phil Firsenbaum

Educational Consultant/Student Robotics Specialist, New York City Area

Since retiring from his career with the New York City Public Schools, Phil Firsenbaum has been an educational consultant, handling a variety of curriculum areas and specializing in student robotics. His experience with LEGO Robotics is a result of a very positive, career-changing experience he had attending Vision Education & Media's Stonington Student Robotics Retreat, where he was exposed to practical classroom applications of Seymour Papert's work with LEGO Robotics and the LOGO programming software he developed for it. He runs an after-school LEGO Robotics group at PS 87 in Manhattan.

Mark Gura: How would you recommend newbie teachers get themselves up to speed easily in using this resource, particularly teachers who are not tech or science geeks?

Phil Firsenbaum: Hands-on experience is absolutely necessary. Begin by acquiring some materials and investigating them. I would recommend, depending on the style of the person, getting a book, and there are a great many of them out there—this would be great for an overview. But other types of people might need some face-to-face mentoring. For many, a curriculum like the one developed at Carnegie Mellon would help greatly. Something like that, which gives a step-by-step approach and has some thoughts on classroom management, would probably help a great deal.

Gura: Is this something that pretty much anyone can learn to do?

Firsenbaum: Well, anyone who's motivated. Some people would pick it up faster than others, but pretty much, yes, anyone can learn to do this.

Gura: Do teachers need to know the workings of this resource, know it better than the kids, and be ahead of them?

Firsenbaum: For those who are real novices, I would recommend that they not let their egos be too involved with it, because the kids are going to learn it a lot faster. I think if one were to be successful, go with that reality. Learn from kids, because they pick up on it easily. They fly with it. I think of the teacher as the gatekeeper. The kids are ready for this stuff, and the teacher has to allow them the opportunity.

Gura: Why is that? The kids aren't smarter than the teachers or better educated than the teachers. So what is it they have or don't have? Is it that they're not inhibited? They're not worried?

Firsenbaum: Right! They don't have the fear. They're not worried that they're going to break things. They're eager to experiment. A lot of teachers and adults have to feel very secure. They need to know what's going to happen. Getting involved in something like robotics, you're not going to know what happens until you try it. When kids want to build something or design something, they're fine with just trying it out—do this or make a program. We don't know what it's going to do until we try it. Kids are totally comfortable working this way, and unfortunately, many adults aren't.

Gura: Any recommendations for activities for teachers who are just beginning to start running classes/groups?

Firsenbaum: Use building instructions that come with kits or that can be found on websites and books before allowing free-form designing and building.

Gura: OK, Let's say I am familiar with the materials. How do I run my class?

Firsenbaum: In an ideal situation, you'll have enough materials to break the class up into small, collaborative groups of three who will share the materials. If it's a science or math class, you might want to have some basic bots built—because that alone will take up a good deal of time. And then you need to present a challenge for the students to work on, and the students must be clear on what that challenge or task is. When they are not working in *hands-on* mode, you would work with the students in whole group instruction so they understand what to do, how to handle the materials, how to do the programming for instance, or whatever else they may be tasked with. Then they are given an opportunity to work in small groups, where much of the value is to be had. A good thing to do is to have an end-of-the-day's-work debriefing in which the students relate their experiences.

Journaling is a written variety of the verbal debrief. Have them keep a journal where they write their reflections, what their difficulties were, what they want to do next time.

Gura: How might the teacher and the students use entries on the difficulties they had?

Firsenbaum: Through sharing and reflecting, there is much to learn from one another's problems and mistakes.

Gura: Any classroom organization/management suggestions for newbies you'd like to share?

Firsenbaum: Sure:

- Get plenty of containers to store parts in as well as bots in progress.
- Encourage kids to return unused parts to their bins.
- Monitor groups to ensure that everyone is participating.
- Promote sharing at the end of each session.

Gura: What should they avoid? What sources of problems should they prepare for?

Firsenbaum: Clearly, you need to be somewhat confident and have some classroom management skills in order to succeed. Set parameters and set rules and try to figure out a little ahead of time what the students are going to encounter, so that you can predict problems.

And one of the must-do things is to try out the challenge and solutions to it with the robotics materials yourself. What you assign to the students you try on your own, make sure it's doable, where might it frustrate them, what to anticipate, and so on.

Gura: What about the logistics of robotics in the classroom?

Firsenbaum: You need to be mindful of the time factor. You have to manage all of the little parts that the students will use in building their bots. You need to have a set of eyes on the materials so that they don't get lost, damaged, stolen, or mixed up. And, of course, you can assign monitors to take on some of this responsibility. Robotics activities are the kind of thing that you would prefer to do during a double period.

I once observed a classroom setup for this that had a great system with bins that had pullout drawers. On the outside of the drawer there was an example of the type of part to be stored inside that was glued on to the outside. And so there was no confusion about where things were supposed to go.

Encourage kids and groups to return unused parts and to do so promptly. You don't want them hogging parts they aren't using because other groups may seriously need the ones not in use. They may grab parts during the session, but they should put them back so that others who need them can use them. If parts aren't available, the students will become frustrated. Another approach would simply be for the teacher to distribute the parts. Figure out what parts the students will need and distribute them so you are sure they can succeed.

Storing bots partially completed safely is important, so that students get them back the way they left off when the class ran out of work time. They are delicate and vulnerable before being finished.

Gura: How about managing participation of the students?

Firsenbaum: Yes, it's important to monitor the participation of all members of the groups. Some kids will be more assertive, some are willing to put in more effort, some less, some may prefer to hang back, but you want to let them know your expectation is that they all participate fully. Giving grades ensures a degree of participation and the log or the journal is an indicator of who's doing what.

Gura: Anything else you'd like to offer or suggest?

Firsenbaum: Yes, Concerning RCX vs. NXT:

- The RCX version of LEGO Robotics seems to be perceived [by kids] as friendlier to more open-ended building than the NXT.
- Which platform is best for open-ended building? The NXT is great if you are following some sort of prescribed building or model, but there are kids who really love to do free-form, experimental building. The NXT is less flexible and less adaptable for that purpose than the RCX version. One of the reasons is that there are a limited number of ways to attach important things like motors. There aren't so many ways to do it with the NXT. You are locked in to certain ways of using the material to a high degree. But there are so many ways to attach motors and wheels and all kinds of things with the RCX, and some kids find it more attractive as a result. In a way RCX is more "LEGO-like," something kids seem to really like.
- NXT's components seem prone to hardware failure, whereas RCX's seem to last forever.

And some things to be aware of about the programming aspect of LEGO Robotics: Some kids love to build, some to program, and some love to do both. Last semester, for instance, I found that roughly half the kids were into programming, but it's certainly never all of them. In an informal [e.g., after-school club] setting, some kids are very happy to never program their bots, while others embrace programming. Some kids love to build bots that aren't even programmable, and they use a simple, portable power source to run their RCX machines, for which they didn't even include a programmable brick in their design. Kids (especially those who aren't eager to program) love these battery packs, which are a useful addition to the classroom's equipment collection.

Gura: What about data collection?

Firsenbaum: Both the RCX and the NXT have data collection abilities. And kids at virtually all levels are supposed to learn how to collect and analyze data! I'm a firm believer in having kids design their own data collection projects. When it comes to analyzing such data, they can talk about the data from a personal perspective. The folks up at the MIT Media Lab would talk about a set of data as a story waiting to be told.

In the past, I did some wonderful data collection projects using LEGO Robotics. For instance, once I did a project with a class out at Orchard Beach in the Bronx. We took some RCX materials and used them to collect temperature data at various places along the beach. I had never realized personally how much difference there was between the area along the water and the rest of the beach. We were using temperature probes that were connected to the RCX brick, which is a microprocessor. In fact, you can make this part of a mobile bot that's moving about and taking and recording data sets.

You might create a little mobile bot, put a temperature or light probe on it, and then program the bot to visit each classroom on the floor to see the data it collects throughout the school.

Another idea I liked, again with the RCX and temperature probes, was to have the students measure their own body temperature to see how physical exercise affects the temperature outcome. The RCX was great for this because it has three motor ports and three sensor ports, so you can connect up to three different sensors to it.

INTERVIEW F

Corbett Beder

Student Robotics Specialist/Staff Developer, New York City Area

Over the past several years, Corbett Beder has been doing professional development workshops to train teachers with groups of students who will participate in FIRST LEGO League. He has also directly taught students in after-school robotics programs in the New York Tri-State Area.

Mark Gura: How did you get into LEGO Robotics?

Corbett Beder: I was exposed to it when I started working for Vision Education [& Media, New York City], a provider of professional development and direct services to students. I taught animation and computer design courses and was then exposed to and trained in robotics. I dove in to it. I got myself a kit quickly and read up on it and have been deeply involved in it for five or six years. Vision needed someone to be the content expert for their support of schools in FIRST LEGO League. My area of expertise was originally computer animation and then digital video. But finally, I settled on LEGO Robotics.

Gura: How many teachers have you trained or worked with in LEGO Robotics?

Beder: Around 300.

Gura: So you've shown teachers how to use the RCX and NXT materials and how to participate in FLL and to integrate LEGO Robotics into the classroom, as well?

Beder: Yes!

Gura: What's your advice about how to get started with LEGO Robotics to a teacher who is not necessarily a science teacher or an industrial arts teacher, maybe someone who's a social studies teacher? Let's say this teacher's school has already purchased the robotics kits, and the principal has strongly requested he begin a robotics program for the school sometime soon. Maybe this person is looking forward to taking this on as something new and interesting but doesn't know what to do to get started—doesn't know what he needs to know—or where to begin.

Beder: Well, if you are looking forward to it, enthused about the possibilities, that's half the battle. I've prepared a great many teachers for this, and I've had to work with some teachers who have been thrown into the responsibility of doing it and not enjoyed their initial experience. But I think once teachers start working with this, they pretty much become instant converts. Even if the class they have to run isn't running smoothly, the possibilities this technology presents are very apparent once one begins working with it. So, specific to the social studies aspect, I would point out that there are ways and resources that connect robotics to English and social studies content and standards. Robotics means many, many different things, and there isn't really a field or an industry that isn't connected in some way to this kind of thinking or these kinds of processes.

So, If I was talking to such a teacher, I would start talking about how robotics relates to the Industrial Revolution, how your students would be able to recreate factory systems with it and really understand how autonomous systems can work—and really to look beyond robots as some very technical "sciency" thing that looks like WALL-E or R2-D2, and to understand that they actually surround everyday life. Robotics is a good focus if one wants to understand economics, social movements, and everything up and down the line from advanced political theory to how a supermarket functions. The ability to sort of look beyond or inside the box at inputs and outputs and ways things are programs and ways data is collected is something that LEGO Robotics can really bring out.

Gura: So you would look for a curriculum connection as an entry point?

Beder: If the issue is that the teacher is coming to this and is not necessarily a science or math teacher, yes, I would try to get the person to find the curricular connection.

Gura: Many teachers who are contemplating bringing robotics into what they do with students are uneasy with the idea. What about the average teachers' mindsets are counterproductive to their comfort with robotics? What do they just not get? Even if they think "Ooh, that's cool. My kids will love it and I teach Social Studies and there's an obvious connection to the Industrial Revolution." What don't they get about the robotics that would make it easy for them to embrace it?

Beder: I think it's the shift into project-based learning that can be the biggest problem because the kids need to have the freedom to tinker, and they need to have a question posed to them that can have multiple solutions—and the teachers need to understand that there isn't just one right answer. For instance, I ran one workshop where there were a couple of teachers who were very, very resistant to the notion that if the prompt is "create a robot that can move forward 2 feet," there are genuinely different ways to do that. They kept reiterating, "Well, just tell me the correct answer. Don't ask me a rhetorical question; just tell me what is the right way to do this because I need to know what the one correct solution is." And LEGO Robotics really is a platform that doesn't have one correct solution. The correct solution is that the kids are playing and they're learning and they're innovating and finding different ways to solve the same problem.

A great activity I've run is to set up a prompt where, perhaps it's a scavenger hunt or an obstacle course, they have to design a robot that can get through that. And then I give them the exact same prompt but tell them to redesign the robot to solve the challenge in a different way. And I think this is very inherent in LEGO Robotics. A lot of teachers coming in from more traditional practices have a hard time with this—if you are teaching the multiplication tables, well, 12 times 12 only has one answer—but sometimes when you are working with robotics, you have to be prepared to accept that there are different answers and that kids will be allowed to have them. You create an environment in which kids are allowed to learn different things and to experiment in different ways, and at the end of the day, there will be various right answers to what you are working on. Robotics can present a very difficult sort of watershed moment for teachers, to accept that there isn't an answer key and there isn't one answer only; there are actually a variety of solutions that are acceptable.

Gura: What type of projects should teachers new to robotics begin with?

Beder: I think when you are brand new to robotics, your first project really has to be some kind of a vehicle. The way kids think of robots is that they move and move autonomously. There are hundreds of books out there and so many sources of blueprints. It depends on how much time you have with the students, but if you have something like a 10-week window and meet with the students one day a week for an hour and a half, for instance, you'll want to spend a couple of sessions on a vehicle project, building and programming—so it can move forward and backward, it can make some turns, and students learn how to incorporate the sensors that come with the kit. The next project you should do, and this is what I think is key, has to be a stationary robot—some kind of a factory, an elevator, an alarm system, a trampoline—it doesn't matter what the specific project is so long as they move out of a vehicular understanding of robots. You have to move from what the students think a robot is from their experience with science fiction into an understanding that has to do with real life.

And finally, students should also have the opportunity to design their own projects. That's where the cycle should take them. It gives them the full range of experience and lets them understand there are many different ways to use robotics and sensors.

Gura: An approach you've used well is to start with building robots from blueprints, and from there you move them into building their own constructions?

Beder: Another important element is for the teacher to introduce a theme for a final project. The kids start off with blueprints to get them ready. The second stationary project I assign without blueprints. The final project centers on a theme that supports and encourages kids to come up with their own designs. For instance, The Circus, like Calder's Circus sculptures or The Industrial Revolution are great. There's a book that recreates Da Vinci's experiments; but with LEGO Robotics that's excellent, particularly for more advanced builders. They can do this without the blueprints, either expanding on an existing design or creating their own designs.

My work often has me running after-school robotics groups, usually 12 weeks, one two-hour session per week. You do the vehicle first because that's what the kids are expecting. They are usually a little quicker to get these constructed. That's good because you don't want to wait too long before getting the kids in front of a computer to program the robot. And then we walk them through a series of programming challenges, like backwards and forwards, or have the robot travel in a perfect square. Or if they are a little advanced, this is a good point to have the robot follow a line or engage in "bumper bots" with touch sensors. The purpose of the stationary project, generally a short project, is that it gets the kids to see how robotics fits into their everyday lives—things like escalators or doors at a supermarket, things that have sensors to control their movements. And then in the final project, depending on the theme, the students will follow a worksheet to guide them through identifying a robot they'd like to build: how it ties into the theme, what kinds of parts they think they'd need, and sensors they think they're going to have to use. Then they build and program it. That usually takes from four to five sessions.

Gura: Where does the theme come from?

Beder: Generally, it's a combination of the instructor's interest and feedback from the kids. If they're really into video games, then you might want to use the NXT kits to design and build something like that. When we do the Calder's Circus theme, we sometimes show videos of Calder's constructions.

For first-time teachers who are looking for tips and support, I suggest that they use Google as their friend. There's a huge community of educators working with the NXT platform. The programs that really succeed often capitalize on this. Or even better, have the students research LEGO robot designs before beginning. The "NXT STEP—LEGO Mindstorms NXT Blog" (http://thenxtstep.blogspot.com) is really well-known, but there are many others to investigate. I think it can be very healthy for students to research this. If they want to do a robot that looks like a black widow spider, put "NXT" and "black widow spider" into Google, and they'll get different kinds of blueprints as well as photos and videos that explain designs, and they can modify or learn from these.

One of the dynamic things about FLL is that often there's a tremendous stress on innovative design. The kids are supposed to do their own work, but that can mean practically doing it in a vacuum. The kids are supposed to come up with a great robot without having any prior experience, and possibly their coach has no prior experience. That can be really daunting, but I think an approach to this is to have the students do online research; they can base their hypotheses about the type of design to develop on that research.

Gura: What about integrating LEGO Robotics into an existing course? Math, perhaps?

Beder: More than anything, that's an essential issue and the teachers I've seen try this were all hoping that a robotics activity would allow them to completely replace a book-driven module in a curriculum. They were hoping that the robotics might completely replace the lesson on fractions, for instance, and the kids would be able to walk away from that and receive a good score on a standardized test. That's not the case. Yes, the kids will be working with fractions, and if reflections are done really well, you'll be able to draw out what the kids have learned and provide ways for them to internalize and really use mathematics concepts that otherwise they would just have to memorize.

A good example is gearing ratios to increase speed. The circumference of a wheel for a vehicular robotics project can have a great influence of the speed of a robot. If you increase the circumference, the robot will be quicker because the motor does the same amount of work, but it physically travels further in the real world. Students can also do this on the computer and increase the speed through the programming. Those are both valid solutions if the prompt is to make a faster robot. What the students often find is one solution that they gravitate toward, but most likely if they do full projects, they'll be exposed to both. So, the questions are: How do you present this? Do you make sure that each student understands the totality of robotics? I've never heard of an approach to presenting robotics to students that accounts for every possible scenario and allows for each participant to get the same content knowledge. I think that's where a lot of the discomfort teachers have with robotics comes from. You really can't cover everything with robotics the way you would with books. You may not cover fractions or ratios as thoroughly with Class B as with Class A because Class B had a robotics module to replace some of the book learning, and their scores might not be as high as a result.

The Carnegie Mellon curriculum is really worth looking at in this respect, as it specifically tries to address this issue by walking the students through each step: "Take out a wheel, measure the wheel's radius, now determine the wheel's circumference—what is your hypothesis about how quickly the robot will travel from Point A to Point B?" It's great, but to a degree certain aspects depart from the project-based learning approach that robotics is noted for. I'd prefer it look more like "Here's a robotics kit; can you make a robot with it that can perform a search and rescue mission?" That's the prompt, and the students will arrive at the knowledge needed. They'll figure out that they need to increase the circumference of the wheel, for instance, and the value in the experience is that they have been given the opportunity through a real-world model.

INTERVIEW G

Laura Allen

CEO/President, Vision Education & Media, New York City (VEMNY)

Laura Allen heads up Vision Education & Media, a New York City–based service provider to educators and schools. Vision has provided training for teachers in LEGO Robotics for over a decade on a variety of bases, including FIRST LEGO League, special trainings arranged by school districts, and classes for teachers.

Gura: Teachers who have no science, engineering, or technical background are increasingly interested in making LEGO Robotics part of what they do with students. How do you get teachers up and running with robotics from nowhere?

Laura Allen: There are two approaches you can take. First of all, you need to make the assumption that they're intimidated by the equipment. I mean actually building robots with LEGO pieces, motors encased in the LEGO bricks, and the little computer, either the NXT or RCX brick. Eighty percent of the time this is the case. One approach is to jump right into programming, so that they don't even look at building at all. They just see how you can very simply take a motor connected to a brick, put an axle and a beam on it so it's like a little windmill, and how you can program something to happen. You sort of hop over the building part of it. So one approach is to get them good at that; get them to understand how to program robots, to add sensors, and so on.

Gura: That's all centered on the software.

Allen: Yes, that's centered on learning the capacity of it. And sometimes we give them some pre-built, simple bots so they can learn by programming those.

The other approach is to have them build a simple bot and then program it. And there are advantages and disadvantages to both approaches. Either way you go, you have to gauge your audience. For many people over 40, building with LEGO is unlike anything they've ever done, especially for women who have no experience they can draw on in building. In a way it's good—they get a blueprint they can follow step by step—it works well.

Gura: What are some of the simple bots that educators who want to teach themselves might use for this purpose?

Allen: A windmill, a paper cruncher [a little machine that will take a strip of paper and fold it into little pieces], simple projects like a lighthouse, things like that .

Gura: Are there places people could go to for instructions on how to do this?

Allen: You can find material online; Carnegie Mellon is one good source.

The NXT kit sold to schools comes with a pretty good tutorial on the basics of programming. The NXT itself, the robot's core/onboard computer, has a little LCD screen and three or four keys, so you can key in commands right on the robot, although it can be a little bit difficult to follow it this way.

Gura: Thinking about the LEGO Robotics equipment teachers will have to work with, schools now buy the NXT materials, but a great deal of legacy RCX generation materials are still in use or in storage in schools. Sometimes kids prefer to use the RCX over the newer NXT–why do you think that might be?

Allen: They find the RCX to be a lot less bulky. And the NXT is all about beam building, beams and connector pegs together ... because all the ways you connect to the NXT brick and the motors are through axles and connector pegs. The RCX, however, is more about building with LEGO blocks, and they like that because kids are familiar with LEGO blocks. They find the RCX stuff to be more warm and friendly. The NXT comes off as a little bit overly high tech to younger kids.

Gura: So, you show newbie teachers programming first, maybe a little bit of construction to support that, and then where do you take them?

Allen: I like to tell people about sturdy building because, first of all, it's very important to let people know that things fall apart very easily. You have to set your frustration threshold appropriately. So, for instance, I show them stuff like the difference between a gray and a black connector peg; one is tight fitting and one is loose fitting. We look at how many "plates" it takes to equal a brick–three on top of one another equal the same thickness as a brick. We learn why to use cross beams or diagonal supports–because the constructed robot is much, much stronger that way–and so on.

In the Inventions curriculum I taught to [New York City] Board of Education teachers, we had them make something without blueprints, which was an incredibly difficult challenge. Everyone thought we were crazy. The teachers were mad at us because we wouldn't give them blueprints. But the interesting thing is once we did it, they realized we were right because the blueprints can be very limiting. It's always tricky when you use blueprints to show teachers what LEGO Robotics is all about. The thing about LEGO is it doesn't have a soft, gentle learning slope. It's a pretty abrupt learning slope to do things elegantly in LEGO. It's hard ... and so, everything you are asking the teachers to do is hard for them. They're using materials they never used before, and most of them have never programmed before. For many teachers, it's just not an intuitive thing. It's kind of like going mountain climbing and tackling the Matterhorn first. That's how it feels to them. So once you give them the blueprints, they hold on to them like a lifeline. But when you actually show them some basic ways of putting things together without blueprints, it really opens things up.

The windmill tends to be a really good starter project because it doesn't have to look like a real windmill. You basically need to have a couple of beams, an axle, and a connector peg. You build a little tower, you stick an axle through the top of one of the beams, you add another beam that will rotate around, and then you can connect the axle to the motor. Very quickly you can put together a little windmill, and then you can control it with a touch sensor. You can program it so that if you touch one of the sensors, it goes forward, and if you touch the other, it goes backward. You can add a light to it. You can do a lot of the basics without doing a lot of the building.

One of the things to do is to give the teachers a choice: either build for five minutes and then program OR build for an hour and then program. You are leading people off the precipice of robotics. You have to get them engaged; often the teachers are dying to get started building, but programming can be a great place to start. So, which to learn first is a chicken and egg situation, building or programming?

Gura: What are some of the things that just don't click for people?

Allen: Following blueprints can be a very new experience for people. A blueprint involves taking something in two dimensions and expressing it in three dimensions. It does seem to go easier with younger teachers. Like kids, they are more likely to experiment and mess around.

Teachers should let kids mess around with the LEGOs first thing but set some parameters. So, if you are working with kids you might say, "You can make whatever you want, but I want you to include the following pieces: a motor has to connect to an axle, and you have to have a light in your creation." Then you get super buy-in from the kids because it's their creation into which they put the required pieces you assigned.

LEGO sells the material in kits with all of these different compartments to hold different pieces. The kits are wonderfully organized, and it takes a tremendous amount of time to keep them that way. In the U.S., where the average class time is about 45 minutes, this is a problem. Just forget about the organization of the kit, get rid of the compartment dividers, and dump the whole thing into the kit because the students will spend the last 10 minutes of the period straightening out the kits, putting everything back into the right compartments. This is hard for teachers to do because they like the order, but you'll lose a lot of time doing this. One way to do this is to have kids do certain jobs, like have the motor collectors do just that. You make sure you are collecting all of the expensive pieces, but then mix up all the other types of pieces. We have mixed bins, and we have electronic bins. This can all be intimidating, but you have to own the situation to get past this concern.

Gura: What would you say to a teacher who's going to teach herself LEGO Robotics?

Allen: You might want to find a couple of kids and tell them that they should learn it and teach it to you. Give them all the stuff and observe what they do with it. Also, NXT materials for getting started are good. There's a tutorial disc included, for instance.

Building, though, you learn a lot from watching the kids. It's very intimidating because you think, "I'm the teacher; I should know all this." But it's really that you are an adult, and you are coaching the students. Of course, you are going to prevent them from eating the LEGO pieces and from throwing them or themselves out the window. In other words, you manage the students and coach them. Typically, you'll get one 11-year-old who's just brilliant at this, and no matter how hard you might try, you're never going to catch up to this student. So you have to resign yourself, realizing that what you are doing essentially is giving the students brain candy. Let them go with it. Stand back and admire their learning. Don't feel like you have to know it all. And get yourself up to speed by partnering with another teacher—make a team of yourself, your peer learner, and two students each.

Gura: What other advice do you have?

> "So you have to resign yourself, realizing that what you are doing essentially is giving the students brain candy. Let them go with it. Stand back and admire their learning. Don't feel like you have to know it all."

Allen: School purchasing guidelines and salespeople always encourage you to buy everything all at once. But why not start with just one or two kits? Perhaps do it the June before the September that you actually begin with LEGO Robotics. You may not want the second kit in exactly the same configuration that the first one came in. There's some flexibility. Get some insights into what you really need and can use and only then talk to the sales department as an informed customer.

Another piece of advice is that you can always use lots and lots and lots and lots of the basic LEGO pieces. We have done LEGO drives to collect pieces from students' homes. So many homes have some of the basic pieces in their closets or attics. They are very happy to help out by donating them and getting them out of their spare spaces. With the NXT sets there are uses for the basic LEGO blocks and pieces, even though the electronic pieces aren't compatible from the RCX to the NXT sets.

INTERVIEW H

Luke Laurie

Middle School Science Teacher, El Camino Junior High School, Santa Maria, California; Director, RoboChallenge

Luke Laurie is a science teacher at El Camino Junior High School in Santa Maria, California. He teaches eighth grade robotics-based science classes, science classes for English language learners, and seventh grade science. He is the director of the RoboChallenge program and also works as a MESA (Mathematics, Engineering and Science Achievement) advisor. In 2000, he received the Venoco Crystal Apple Award and in 2005 the Amgen Award for Science Teaching Excellence. In 2006 Laurie became an Albert Einstein Distinguished Educator. In 2008, he was named Santa Barbara County Teacher of the Year.

Mark Gura: How did you become a science teacher?

Luke Laurie: I had a lifelong interest in playing LEGOs. In high school I moved away from this and was more interested in theater and band and things like that. I went to Cal Poly in San Luis Obispo, where my major was liberal studies with an emphasis in physical science. But I still had a knack for things physical and physical science related and had some background in technical things, like auto mechanics and building things. I started out as an elementary school teacher, a generalist, and later acquired the credential to teach any level of geosciences.

I also always had an interest in technology, creating websites and programming, that sort of thing. But I had never built a robot until I was given the LEGO Robotics materials for my class back in 2000. I didn't just approach the LEGO robotics as something I was going to give to my students to use. I took it to heart that I was going to try to master these things so that I would have more to teach and share with the kids. I bought some of my own kits, started learning the programming, and entered amateur robotics competitions. I learned what worked well and what the materials were well suited for and what they weren't well suited for. That led me to adapt the materials to activities that made sense for my students instead of trying to stretch the materials and students to meet some abstract concept.

Gura: What was your teaching like before you brought in robotics? What convinced you of the advantages of robotics for teaching students?

Laurie: I transitioned from using robotics as an extracurricular activity to a full-blown robotics science class in 2003. I was finding that I was working very hard to provide activities in technology, applied science, and mathematics through robotics in my work with MESA. I was doing a lot of extra work at lunchtime and after school, demanding a lot of extra time from my students, and I realized that so much of what I was doing was overlapping with the kinds of things I was doing with my eighth grade science class. Robotics is well suited to the curriculum for eighth grade science. I have a chart that shows this on my website.

I went to the principal of my school and told him that I was doing a great deal of robotics with the students after school and it really fit with what I was doing in eighth grade science. I proposed that we meld the robotics into the eighth grade science class and offer it as an option for students who wanted to do something that was above and beyond the standard course. I had to explain that I was still teaching these kids the science class and that the science instruction was actually enhanced. In addition, I was giving more students the opportunity to work on robotics than were able to do so strictly through the extracurricular robotics program.

The course I created is called Robotics Science. It's eighth grade science using robotics. Ours is a medium/large junior high school, about 650 students. There are multiple teachers giving the eighth grade science class. And we offer the robotics science course as an option. Students can take either regular eighth grade science or the eighth grade robotics science.

We have enough sections of this class so that we don't have to turn away any of the kids who want to take it. We have no requirements to be in the course other than intrinsic motivation. We have students who are ELLs [English language learners] and students who are special ed students, and certainly plenty of kids who do not have outstanding academic records. This makes for an interesting blend. The common thread is that all the kids who sign up for the class are interested in robotics and want to learn this way.

There have been some years when we had trouble recruiting girls but usually not. We average almost 50 percent girls and one year had more girls than boys. One thing that is inevitable, though, is that most of the students who opt to sign up for the class tend to be higher achieving, probably because they hear ahead of time that this is more work than the regular class. They are expected to do more independent work, and in some respects they receive less direct instruction in some of the content. They have to be willing to accept increased difficulty to be in the course. Still, we have some challenged students, oftentimes with attention issues or other learning disabilities. In fact, the kinds of hands-on things we do are very well suited for our students who may have trouble in a more traditional setting.

Gura: And how do the robotics students do on their standardized tests?

Laurie: Well, here in California we look not only at performance on tests but how the performance changes from year to year. Science achievement is tested in eighth grade, and in general the robotics students do as well or better than their nonrobotics peers. Another factor we've looked at is the LA and math scores. The robotics students tend to outperform their traditional science course peers, not just in raw scores in these areas but also in growth. They show greater growth in those subjects that we can check year to year.

Gura: How much of Robotics Science, which serves as the only eighth grade science course the students take, is devoted to hands-on learning with robot materials?

Laurie: There's a tremendous amount of hands-on learning. For example, this week in the robotics science class, we're learning about forces and friction, and at the same time the students are working on the first physical structures that they get to design. They've built two robots so far from instructions, but now they're going to come up with their own design for the Tug of War robot. And in doing that, the guidance that I give them is to build on the knowledge of forces that we've been learning—to think about how friction will play a role in their robot's performance, about how forces, mass, various things related to tension, and compression—things like that.

Gura: Do you find that as a teacher you are able to create your own curriculum as you need it, and does that relate to your ability to integrate robotics fully into your science teaching?

Laurie: I would even go as far as saying that I'm not really good at following other people's instructions. I really prefer to contemplate the content and come up with my own ideas. And I think that relates a lot to the way teachers approach robotics.

Gura: So there are actually plenty of opportunities to apply robotics to the California science curriculum and standards. You simply have to be a little creative about how to structure that with the robotics for your students?

Laurie: I've looked at the elementary science standards and the elementary math standards as well as the technology standards. And they seem to fit with robots in many categories.

Gura: Have you written your own curriculum?

Laurie: The curriculum I use is a combination of the traditional eighth grade science curriculum and the robotics activities that I've created to go along with it.

Gura: There are big concepts in the eighth grade standard curriculum. Do you go over these traditionally and then use the robotics activities as a way to illustrate, apply, and understand them?

Laurie: I use a lot of traditional teaching methods. My students read from a science textbook, they take notes, and I deliver lectures using electronic slide shows. We engage in demonstrations using science apparatus, and we do some traditional labs, but then a lot of that is truncated. One important point is that you have to be honest when you approach something like this, in that when you add something else to the curriculum, something else is going to be taken away. Sometimes I hear descriptions of artificial approaches where some teacher says, "Well, you can just integrate it all and it's all going to work out fine!" But, to be successful, you really have to think, "Where can I cut? What can I shorten? In order to create time to let my students experiment with robots and programming and the engineering process, I spend less time on direct instruction. I may give them notes and demonstrations that may be shorter than what I give to another class. They may receive fewer examples and less practice.

It's my belief that the higher-order thinking they are doing with the robotics makes up for some of the shortages in lower-order thinking activities that are more directly related to the traditional curriculum. These may not be as stimulating to the students' brains or offer them as much growth as working with the robots does. At the end of the day, I do manage to cover just as much in the robotics science class as I do in the traditional science class.

A whole host of mini-lessons happen [in the robotics classes] that I haven't necessarily planned. These relate to content things, but they also can relate to technical things. One of these is gears. For example, "What do you use gears for?" and "What's the effect of gears when you take a big gear and a little gear and put them in sequence?" Working with gears is not something I usually teach in advance. I point the students to the resources on this on my website. Usually this comes up when students start to use gears and make observations about what goes on when they put different kinds of gearing together and they observe the differences in speed or the torque or power of the robot. Robotics provides an opportunity on the spot to demonstrate this particular concept, and that allows it to sink in much better than showing slides and talking your way through the concept.

Gura: And that sounds like the teaching is a lot more interesting for you, the teacher—a more interesting and spontaneous experience than a book-driven course.

Laurie: Exactly. In fact, often if you were you to look at my lesson plan, you'd see a couple of lines, but if you were to chart out what actually happened you'd see a very complex web of interactions with kids and content.

Gura: And what about the social aspect of learning in your robotics science course?

Laurie: The social aspect works on many levels; this is actually the part of the teaching that can be the most challenging. A lot of the time when you would look at what's going on in my class, on the surface you might think that nothing's happening, that they're not really working that hard, that they can't be because they're talking too much. But, in fact, oftentimes the conversation and camaraderie that are going on is related to the work or the kind of social learning that helps students be productive. I watch students, and in a way I play puppeteer with their social interactions. I'm careful about grouping students and planning which ones work together. Inevitably, there are some groups that can be dysfunctional. Their social ties are so strong that they override any sense of duty to accomplish the task. A lot of the time if the challenge is interesting enough, they don't care if it's graded or not; they just want to succeed in the task.

Gura: So, in essence, what you've developed is a course in which you talk to the kids and have discussions; you use books and have discussions, demos and lectures, and interwoven throughout all of this, consistently from start to end, is robot design, building, and programming.

Laurie: That's right!

INTERVIEW I

Mike Koumoullos

Teacher, Aviation High School, New York City

Michael (Mike) Koumoullos has been a teacher for seven years at Aviation High School in New York City, teaching aircraft maintenance and ninth grade pre-engineering courses. He holds a New York state teaching license in aircraft maintenance education, a specialized license offered by the New York State Department of Education. Previously he was a vocational education assistant, working simultaneously in industry and teaching school as he did an internship that split his activities between school and working in the aviation industry. He was the coach/teacher of the school's FIRST LEGO League team for high school freshman (FLL U.S. includes students up to age 14) for three years. He then became the Queens Regional FIRST LEGO League coordinator. In that capacity he organizes and runs the Queens FIRST LEGO League Qualifying Tournament.

Mark Gura: How did you find out about LEGO Robotics?

Mike Koumoullos: An assistant principal at my school started the FIRST Robotics Team for older students, and so we extended the program to include FLL for the younger kids. Our school's path to LEGO Robotics was through FLL, which we came to through the upper-level FIRST Program. I then became a robotics staff developer for our community school district in NYC. We had seminars on robotics for different teachers in how to work with the LEGO Robotics materials.

Gura: What's your impression about how the teachers you trained in robotics would use what you taught them?

Koumoullos: About a third of them would integrate it into their teaching, some had already integrated LEGO Robotics into their regular daytime curriculum and wanted to learn more, and the remainder wanted to participate in FIRST LEGO League (FLL). Over time, these numbers changed. In the beginning, most were involved in FLL and eventually more became interested in curricular integration.

Gura: Is LEGO Robotics something that the average teacher can do? I mean, someone who is not a science teacher or has no particular affinity for things mechanical?

Koumoullos: The only prerequisite you need is that you can't be afraid of computers. If you're a person who's still struggling with email, you will need a great deal of support. If you're comfortable installing programs in a computer, can do email, know how to save files, and are comfortable playing with it a little bit, that's about the comfort level you need. Then you'll be able to figure it out. If you're afraid of the computer, you'll need a lot of support. But actually, if you had that support, someone to visit you at your school every couple of weeks for an hour, you could run the group even if you're afraid of the computer. And it's even easier now with the NXT system. With the old RCX, it was much more difficult; the programming was more challenging with a slower learning curve.

One of the first things you need to do at the beginning of the FLL season is take advantage of the CD that comes with the FLL basic materials kit. This has a bunch of PDF files that show you how to build the playing field that the robots operate on.

Gura: How would you advise newbie teachers to get started with LEGO Robotics?

Koumoullos: How to get started? If you are entering LEGO Robotics through FLL, you need a local tournament to get yourself immersed in it—and you can go to the FLL website and find one.

The NXT kits come with instructions to build a "demo bot." If you are going to be part of FLL, my suggestion is build a demo bot, follow the instructions, and in four or five hours, you'll have one finished, one you could actually use for a LEGO Robotics tournament. It'll look like the other rookie teams' robots, as many will have exactly the same demo bot, but you could use it if you wanted to. This was not the case with the old RCX kits. These were very difficult to get started with. Once you've built your demo bot, then you have to program the robot, another issue.

If you want to integrate robotics into your classes, you'll find that LEGO sells curriculum for it.

If you are going to do FLL, when you register, get a coach's handbook that will help. And whoever is running your local tournament will be able to find someone who can guide you. You have to piece together bits and pieces of information and support.

Gura: Do you have any suggestions for managing and guiding students as they're learning robotics and learning with robotics?

Koumoullos: Yeah, kids have a tendency to want to tear their robot apart and start all over as soon as they get frustrated and see that their initial idea won't work. I think it's best to encourage them to press through their problems and learn from them—fix the robot and its program, don't start over or you'll never finish enough to get to the next level.

Gura: Any advice about dealing with the classroom itself?

Koumoullos: If you are doing LEGO Robotics for FLL you need a lot of space. You have to set up "the field" and keep it set up for a while, that's space intensive. If you're not involved in FLL, the space requirements are much less intensive.

Also, make sure that the students build something that's stable. You won't be able to build something sturdy in exactly the way you would that's not stable. But encourage this because there's nothing more frustrating than building a beautifully designed robot that will perform in a challenge to solve the problem and then watch it fall apart soon after getting it going. This is the same issue professional robot designers have in the real world and it's a perfect issue for students to learn from as they deal with it, too. Above all keep it simple and leave room to alter the design when needed.

INTERVIEW J

Chris Dudin

Robotics Teacher, New York City

Chris Dudin is a licensed physical education teacher but teaches robotics primarily at his school. Chris designed a daytime robotics program that has been expanded to eight regularly scheduled classes, which he teaches in addition to coaching two FLL teams at the school.

Mark Gura: Was it hard for you to learn LEGO Robotics, both understanding the material and how to use it with the students?

Chris Dudin: When I first started, an advisor from FIRST LEGO League came in to work with another teacher and me. He showed us a little about the program and how the robots work. I said to the other teacher, "I'll take on the robot building and designing with the students because I enjoy that, if you'll take on the research part of the program." We split the duties, and after the first few seasons she moved on, and I did the program by myself. And actually, building things with LEGOs, not LEGO Robotics, but simple LEGO bricks, was something I did as a kid, so that part of it seemed natural to me. Having that experience helped.

FIRST LEGO League in NYC had some workshops that teachers could attend. They'd have us build some robots, just so we could see how the robots and parts worked and moved. Not that they really wanted us to build anything for the kids. One of the FIRST LEGO League values is having the kids do the work and doing the discovering.

One of the things they taught me was programming, how to program the robot. But still, I have to say that my students know far more about this than I do. They know far more about it because they do it day in and day out, and I supervise. One of the core values in my classes has been problem solving. I want my student to learn how to solve problems, not just with the robots or the research project of FLL, but everyday problems. So whenever I have an opportunity I give them a problem to solve. Sometimes I throw a monkey wrench in their work. Just a couple of weeks ago, I gave them a faulty motor and I watched them work for a long time trying to figure out what was wrong. It was difficult for them, but they did all the necessary things to find out what was wrong with it. They were frustrated, yes, but in the end they learned.

Gura: How long was it from the time you began with LEGO Robotics until the time you felt somewhat competent—how much time passed?

Dudin: It didn't take too long. I'd say maybe a couple of months, watching the students use the materials and putting in a little practice on my own. But as far as building robots, you don't need to have the higher skills yourself. It's not really necessary. It might help, but I don't have those higher skills because I don't really do it; the students do. It's good to know—maybe how gears work, so you might have a little bit of science background or you might look it up. As a teacher, you should be able to learn by yourself how certain things work. I might say to the students, "Is that gear ratio right?" or "Is there something you can do to speed the robot up or slow it down?" Then you let them figure out how to put it together, and in the end they will. They'll find a way whether they have to read a book or look it up on the web. They'll find a way to do it, or they'll go another route and find another way.

Gura: And do you find that they pick one another's brains and help each other?

Dudin: Oh, absolutely!

Gura: What would your advice be to teachers who are thinking of doing LEGO Robotics or just about to get started? They'd like to have a class and/or an FLL team. The teacher is wondering, "Can I do this?" and "What should I do?"

Dudin: My best advice would be to plan! Come up with some kind of a game plan. If you don't know anything about it, talk to other teachers and find out what they might do, but have a plan when you go into the classroom. Know where you want to go with it. That's my best advice. That summer, when I knew I would be doing LEGO Robotics as a regularly scheduled class for the first time in the fall, I spent a lot of that summer thinking, "Where do I want to go? What do I want to do? What are my goals for the students and myself?" Having coached FLL for a couple of years before really helped because I knew a little more about it and had that advantage. If someone were just coming in to do robotics for the first time, I'd say it would be a little more difficult for them if they don't have any experience with the materials. But certainly, taking some time to plan what you're going to do is essential.

> "What I love about LEGO Robotics is that, in a sense, the kids are self differentiating. They give themselves their own challenges. You don't have to do it; you simply have to encourage it."

Plan how to organize the students. For the most part, you have to have them work in groups. I don't see any other way. Working in groups is not only practical, but it's a good thing to learn. One of the big concepts now is differentiation. My supervisors have asked me how I'm differentiating robotics in my class. My understanding of this is that every student has a different set of abilities. One student may be stronger at programming, while another is stronger at building, and a third is stronger at research. So I would plan my work groups so that I would have someone strong in each area in each group. For new teachers, though, they might have to find this out on their own. What I do is survey the class first to see what they enjoy most, and, therefore, probably are better at. I have them write in the survey what their experience is with robotics.

I try to group them so that there's a little bit of strength in each area that we are going to have to learn in and use. What I love about LEGO Robotics is that, in a sense, the kids are self differentiating. They give themselves their own challenges. You don't have to do it; you simply have to encourage it. I can just sit back and watch the learning take place and support it, which is what every teacher wants to do.

Gura: Is your class an elective? Is it part of the science instruction?

Dudin: We call it applied science. Actually, robotics is just part of the applied science program we've developed, because there is a big research element of it, in which we do a lot of English language arts. We follow a lot of the ELA curriculum.

INTERVIEW K

Mark Sharfshteyn

Chairperson, New York City FIRST LEGO League Planning Committee

Mark Sharfshteyn has taught students how to "do" LEGO Robotics and has taught New York City public school teachers how to teach their students robotics. His perspective is different from that of other robotics-using teachers, though, because he is a professional computer engineer. He holds a degree in computer engineering from Polytechnic Institute of New York University in Brooklyn and is pursuing an MBA. As an engineer, Mark sees the things students learn with LEGO Robotics as real engineering. Among his experiences with LEGO Robotics, Mark taught teachers how to coach an FLL (FIRST LEGO League) robotics team—as part of the teacher training workshops offered every year by Polytechnic Institute of NYU. This included showing them how to use LEGO robotics kits and how to teach students to use them.

Mark Gura: What would you recommend for teachers just getting started with LEGO Robotics?

Mark Sharfshteyn: My first thought is for you to get a LEGO Mindstorms kit. Open the box, play around with it, build a small, simple robot and see how it works. You know, there's a plethora of published curriculums available for sale. There's actually a large community out there of teachers who integrate LEGO robotics into their classrooms. But I suggest you get and experiment with a kit, because I don't think that until you are comfortable with it you'll be able to implement any professionally created curriculum with the students.

Gura: Could a typical teacher, someone without an engineering background, learn a kit this way?

Sharfshteyn: It's very intuitive. I see rookie teachers who come into FLL looking for support. They've never even remotely touched anything like a robotics kit, no experience whatsoever. You know what? I've come to the conclusion that it's really a matter of just taking the first step and saying, "Yeah, I will try it!"

Gura: Supposing a teacher takes your advice and in a leisurely way gets comfortable with how the kit and the materials work. What else is good to do to get ready for using robotics with students?

Sharfshteyn: Well, I definitely wouldn't try to do this from scratch on my own. Look for simple exercises. You're not all of a sudden going to start up a full robotics class. But you can start implementing facets, small bits and pieces of what you're teaching in the classroom, through using the robotics sets. And you might want to look for some of the starter sets at LEGOeducation.com designed to complement what's being taught in class.

The other thing to understand is that some teachers will start with FLL—after you register a team and are ready to get started, you wonder what to do first. To me it's always about getting a foot in the door, even if it's a small crack, and then prying the door open.

Gura: What do you think would be more difficult, to start an FLL team—say with 12 kids—or to try to bring some robotics into a regular science class?

Sharfshteyn: Well, for the first year I think some simple integration of robotics into some aspects of what you are teaching would be better. This way you'd build up momentum and maybe be ready to coach the team the following year.

And by all means, think about what you could bring into the classroom with the kit that you couldn't have done before. That's real important. You definitely have to show the kids the greater meaning of robotics. That goes beyond the LEGO kits. Show them videos of real-world robots, and talk to them about what the robots do and why they do it.

Gura: You've worked with both the RCX and NXT versions of the LEGO Robotics materials. What are your impressions of their differences and similarities?

Sharfshteyn: Both the RCX and the NXT platforms are great. I started with the RCX. I thought it was a great tool because I could see that it was so interactive and accessible for someone who isn't an engineer or doesn't have that mindset.

Obviously, the NXT brings a lot of advantages to the platform, things like expanded memory, Bluetooth capability, and additional motors with rotation sensors built in—all those things are good—but to me the fundamentals of both the RCX and the NXT are one and the same. To me the NXT is like an upgrade of RCX.

One of the things that did change with the NXT is the actual pieces that come with the kit. The connections are different. To me, from a structural standpoint, NXT is a little harder to grasp. And maybe kids who haven't seen the older, RCX version would think this is fine, but for someone who's used both, the RCX version was a little easier to get started with.

Gura: Why do you think that is?

Sharfshteyn: Well, maybe because I observe kids who are used to the older RCX. For me, at least, making sure everything was structurally sound and wouldn't break apart seemed to be a little easier with the RCX version.

Gura: You mentioned rotation sensors.

Sharfshteyn: A rotation sensor is something that used to be separate from the motor [in the RCX version]. Now it's incorporated into the motor [in the NXT platform]. This sensor counts the revolutions that the motor makes. When you program the brick, rather than directing the bot to go for a certain time, with the sensor you can direct it to go a specific number of revolutions before it stops. The rotation sensor is a little more accurate in NXT because things like battery strength, something that can influence this sort of thing, won't throw your calculations off.

Gura: As you've observed kids' reactions to the two versions, RCX and NXT, what have you observed? Do the kids like either version more?

Sharfshteyn: I haven't noticed a difference with the kids. I have noticed a hesitance to change over from one version to the other on the part of teachers. This was true especially the first year the NXT came out, and many teachers voiced that they didn't want to have to learn two completely different systems. But I pointed out to them that that's actually not true. The new one is an extension of the old. For all intents and purposes, if you know the RCX, you know much about the NXT.

Gura: In what ways do you think LEGO Robotics has an educational payoff for students?

Sharfshteyn: It's applied learning, applying what kids learn in the classroom to real-world experiences. When I was going to junior high school in NYC, there was a big disconnect—you'd sit in a math class but wouldn't conceptually see what it was you were learning. We were studying really just to pass the class. This is where we start to lose a lot of kids because they can't see an end result.

When I was a sixth grader sitting in math class, it was clear to me that I was there because I had to be there. If you had asked me was I eager to go to class because it was interesting or because I loved learning algebra or trigonometry, the answer would have been "No." I think if you ask most kids [the same questions now], they'd tell you they'd prefer to do something else. What the LEGO robotics program does is show them how the fruits of their learning can have an end result, and it's as close as pushing a button after you program a robot on the computer and actually see it work.

Gura: And you assert this as a person who clearly has an aptitude for math. You were a good math student, and it comes naturally to you. You majored in computer engineering in university.

Sharfshteyn: Yes, absolutely!

Gura: When did you first come into contact with LEGO Robotics?

Sharfshteyn: Actually, it was when I was recruited to FLL as a freshman at Poly Tech; one of my professors asked me to help.

Gura: What did you think when you first saw the LEGO robots?

Sharfshteyn: At that point, it was all new to me. I had no idea that LEGO put out these robotics kits. The technology seemed incredible, something that small but that powerful was mind-boggling to me. I used the LEGO Mindstorms materials in my freshman engineering class and experienced them as a student.

Gura: What about the opportunity that students get from robotics programs to meet people they wouldn't otherwise become acquainted with?

Sharfshteyn: I worry about where education is going and some of today's problems, things like the dropout rate from middle and high school; in some places it's a never-ending cycle. Something needs to be interjected that can make a difference. Unfortunately, in today's crowded classrooms, this is hard to do. Often there isn't much teachers can do to deeply influence the life paths of students.

The question is: where can an intervention come from that will show kids something else? The answer is *someone else*—someone who is not like them, not like their parents, someone who is completely different from the types of people they are used to seeing. In a program like FLL, this happens. Students are directed to focus on real-world problems as part of the robotics challenge. And through that, they start to think about men and women working today who are trying to solve these problems. When they compete in FLL tournaments, they actually meet them. Often the adults who volunteer for these events, coaches and judges, are such people. Even through a simple conversation, such adults can be an important positive influence on kids. The students interact with successful adults because of a common interest in robots.

I'm a good example of this when I meet with young kids to coach them; I ask them big questions. When kids become involved in FLL, they take on a new and different set of responsibilities—being accountable to do real things in the real world.

When these kids turn on the TV, they see music stars, movie stars, and sports stars, and those are the only types of role models they aspire to be. From a practical perspective, how many of those famous people are involved in solving real-world problems? And, of course, very few people can have careers like that. FLL gives these kids some real options.

APPENDIX A

Classic Robotics Projects

For each resource, the title, source, URL, and a brief description are provided.

A. Sumo Bots

C.V.D. (Combative Vector of Danger)

LEGO Mindstorms:
http://mindstorms.lego.com/en-us/Community/NXTLog/DisplayProject.aspx?id=7ea238af-3de5-4088-917f-68d7e5a9d75d

Photos, descriptions, and explanations of this battle bot.

iBot

LEGO Mindstorms:
http://mindstorms.lego.com/en-us/Community/NXTLog/DisplayProject.aspx?id=7e065be6-6460-4895-9732-a1af85208ade

Easily modified by adding attachments such as rams for sumo.

Introduction to LEGO RCX Robotics and Robot Sumo

C. J. Chung:
www.docstoc.com/docs/2687516/Introduction-to-LEGO-RCX-robotics-and-Robot-Sumo

Slides and a paper from a robotics workshop that focused on sumo.

Mini Sumo Bot

Nxtprograms.com, Dave Parker:
www.nxtprograms.com/mini_sumo/steps.html

Detailed, photo-illustrated directions and material on programming and challenges.

Sumo Robots

Luke Laurie, El Camino Junior High students:
www.youtube.com/user/lukelaurie

YouTube video of students and robots in action: "These were the robots of the Robotics Science Class 2008. This is their final competition."

Sumo Robot Competition (2008 Guide)

Wichita State University:
http://webs.wichita.edu/depttools/depttoolsmemberfiles/mindstorms/Fall%20Kick-Off/Fall2008SumoCompetition_Ver2.pdf

Text description of how to organize a sumo robotics event.

Sumo Robot Contest (including how-to videos)

Geekzone:
www.geekzone.co.nz/BlueToothKiwi/4249

A set of resources that includes how to build a sumo robot, sumo ring, and stage a sumo bot contest.

Sumo for Lego NXT-G MindStorms Robots!

Graeme Faulkner:
http://drgraeme.net/DrGraeme-free-NXT-G-tutorials/Ch46/SUMO-G/

A comprehensive site with examples of sumo robots built by students, a mentor's guide, lists and links to related robot activities, and more.

UniS Lego Mindstorm Sumo Robot Fights

LLPaddyP (screenname):
www.youtube.com/watch?v=AXMNYiwYnMA (part 1);
www.youtube.com/watch?v=Wb28-TAoBjQ (part 2)

Two of many examples of sumo bot videos to be found online. These give a taste of the completed robots in action, doing what they were designed, built, and programmed for.

B. Tug-of-War Bots

Getting Started with Tug O' War Robots

Luke Laurie:
http://homepage.mac.com/mrlaurie/robo/tugowartutorial.html

Comprehensive guide (enhanced with videos) to TugBot activities, with rules, description, building directions, design ideas, resources, assessment rubric, and more.

Tug-o-War

LEGO Education:
www.legoeducation.us/sharedimages/resources/TugoWar.pdf

An overview of the tug-of-war activity based on the use of LEGO Robotics materials.

Tug-of-War!

Graeme Faulkner:
http://drgraeme.net/DrGraeme-free-NXT-G-tutorials/Ch40/Ch40V1BCG/

Thoughts on tug-of-war robot activities for students with photos and links to videos.

C. Drawing/Art Bots

ArtBot (Build It!)

LEGO Mindstorms NXT log:
http://mindstorms.lego.com/en-us/Community/NXTLog/DisplayProject.aspx?id=f88ab5a7-e42f-4fdb-b76e-e2ed333e19e4

Photos and descriptions of a classic robot that draws random pictures.

Draw Bot

LEGO Mindstorms NXT log:
http://mindstorms.lego.com/en-us/Community/NXTLog/DisplayProject.aspx?id=7d84c9ff-39d3-4c7f-b345-910c1cc484bd

Photos and descriptions of a LEGO Mindstorms NXT robot that draws pictures with a pencil.

D. Mobile/Vehicle Bot Performance

Bumper

ROBO–ZONE:
www.amblesideprimary.com/ambleweb/robotzone/bumper/bumper.htm

Photos and descriptions of mobile robots.

Great Robot Race

NOVA Teachers, Veryl Greene:
www.pbs.org/wgbh/nova/teachers/ideas/3308_darpa.html

Complete lesson plan for LEGO Racing Car robots.

Robot Racing—Around the Bends

Graeme Faulkner:
http://drgraeme.net/DrGraeme-free-NXT-G-tutorials/Ch22/Ch22V1BCG/Challenge22Robot500Level1V1.doc

Illustrated (word document) description of student activity.

E. Line-Running and Line-Following Bots

Josh Bot (Line Follower)

Ambleside Primary School:
www.amblesideprimary.com/ambleweb/robotzone/Joshbot/joshbot.htm

Photo and description of a student line-following robot.

LEGO Robotics and Medibotics

Digital Extremities:
http://extremities.com/rbt/

Scroll to Lab 0: Following a Line.

SteerBot

Gus Jansson, LUGNET:
www.lugnet.com/~726/SteerBot

Photos, descriptions, and instructions on steering a robot.

F. Fetch Bot—Gather Bot—Harvest Bot

Barrel Collector Robot *(built as an application for the Laser Target Finder sensor)*

Philippe Hurbain / Extreme NXT:
www.philohome.com/picker/picker.htm

Photos and descriptions of a robot built by a professional engineer with LEGO offer information and/or inspiration for younger students pursuing the same type of robot.

The Grabber Arm

Thomas Waadeland:
http://folk.uio.no/thomasw/robotics/grabberarm/grabberarm.html

Photos and descriptions of a robot built by a professional engineer with LEGO offer information and/or inspiration for younger students pursuing the same type of robot.

Grabber Mechanisms

Gus Jansson, LUGNET:
www.lugnet.com/~726/GrabberMechanisms

Blueprint instructions on how to build grabber(s) for LEGO robots.

LEGO Mindstorms NXT Model Building Instructions

Active Robots:
http://www.active-robots.com/products/mindstorms4schools/building-instructions.shtml

See RoboArm T-56 (machine) and TriBot (vehicle) PDFs in particular.

NXT Competition Idea: Can Grabber

http://nlrobotics.blogspot.com/2008/02/nxt-competition-idea-can-grabber.html

Video of a LEGO robot that grabs and retrieves beverage cans.

Simple Grabber

LEGO Mindstorms NXT log:
http://mindstorms.lego.com/en-us/Community/NXTLog/DisplayProject.aspx?id=a3405247-d06a-4204-b2e7-c58163c6b09f

Photo and description of a student robot grabber with an automatic flashlight.

Soda Grabber

NXT log:
http://mindstorms.lego.com/en-us/Community/NXTLog/DisplayProject.aspx?id=8c96ad2c-b28a-4ba8-8989-2fade1945cc2

Photo and description of a student robot.

Volcanic Panic Sample Container Practice

Linda Hamilton, Davis Creek Elementary School:
http://daviscreek.cabe.k12.wv.us/legograbber10mm.htm

Photo story of students at work on programming a "grab" robot.

G. Maze Challenge

Building Instructions: Maze Robot

David Wang:
www.mit.edu/~kristina/Lego/UnifiedF04/Build%20Instructions/Maze%20Robot%20Instructions.pdf

Detailed, illustrated directions on building this robot.

Teenage students develop LEGO robot that solves a maze

Gizmowatch:
www.facebook.com/note.php?note_id=323941430724

Short article.

Maze Robot

ROX Software:
http://roxsoftware.com/legos

Step-by-step instructions in sequential photos for a maze-following robot (scroll down to maze robot).

Mindstorm Mazes

University of Hertfordshire, UK:
http://dragon.herts.ac.uk/~eleqdcl/lego.html

Descriptions, photos, and videos of maze bots.

Mindstorms MazeWalker

Hempel Design Group:
www.hempeldesigngroup.com/lego/mazewalker/

Descriptions, photos, and tutorial on building this more advanced robot.

H. Robot Zoo

How to Make a Lego Robot Spider

RobotShop blog:
www.robotshop.com/blog/how-to-make-a-lego-robot-spider-164

Explanation of how to create this robot as well as video of it in action.

LEGO Mindstorms Crocodile Robot

Gronbaek.net—A public note book:
http://gronbaek.net/2007/11/24/lego-mindstorms-crocodile-robot/

Detailed explanation and instructions for a complex robot.

LEGO Mindstorms NXT ZOO

No Starch Press, Fay Rhodes:
http://thenxtzoo.com/zoobook.html

Illustrations of completed NXT animals and general information about them.

Robotic Zoo Activity Guide Using LEGO Mindstorms NXT

Technically Learning:
http://technicallylearning.org/ActivityGuides/RoboticZooActivityGuide.pdf

Ten lessons guide students through the creation of robots inspired by animal behavior. Rates difficulty at Grades 6–8.

The Waddling Penguin

NXT log:
Toothpaste35: http://mindstorms.lego.com/en-us/Community/NXTLog/DisplayProject.aspx?id=ba229cb3-fc3f-4f2a-b1da-7d7b443d5ffb

A simple robot that walks.

APPENDIX B

Robotics Resources

This icon precedes resources that are highly recommended by the author.

A. Getting Started with LEGO Robotics

A Crash Course in LEGO Robotics—Getting Started

Meri V. Cummings:
www6.cet.edu/cet/robotics/RoboticsGettingStartedNAA.ppt

A detailed, proposed plan and overview of a new robotics program for school age participants.

Getting Started

2010 Center for Engineering Education and Outreach, Tufts University:
http://legoengineering.com

Four very worthwhile sections: Introduction to LEGO Engineering (building with RCX and building with NXT), Intro to Programming (with NXT-G and Robolab), Intro Activity (NXT Snail Car), and Hints for the Classroom (Managing LEGO Learning).

How LEGO Mindstorms NXT Works

National Instruments:
www.ni.com/academic/mindstorms/works.htm

A brief overview of the Mindstorms software and programming–NXT oriented.

Introduction to LEGO Mindstorms for Schools

S. Rhodes:
www.docstoc.com/docs/20929226/Introduction-to-LEGO-Mindstorms-for-Schools

An overview of the Mindstorms system and how it works—RCX oriented.

The NXT Classroom

Damien Kee, editor; James Floyd Kelly and Fay Rhodes, senior contributors:
www.thenxtclassroom.com

The NXT Classroom is a community dedicated to supporting teachers who are using the LEGO Mindstorms system in their classrooms. A rich repository of various types of resources for robotics teachers, including building plans, eJournal, lesson plans and ideas, and more.

The NXT STEP Forum

The NXT STEP—LEGO Mindstorms NXT Blog—Various contributors:
http://thenxtstep.blogspot.com

A blog with a forums area that supports colleague-to-colleague collaboration and mentoring.

Robotics Education Project

NASA:
http://robotics.nasa.gov/edu/9-12.htm

A page of links to a rich body of robotics resources, many LEGO specific.

Steps to Starting a LEGO Robotics Program

Carnegie Mellon Robotics Academy:
www.education.rec.ri.cmu.edu/downloads/lego/get_started/Steps%20to%20starting%20a%20LEGO%20robotics%20program.pdf

An outline of general ideas and to-do items to start a school robotics program.

Teaching Robotics

LEGO Education:
www.lego.com:80/eng/education/mindstorms/default.asp

LEGO's own support to teachers using robotics includes sections on NXT Concept, LEGO Mindstorms for School, and After School Programs and Competition.

Team Resources (FIRST LEGO League)

FIRST LEGO League (U.S.):
www.usfirst.org/roboticsprograms/fll/content.aspx?id=786

An extensive body of resources on themes like preparation (coaches' handbook), programming, building resources, curriculum, team-building activities, and more.

Tomb Raider

LEGO Engineering:
www.legoengineering.com/index.php?option=com_community&Itemid=59&c=item&id=328

Complete instructions for a short activity/challenge where students use an RCX and a light sensor to trace the tracks of an Egyptian tomb raider.

B. Curricula

Artbotics: Combining Art and Robotics to Broaden Participation in Computing

Holly A. Yanco, Hyun Ju Kim, Fred G. Martin, & Linda Silka, University of Massachusetts, Lowell:

www.cs.hmc.edu/roboteducation/papers2007/c39_yancoArtbotics.pdf

Children's Storytelling and Programming with Robotic Characters

Kimiko Ryokai, Michael Jongseon Lee, & Jonathan Micah Breitbart, School of Information, University of California, Berkeley:

http://students.washington.edu/mjslee/content/pleo_ACM_C&C2009_042709_final.pdf

Creating Appropriate Student Challenges for an Elementary School Robotics Curricula

David VanEsselstyn, Assistant Professor, Department of Educational Technology, School of Education, C.W. Post Campus, Long Island University; & Shawn Mishler, Director of Technology, the School at Columbia University:

http://center.uoregon.edu/ISTE/uploads/NECC2005/KEY_6851156/VanEsselstyn_final_lego_robotics.pdf

Designing Technology Activities that Teach Mathematics

Eli M. Silk, Ross Higashi, Robin Shoop, & Christian D. Schunn, Technology Teacher, December/January 2010:

www.lrdc.pitt.edu/schunn/research/papers/silk-etal-techteach2010.pdf

5-Week Lesson Plans

High Tech Kids, a 501(c)(3) nonprofit that supports Minnesota FIRST LEGO League teams, coaches, and volunteers:

www.hightechkids.org/5-week-lesson-plans

Learning by Stealthrobotics in the Classroom

Ian Maud, *Teaching Science*, December 2008:

http://findarticles.com/p/articles/mi_6957/is_4_54/ai_n31161076/

Robotics Across the Curriculum

Elizabeth Sklar, Simon Parsons, & M. Q. Azhar, Department of Computer and Information Science, Brooklyn College, City University of New York; Presentation to the American Association for Artificial Intelligence, 2006:

www.cs.hmc.edu/roboteducation/papers2007/c46_sklar_rac.pdf

Robotics in Child Storytelling

C. R. Ribeiro, M. F. M. Costa, & C. Pereira-Coutinho, Instituto de Educação e Psicologia and Departamento de Física, Campus de Gualtar, Universidade do Minho, Braga, Portugal; Presentation to the International Conference on Hands-On Science, 2009:

http://repositorium.sdum.uminho.pt/bitstream/1822/9979/1/HSCI20091.pdf

Robotics in the Classroom Introduction to Robotics: A collaborative unit for 5th and 6th grade students in science, math, and language arts

This publication was developed for Wright Patterson Air Force Base with the assistance of educators from the Teachers in Industry for Educational Support (TIES) Program and professionals from WPAFB under direction from the Educational Outreach Office:

http://edoutreach.wpafb.af.mil/Robotics/media/resources/intro_robotics_5th.pdf

Robotics Learning as a Tool for Integrating Science-Technology Curriculum in K–12 Schools

Eli Kolberg and Nahum Orlev; Presentation to the ASEE/IEEE Frontiers in Education Conference, 2001, Reno, NV:

http://citeseerx.ist.psu.edu/viewdoc/download?doi=10.1.1.16.2894&rep=rep1&type=pdf

The Use of Digital Manipulatives in K–12: Robotics, GPS/GIS and Programming

Gwen Nugent, Brad Barker, Neal Grandgenett, & Vaicheslav Adamchuk, University of Nebraska; Presentation to the ASEE/IEEE Frontiers in Education Conference, 2009, San Antonio, TX:

www.fie-conference.org/fie2009/papers/1041.pdf

The Use of Robotics to Teach Mathematics

Eli M. Silk & Christian D. Schunn, Learning Research & Development Center, University of Pittsburgh; Ross Higashi & Robin Shoop, Robotics Academy, NREC; Al Dietrich & Ron Reed, Shaler School District and Pittsburgh Public Schools; Presentation to Robotics Educators Conference, Butler County Community College, 2007, Butler, PA:

www.elisilk.com/research/SilkEtal2007a-RoboEd-Presentation.pdf

Using Robotics to Teach Mathematics: Analysis of a Curriculum Designed and Implemented

Eli Silk & Christian Schunn, Presentation to the American Society for Engineering Education, 2007:

www.elisilk.com/research/SilkSchunn2008a-ASEE.pdf

C. Background Reading

The Art of LEGO Design

Fred G. Martin:
www.cs.uml.edu/~fredm/papers/artoflego-printfix.pdf

Originally published as an article in *The Robotics Practitioner: The Journal for Robot Builders 1*(2, Spring), 1995. Copyright © 1995 by Fred G. Martin. A comprehensive manual on constructing with LEGO, 19 pages.

Developing a Research Team for the R&D Challenge

Linda Reynolds:
www.botball.org/sites/default/files/page-files/53/Resarch_Team_Dev.pdf

Colleague-to-colleague materials for implementation, 10 pages.

From the Logo Turtle to the Tiny Robot Turtle: Practical and Pedagogical Issues

Moro Michele & Alimisis Dimitris:
www.terecop.eu/downloads/gre/ErgasiesSyrou2009/Moro_Alimisis_Syros2009_paper.doc.pdf

Academic paper, 6 pages, describes how students learn to construct and program a Logo Turtle using a LEGO Mindstorms NXT set. Knowledge areas are technology, informatics, and mathematics.

Motivating Students with Robotics

US FIRST/*The Science Teacher;* Brenda Brand, Michael Collver, & Mary Kasarda, *The Science Teacher 75*(4, April/May), 2008:
www.usfirst.org/uploadedFiles/News/Science_Teacher_2008_Reprint.pdf

Article, 6 pages.

Using Educational Robotics to Engage Inner-City Students with Technology

Rachel Goldman, Amy Eguchi, & Elizabeth Sklar:
http://citeseerx.ist.psu.edu/viewdoc/download?doi=10.1.1.83.9302&rep=rep1&type=pdf

Academic paper, 8 pages, on a pilot project (summer 2003) developed to enhance teaching of standard physics and math topics to middle and early high school students in inner-city schools in New York City. Lessons used the LEGO Mindstorms robotics kit and the Robolab graphical programming environment.

D. Videos

2003 TCEA Promotional Video (Texas Computer Educators)

Irving ISD Robotics:
www.irvingisd.net/robotics (link near top of page)

Many other valuable student robotics links are on this and adjoining pages of this site.

A highly illustrative video, directed at teachers contemplating using robotics, shows the value and variety of learning involved in a school robotics competition (3½ minutes).

How to Program the Light Sensor on a LEGO Mindstorms Robot

Wonder How To, video created by ortop.org, Oregon Robotics Tournament and Outreach Program (ORTOP):
www.wonderhowto.com/how-to-program-light-sensor-lego-mindstorms-robot-79059

Screencast-based video with good explanations and instructions for NXT (6 minutes).

KIPR Botball!

Botball promo and information; KISS Institute for Practical Robots (KIPR) is a not-for-profit organization that uses educational robotics programs to actively engage students in science, technology, engineering, math, and project management:
http://files.kipr.org/botball.org/movies/2007BotballPromo-320x240.mov

Botball pictures and video links:
www.botball.org/pictures_video

Introductory promotional video and photos for Botball, an international competition for middle and high school students, emphasizes math and engineering integrated into robotics activities.

LEGO Claw Tank Bot

NotSoSiniSter:
www.youtube.com/watch?v=hllLodFuM-A

A masterpiece LEGO Robot built by a young student.

LEGO Mindstorms NXT: A Brief Introduction & Tutorial Parts 1 & 2

Chad Cardwell: Part 1—Overview (8 minutes)
www.chadcardwell.net *also* www.youtube.com/watch?v=l0vqZQMF0A4

Chad Cardwell: Part 2—Programming (8½ minutes)
www.chadcardwell.net *also* www.youtube.com/watch?v=AzRRulYvVdY

Part 1 contains a brief introduction and tutorial to LEGO Mindstorms NXT which discusses (1) what is included with the NXT robotics kit and (2) how to build a simple NXT robot. Part 2 shows how to (3) program an NXT robot and (4) test an NXT robot.

Very good overviews, clear explanations, and demos of the LEGO NXT Robotics system.

LEGO Mindstorms NXT Biped Walker

Laurens200 (screen name):
www.youtube.com/watch?v=oHf0QiIUleU

Short video of a particularly successful design for an NXT navigating robot.

LEGO NXT Dog

Soupjvc (screen name):
www.youtube.com/watch?v=D3JX9-5GfDg

Very short video of a particularly successful design for an NXT navigating robot.

LEGO Mindstorms NXT Gorilla

Matthias Paul Scholz:
wwww.youtube.com/watch?v=WNTFXmmW6p4

Video of NXT gorilla bot rebuilt from the book *Robots Alive! Endangered Species* by Fay Rhodes. Illustrates the construction and performance of the robot.

The video shows a gorilla bot.

LEGO Mindstorms NXT Hopper

Laurens200 (screen name):
www.youtube.com/watch?v=sAQS4NLEnEw

Very short video of a particularly successful design for an NXT navigating robot.

My LEGO Mindstorms Creations

Teambolz, Brent Hunter:
www.youtube.com/watch?v=gXiql8Fm64A

Excellent short video by an experienced builder shows what's possible with LEGO Robotics materials; it would make a great introduction for students.

NXT Ribbit Jumping

Simpfan4 (screenname):
www.youtube.com/watch?v=fko_gqcnN68

Short video of a simple NXT hopping robot.

NXT Segway with Leaning Rider

NXT programs.com:
www.youtube.com/watch?v=q9ZONn3p1LI

Video of a slightly more advanced bot (programmed in NXT-G): This is the "NXT Segway with Rider" project for NXT 2.0 from nxtprograms.com. See free building instructions and programs at www.nxtprograms.com/NXT2/segway/

NXT Tank Test

RacerXRS:
www.youtube.com/watch?v=_l4mFJXgJ78

Short video of a well-designed and constructed robot.

Robofest

Dwayne Abuel:
www.highlands.k12.hi.us/robofest/2010robofest.mov;
www.highlands.k12.hi.us/robofest/newsapril192009.mov

Videos of the Robofest Hawaii sumo robot competition and a TV news clip of Robofest.

Robot Pals

Scientific American Frontiers on hulu:
www.hulu.com/watch/23328/scientific-american-frontiers-robot-pals

Full *Scientific American Frontiers* episode (26 minutes), an engrossing TV program on robotics applicable for upper elementary students through adult audiences.

Students Participating in Robotics

Hatboro-Horsham School District, Horsham, PA (a suburban area near Philadelphia):
www.hatboro-horsham.org/425920102614325990/lib/425920102614325990/Lego%20Robotics%20w%20voice.wmv

Overview of a school robotics program shows various aspects of learning and doing and captures the flavor of a school-based program (11½ minutes).

TurtuleBot LEGO Mindstorms NXT

www.youtube.com/watch?v=G5beI17qWRw

Short video of a particularly successful design for an NXT navigating robot, TurtuleBot, that looks and acts like a turtle.

Using LEGO Robotics to Promote Math and Science

Think Tank article by Robotics Resource Center, Worcester Polytechnic Institute, Worcester, MA: http://thinktank.wpi.edu/article/151

Bill Johnson, math professor, Scottsdale Community College, AZ: http://media.wpi.edu/News/Events/Robotics/First/2009Conference/2009CON_Promoting_Via_Robotics_Johnson.wmv

Video presents an overview of student robotics by an educator (retired engineer) who found that students who hate math can have fun learning it by building robots.

E. Events and Competitions

EARLY Robotics (Engineering and Robotics Learned Young)

www.earlyrobotics.org

EARLY exposes youth to engineering, providing 7- to 12-year-olds opportunities to participate in a robotics competition every fall and spring. Provides links to many resources and materials.

FIRST LEGO League (FLL)

www.firstlegoleague.org

Official FLL International Information site.

High Tech Kids: MN (Minnesota) FIRST LEGO League

www.hightechkids.org/home

Many FLL and LEGO Robotics resources.

Robofest

http://robofest.net

Home/informational site for Robofest competition.

F. Ideas for FIRST LEGO League Challenges

Creating Appropriate Student Challenges for an Elementary School Robotics Curriculum

David VanEsselstyn & Shawn Mishler (posted on ISTE's website, NECC Research Paper Archive):
http://center.uoregon.edu/ISTE/uploads/NECC2005/KEY_6851156/VanEsselstyn_final_lego_robotics.pdf

Research paper on the integration of robotics into the instructional program.

Elementary and Middle Schoolers Accept the Robotic Challenge

Elise Hasty, College of Engineering, University of Missouri, Columbia, MO:
http://engineering.missouri.edu/news/stories/2009/high-school-student-robotics-comp/index.php

Article with photo of middle school maze challenge.

GC Robotics RCX/Ice Storm Challenge (Robo Challenge Extreme)

Georgetown College:
http://spider.georgetowncollege.edu/peach/robots/videos/2010CoachMeeting.htm

Videos prepared for coaches, covering a dozen elements of the Ice Storm Challenge.

Mini Grand Challenge Contest for Robot Education

Bob Avanzato, associate professor of engineering, Penn State Abington:
www.cs.hmc.edu/roboteducation/slides2007/bobavanzato.ppt

May serve as a model for a scaled-down challenge done with LEGO Robotics.

Missions

US FIRST LEGO League:
http://usfirst.org/roboticsprograms/fll/missions1.aspx#

Mission components from annual FLL challenge for 2010; explanations in text and screencast.

NASA Robotics Alliance Project

NASA:
http://robotics.nasa.gov/students/challenge.php

Information page for robotics challenges that can be replicated at schools: sumo, line running, and line following.

NSF Robot System Challenge

National Science Foundation (NSF) Engineering Research Center (ERC) for Computer-Integrated Surgical Systems and Technology (CISST)—CISST ERC (NSF):
www.cisst.org/K-12-programs

Resource page of a challenge event organized by the Computer-Integrated Surgery Student Research Society (CISSRS) at Johns Hopkins University; middle and high school students compete using LEGO Robotics. CISST Research Society at Johns Hopkins University.

Preparing for Robotics Park

Rhode Island School of the Future:
www.risf.net/RoboPReg.htm

The goal of the Rhode Island Robotics Design Project (RIRDP), an extension of the Rhode Island School of the Future (RISF), is to provide opportunities for students to act like real writers, real scientists, real mathematicians, and real designers; and to develop technological fluency through involvement in robotic design activities.

Information and resource page for one of the country's largest K–12 robotic events. "These challenges were designed to engage and invite all groups of students, especially females, into the world of robotics."

UK Micromouse Championship

Micro Mouse:
http://www.tic.ac.uk/micromouse/toh.asp

A competition for older participants that could serve as the basis for K–12 activities.

Western Kansas LEGO Robotics Competition

Fort Hays State University, Hays, KS:
www.fhsu.edu/smei/Lego-Robotics/

See link to brochure. Brochure with challenge descriptions for April 9, 2010 competition.

Wings Over Mars/NASA Quest Challenge

NASA:
http://wingsovermars.arc.nasa.gov/challenge.html

This web-based, interactive exploration is designed to engage students in authentic scientific and engineering processes and may be used as the basis for robotics activities. The solutions relate to issues encountered daily by NASA personnel.

G. Blueprints and Plans Online

For each project, the platform (**RCX** *or* **NXT**) *or type of project is provided.*

A-Mazing

RCX, Brickshelf:

www.brickshelf.com/cgi-bin/gallery.cgi?f=44231

Sequential photos illustrate the construction of a maze-following robot.

Basic Programming Tips

RCX, Robolab Starter Sheet

FIRST LEGO League (FLL), Robolab 2.5, inventor level 4:

www.usfirst.org/uploadedFiles/Community/FLL/FLL_Assets/ProgrammingTips11.pdf

Suggestions and observations in text format on programming with some links to external resources for greater detail.

www.usfirst.org/uploadedFiles/Community/FLL/FLL_Assets/RobolabStarterSheet11.pdf

An illustrated chart and instructions tell how to get started using the Robolab robot programming software. Instructions for opening a new program within Robolab are given. Programming blocks that a new team is most likely to use first are shown.

Castor Bot

NXT, car/moving robot, nxtprograms.com:

www.nxtprograms.com/castor_bot/

Photo-illustrated building directions and a demo video. This is one of many dozens of projects at this source built with either the NXT over the counter or NXT Education sets.

www.nxtprograms.com/projects.html

Each project on this site gives free, detailed, photo-illustrated building instructions (requiring no parts beyond what comes with the standard kit) and a video of the completed robot. These projects are rated by building and programming difficulty.

Cattbot

RCX and **NXT,** roving mobile robot, Carnegie Mellon University Robotics Academy:

www.education.rec.ri.cmu.edu/products/teaching_robotc_tetrix/setup/buildshows/cattbot.html

This page offers detailed, sequential, photo-illustrated instructions on how to build this robot.

www.education.rec.ri.cmu.edu/content/lego/building/

This page offers building instructions for three NXT-based robot projects, Robotics Educator Model (R.E.M.), Taskbot, and Cattbot.

Comparison of Three Wheelchair Drive Train Models

RCX, Tufts University Center for Engineering Education Outreach and LEGOengineering.com:

www.legoengineering.com/images/stories/curriculum/LEcom_AssistiveTechRobotics.pdf

Robotics: Assistive Design for the Future, Curriculum Resources (Spring 2007 ed.) contains detailed, sequential, drawing-illustrated building directions for three versions of a motorized wheelchair. Scroll to page 77 to begin "Comparison of Wheelchair Drive Train Models."

Constructing a Fan

RCX, stationary construction of a fan, William Conrad:

This is part of the downloadable MSWord LEGO Amusement Park curriculum offered by William Conrad at www.engr.iupui.edu/~conrad/Lego/right.html

Scroll to Day 3, page 9, for this section. This page offers photo illustrations of the completed project, detailed, drawn illustrations of the required parts, and a lesson plan on how to introduce the project. The lesson plans were created by Kenya Taylor-Wash and Alan Mays, fifth grade teachers at Otis E. Brown School #20, Indianapolis Public Schools.

Constructopedia: Swing Set project, NXT Merry-Go-Round! Project, NXT Quick Start Car project

NXT Kit 9797, guidebook with basic instructions, Center for Engineering Education Outreach (CEEO), Tufts University:

www.education.rec.ri.cmu.edu/content/lego/building/media/Constructopedia%202.pdf

This complete, 64-page guidebook tells how to build constructions using the LEGO NXT materials. Scroll to page 51 to begin the section titled "Building Instructions: 15 Minute Building Projects" for these three projects.

Crawler

NXT, crawling robot, Ricquin.net:

www.ricquin.net/lego/instructions/crawler.htm

Gives photo-illustrated, sequential directions for building a crawling mobile robot.

http://ricquin.net/lego/instructions

Official LEGO Mindstorms Forum members have put this site together.

Mindstorms Building Instructions give building plans for five more NXT robot projects.

Domabot

NXT, vehicle, the NXT Classroom:

www.thenxtclassroom.com/build

A simple, quick build that's perfect for getting started in the classroom.

FIRST Place Scooter robot

RCX, FLL:

www.usfirst.org/uploadedFiles/Community/FLL/FLL_Assets/FIRSTScooter11.pdf

Detailed, sequential, photo-illustrated directions to build the FIRST Place Scooter robot.

Also for this robot from the same source:

Light sensor addition:
www.usfirst.org/uploadedFiles/Community/FLL/FLL_Assets/FIRSTScooterLight11.pdf

Touch sensor addition:
www.usfirst.org/uploadedFiles/Community/FLL/FLL_Assets/FIRSTScooterTouch11.pdf

Rotation sensor addition (scroll to page 2):
www.usfirst.org/uploadedFiles/Community/FLL/FLL_Assets/FIRSTScooterRotation11.pdf

LEGO Soccer Player
Parts Chart

RCX, Henrik Hautop Lund:

www.mip.sdu.dk/~hhl/RoboCupJr/Build

Building instructions are given for this robot, constructed in 57 steps, each one a separately drawn illustration presented in sequence.

www.mip.sdu.dk/~hhl/RoboCupJr/Build/partlist.txt

Parts Chart (downloadable) and has a link to a YouTube video of the robot in action.

Lesson 1: Introduction to LEGO Building
Lesson 2: Building a Sturdy Car

RCX, Tufts, CEEO:

www.ceeo.tufts.edu/robolabatceeo

Tufts University Center for Engineering Education Outreach (CEEO) offers a comprehensive, LEGO-related, upper elementary-level curriculum.

www.ceeo.tufts.edu/robolabatceeo/K12/curriculum_units/SimpleMachinesbyDesign.pdf

"Simple Machines by Design," contains Lesson 1: An Introduction to LEGO Building and Lesson 2: Building a Sturdy Car. Lesson 2, a complete, drawing-illustrated set of directions to build a motorized car, starts on page 4.

www.ceeo.tufts.edu/robolabatceeo/K12/curriculum_units/Engineering%20by%20Design.pdf

See "Steps to Build a Sturdy Car with an RCX," page 142 of "Engineering by Design: Lego Based Building Lessons for Grade One."

Maze Robot

RCX, Kristina Lundqvist, MIT; modifications by David Wang:

www.mit.edu/~kristina/Lego/UnifiedF04/Build%20Instructions/Maze%20Robot%20Instructions.pdf

Detailed, illustrated, sequential building directions with full text explanation.

Plotter

RCX, plotting robot, Ricquin.net:

http://ricquin.net/lego/instructions/plotter.htm

Gives detailed, sequential, illustrated directions to build the robot (downloadable) and has a link to a YouTube video of the robot in action.

Robotics Workshop: Advanced Bot Plans

RCX and **NXT,** Convict Episcopal de Luxembourg:

www.convict.lu/Jeunes/RoboticsIntro.htm

Links to many advanced student LEGO Robot plans, ideas, and videos.

Sumo Robot

RCX, ROX Solid Foundation Software:

http://roxsoftware.com/legos/robots/SRis/SRis_Complete_Model-00.html

Each in a series of web pages offers a step in the sequential construction of this robot. Illustrated with drawings. (Pages must be viewed on a computer.)

http://roxsoftware.com/legos/robots/SteerOne/Steer_One-00.html

Similar to the sumo, this design is a line-following robot.

Tankbot

RCX, vehicle, Carnegie Mellon University Robotics Academy:

www.education.rec.ri.cmu.edu/roboticscurriculum/teachertraining/tankbotbldginstr.pdf

Detailed, sequential, photo-illustrated building plans.

Tracked Bumper Bots

RCX, vehicle, Doug's LEGO Robotics Page:

www.visi.com/~dc/bumper/index.htm

Detailed, sequential, photo-illustrated building plans for a more advanced project.

Trusty Bot

RCX, a light-sensor enabled vehicle, O'Reilly Catalog:

http://oreilly.com/catalog/lmstorms/building

Detailed, sequential drawing illustrated plans for Trusty and four other bots. These plans can be used directly from the web pages or downloaded from this site.

H. And More!

The Art of LEGO Design (PowerPoint Presentation)

Carnegie Mellon School of Computer Science:
www.cs.cmu.edu/afs/cs.cmu.edu/academic/class/16311/www/ppp/LEGO_Design_2008.ppt

PowerPoint presentation tells how to build better robots with LEGO Robotics materials: minimize mechanical breakdowns, build easy-to-control bots, use good design strategy, and strive for elegant, clever solutions.

Basic Programming Tips

FIRST LEGO League:
www.usfirst.org/uploadedFiles/Community/FLL/FLL_Assets/ProgrammingTips11.pdf

This four-page paper offers advice to novices on programming, such as program in small steps, take time to learn the basics, save often, and much more.

Botball Curriculum Resources

Borball:
www.botball.org/curriculum

A variety of worthwhile downloads more advanced than basic Mindstorms include navigation, rotation, and distance lessons.

Building LEGO Robots for FIRST LEGO League, Version: 1.0

Dean Hystad, Minnesota FIRST LEGO League:
http://neuron.eng.wayne.edu/LEGO_ROBOTICS/lego_building_tutorial.pdf

A complete, RCX-oriented curriculum, sponsored by Innovations in Science and Technology Education (INSciTE) (www.hitechkids.org), contains detailed explanations, figures, and tables to help teachers and coaches understand how to help students build robots (91 pages).

Canyon Creek Elementary Robolab Curriculum

Belinda Gingrich:
http://pages.sbcglobal.net/gingrich/

Complete lesson plans for Grades 2, 3, 4, and 5 (Winch & Rachet, Bumper Car, Line Follower, and Kinetic Sculpture Garden) use RCX team challenge kits and NXT Mindstorms kits.

Construction Tips and Tricks

Legobot Headquarters, Mike Wampole:
www.geocities.com/legobothq/tips.htm#top
www.reocities.com/legobothq/index-2.htm

Interesting ideas and building directions, primarily for non-motorized robots, such as how to make joints without a hinge, a legobot, stiff joints, and more.

Core Concepts

Carnegie Mellon University Robotics Academy:
www.education.rec.ri.cmu.edu/roboticscurriculum/multimedia/core.shtml

A page of links to core concepts of robotics, each with further links to explanatory content, plus link to teachers' resources.

Curriculum Map for Robotics

Robotics—Galileo Educational Network:
www.galileo.org/robotics/curriculum.html
www.galileo.org/robotics/schools.html
www.galileo.org/robotics/ourrobots.html

Interactive mapping of interrelated curriculum areas having to do with robotics. Materials discuss how robotics is integrated into the regular instructional program in a number of schools and grades. Students' narratives about their robots are illustrated with photos and videos.

Design Challenges (activities)

Carnegie Mellon University Robotics Academy:
www.education.rec.ri.cmu.edu/roboticscurriculum/multimedia/design.shtml

A page of links to a wide variety of student robot activities has brief descriptions, grade levels, and difficulty ratings. Each activity contains numerous links to explanations of essential concepts students will need to understand to complete the build.

Diameters and Circumferences

The NXT Classroom, Damian Kee:
www.thenxtclassroom.com/sites/thenxtclassroom.com/files/
Diameters%20and%20Circumference.pdf

A lesson plan and informational worksheet for students in Grades 6–7 explains basic math concepts needed to build a robot.

EDU F500 Robot Design for Teachers

Jeffrey Nowak and Carlos Pomalaza-Ráez, Purdue University:
http://raven.ipfw.edu/teacher/

A page of links to 11 lesson plans on LEGO Robotics-based learning posted by members of an elementary through high school education class.

Get Set! Go! Robotics

Tad A. Douce, Jerffersonville, IN:

This website is an online textbook for the River Valley Middle School Technology Education/Project Lead the Way class taught by Tad A. Douce:
www.getsetsite.org/robotics/robowellington.htm

A rich source of curriculum, instructional materials, building and programming instructions, activities and challenges, illustrated with photos and videos. Oriented toward RCX-Robolab materials yet of use to all.

Get Started: LEGO Mindstorms

Carnegie Mellon University Robotics Academy:
www.education.rec.ri.cmu.edu/content/lego/start/

Introductory information on NXT hardware and software.

Go, Gadget, Go! Building Robots with LEGO Mindstorms

Science Buddies:
www.sciencebuddies.org/science-fair-projects/project_ideas/Elec_p052.shtml

This instructional resource gives background, supplementary materials, and focused activities on student robotics. The goal of the featured project is to build a fast, lightweight, stable robot.

How Do You Store Your LEGO in Class?

The NXT Classroom:
www.thenxtclassroom.com/sites/thenxtclassroom.com/files/how_to_store_LEGO.pdf

Great ideas on organizing and storing robotics materials in the classroom plus many other worthwhile links on this site.

How Robotics Achieves Outcomes: Information Addressing How This Robotics Curriculum Addresses Content Standards

Carnegie Mellon University:
www.education.rec.ri.cmu.edu/downloads/education_standards/data/robotics_outcomes.pdf

National Teacher Standards connections for science, math, and technology.

Instructional Media Robot Building Instructions

Colorado School of Mines:
http://outreach.mines.edu/cont_ed/courses/robo/media/building/building.htm?CMSPAGE=Outreach/Cont_Ed/courses/robo/media/building/building.htm

A rich source of high-quality, photo-illustrated building instructions plus videos of students at work on robots and demonstrating their robots.

LEGO Design

Ohio State University, School of Engineering:
www.physics.ohio-state.edu/~jdw/LegoDesign.pdf

Comprehensive, 54-page resource shows how to design and build better motorized robots with LEGO robotics materials. Detailed photos and diagrams illustrate numerous tips and explain for what purposes various parts work best.

LEGO Design and LEGO Geartrains

Lego Design by James F. Young, John K. Bennett, Fred Martin, et al., Rice University. LEGO Geartrains by Sergei Egorov. Owl Net:
www.owlnet.rice.edu/~elec201/Book/legos.html

Also (for full-blown engineering students):
www.malgil.com/esl/lego/geartrains.html

Serious engineering of LEGO materials. Meshing Table lists all useful ways to position LEGO gears so they mesh properly (for keen engineering students).

LEGO Mindstorms for Fifth Grade: Amusement Park Theme

William Conrad, School of Engineering and Technology, Indiana University Purdue University Indianapolis (IUPUI):
www.engr.iupui.edu/~conrad/Lego/right.html

Teachers Kenya Taylor-Wash and Alan Mays revised plans for an IUPUI summer camp program for use in their fifth grade classes. The MSWord downloadable plans use LEGO Mindstorms and Robolab software; integrate math, science, and language arts; and cover numerous Indiana state standards.

LEGO Mindstorms Robots by Jonathan Knudsen

O'Reilly Online Catalog: The Unofficial Guide to LEGO Mindstorms Robots: http://oreilly.com/catalog/lmstorms/building

Detailed, photo-illustrated directions for building five different robots (RCX generation materials).

LEGO Robot Competition: A Competition Designed by High School Students for Middle School Students and Fifth Graders

Best Practices of Technology Integration, Farmington Hills, MI, Joyce Tomlinson:
www.remc11.k12.mi.us/bstpract/bpII/Lessons/99019/99019.pdf

An older implementation manual tells how to organize a LEGO Robot Competition from start to finish.

LEGO Robot Pages

Utrecht University:
http://people.cs.uu.nl/markov/lego/

An interesting site with a variety of resources that take LEGO Robotics beyond the basics.

LEGO Robotics: Measuring and Graphing Speed of a LEGO Robotic Car

Maureen Reilly:
www.maureenreilly.com/robotics/; www.teachersnetwork.org/readysettech/reilly/LEGORobotics_MaureenReilly.pdf

Complete lesson plan (Grades 3–6), instructions, students' feedback, photos, bibliography, and links to resources.

LEGO Robotics & Resources

Carnegie Mellon University, National Robotics Engineering Center, Robotics Academy:
www.education.rec.ri.cmu.edu/content/lego/

A comprehensive, NXT-oriented curriculum on how to design, build, and program LEGO robots for middle and high school students. Portions of this, like building instructions, are free.

LEGO Walker, inspired by Theo Jansen's "strandbeest"

Robotics Learning, Steve Putz:
www.roboticslearning.com/jansenwalker/

This video of a remarkably designed and constructed LEGO Robot (RCX) illustrates what's possible with these materials.

Lesson Plans for LEGO Mindstorms Robots

Brooklyn College:
www.sci.brooklyn.cuny.edu/~sklar/er/curriculum/

A short, complete plan for guiding students through learning LEGO Robotics (with RCX-Robolab or Lejos-Java) includes building and programming instructions, programming sensors, and music. Computer science concepts are emphasized, plans for math and science lessons, and more.

Liftoff to Learning: Let's Talk Robotics

NASA Quest:
http://quest.nasa.gov/space/teachers/liftoff/robotics.html

A short-term instructional unit presents the history and theory of robotics combined with a hands-on activity that may be adapted to LEGO Robotics materials.

Line Following

Luke Laurie:
http://homepage.mac.com/mrlaurie/robo/documents/linefollowing.pdf

Instructions and a line-following program for a LEGO robot using Robolab 2.5 in two pages with photos.

Middle School Curriculum

Carnegie Mellon University Robotics Academy:
www.education.rec.ri.cmu.edu/content/curriculum/middle_school/sub_page_999/

Comprehensive curriculum for RCX robotics: Why Robotics? Standards/Benchmarks; Introduction to Robotics; Introduction to Hardware; Introduction to Software and Electronic Control; Introduction to Programming; Design and Mechanics (Introduction to Gears Gears, Speed, Torque); Simple Machines; Sensors (Touch Sensors, Light Sensors, Temperature Sensors, Rotational Sensors); and more.

Playing with Gears

Syngress:
www.elsevierdirect.com/downloads/SyngressFreeE-booklets/Lego/1928994679.pdf

Comprehensive, LEGO-specific material on gears, pulleys, chains, belts, etc., presented on a level appropriate for students.

RoboChallenge Tutorials

Luke Laurie:
http://homepage.mac.com/mrlaurie/robo/tugowartutorial.html
http://homepage.mac.com/mrlaurie/robo/sumotutorial.html
http://homepage.mac.com/mrlaurie/robo/rover.html

Excellent text and video descriptions, explanations, illustrations and demonstrations of "must do" student robotics activities, including Tug O' War, Sumo, and Rover Challenge. Learn to build a robot that can pull another robot in a test of strength. Learn to build a sumo robot that can battle against another robot in a circular ring. Push the other robot out to win (with video). Use two Mindstorms NXT kits to build a remote control and a RobotRover. Send the rover exploring in this challenge similar to robotic explorations of the oceans and other planets.

Robolab Programming Notes

Steve Putz, Robotics Learning:
http://ncafll.home.comcast.net/~ncafll/guides/robolab-notes.pdf

An illustrated guide to programming in Robolab.

Robolab Tutorial

Steve Dakin, Hacienda Robotics:
www.qmate.com/robotics/RobolabTutorialSlides.pdf

A clear and thorough tutorial on programming in ROBOLAB for coaches and parents of kids in the FIRST LEGO League program. Comprehensive, RCX-oriented curriculum in how to design, build, and program LEGO robots for middle school, high school, and some upper elementary students. Content is "designed for teachers using LEGO Mindstorms RCX hardware and Robolab software."

Robot Building Instructions

Colorado School of Mines Teacher Enhancement Programs:
http://outreach.mines.edu/cont_ed/courses/robo/media/building/building.htm

Blueprinted instructions for a variety of robots, developed for Robocamps in 2003–2004, are on this site, plus videos and more.

Robot Turns

Richard Wright:
www.weirdrichard.com/roboglee.htm

A complete lesson plan centers on the challenge to design and build a LEGO robot that turns. This resource offers strategically placed links for hints and illustrations.

Robotics: Assistive Design for the Future

Tufts University Center for Engineering Education Outreach and LEGOengineering.com, Morgan Hynes, Tufts University, and Haruna Tada, TechBoston Northeastern University, contributors:
www.legoengineering.com/images/stories/curriculum/LEcom_AssistiveTechRobotics.pdf

A complete, RCX-oriented curriculum with teachers' guide, lesson plans, building and programming instructions, and student worksheets (173 pages).

Robotics Camp 2000

Indiana University/Purdue University:
http://raven.ipfw.edu/RoboCamp2K
http://users.ipfw.edu/groff/Groff_and_Raez.pdf

Text and photographic record of the activities and results of a summer robotics camp (4 half-day sessions) for kids ages 8–14. The structure of the course, technical instructions, and photos of results illustrate what's possible with LEGO Robotics. This paper describes the thinking behind the camp and other robotics-oriented activities sponsored by the two universities.

Robotics Curriculum

Carnegie Mellon University Robotics Academy:
www.education.rec.ri.cmu.edu/roboticscurriculum/index_to_robotics.htm

Robotics Engineer Hawaii: Online Book

Dwayne Abuel:
https://sites.google.com/site/roboticsengineerhawaii/Home

A complete course in NXT LEGO Robotics taught from the engineering perspective.

Robots 101

ROVer Ranch, NASA Johnson Space Center:
http://prime.jsc.nasa.gov/ROV/library.html
http://prime.jsc.nasa.gov/ROV/vocab.html

A trove of materials for fleshing out robotics activities with academic connections, including factual texts, stories, vocabulary, illustrations, examples of robots, and more.

Robots Alive

PBS:
www.pbs.org/safarchive/4_class/45_pguides/pguide_705/4575_idx.html

Not LEGO-specific—PBS teaching guide intended to accompany viewing of *Scientific American Frontiers* TV show on robotics, narrated by Alan Alda. This is a rich source of curriculum and materials to teach robotics in context.

Also see link to program at hulu:
www.hulu.com/watch/23328/scientific-american-frontiers-robot-pals

Sample Robot Models, Sample Robot Activities, LEGO Robotics Creatures

Robotics Learning, Steve Putz:
www.roboticslearning.com/examples/robots.html
www.roboticslearning.com/activities/
www.roboticslearning.com/activities/creatures.html

Illustrations of RCX and NXT LEGO robots, descriptions of worthwhile student robotics activities and handouts to support them, and examples of activities from creatures challenges.

The Science of Gears: Lesson Plans and Other Activities

The Franklin Institute:
www.fi.edu/time/Journey/Time/Lessons/grlesson1.html

Not LEGO-specific, this material covers the principles of gears.

STEM Lessons Taught Using Robotics

Carnegie Mellon University Robotics Academy:
www.education.rec.ri.cmu.edu/downloads/education_standards/standards_menus/STEM%20lessons%20for%20Immersion%20Units.pdf

Chart of math, science, and technology concepts demonstrated through robotics.

Toeing the Line: Experiments with Line-Following Algorithms

Home School Learning Network, Jonathon A. Gray:
www.homeschoollearning.com/vsf/exhibit/senior/spring-03/01-jgray/01-jgray_report.pdf

Concentrates on slightly more advanced programming, rated for ninth grade (RCX Robolab oriented).

Tutorials (for teachers), Design Challenges (for students), and Core Concepts (for all)

Carnegie Mellon University Robotics Academy:
www.education.rec.ri.cmu.edu/roboticscurriculum/multimedia/tutorials.html

A page of links to self-directed tutorials on essential concepts, like gears and speed, gears and strength, touch sensors, and more. Contains lessons with specific programs to follow.

USS Missouri Robotics

Dwayne Abuel, USS Missouri Robotics Program:
http://sites.google.com/site/ussmissourilearner/home

This comprehensive body of NXT-oriented instructional information and challenges is designed for students on a nautical theme.

YET Robotics Curriculum

Youth Engaged in Technology (YET), The Pennsylvania State University: http://cyfar.cas.psu.edu/PDFs/YET_Robotics_curric.pdf

Penn State's YET activities closely follow the "Robotics Educator" CD from Carnegie Mellon's Robotics Academy with insights into structuring robotics activities and courses.

APPENDIX C

Glossary

accountable talk. Accountable talk is an instructional approach that values student discussions, primarily directed at sharing the thinking, problem solving, strategizing, and decision making underlying their work. In classrooms where accountable talk is part of the learning equation, students talk accountably to their peer co-learners, probing and explaining how their work addresses, satisfies, and expands on learning foci or challenges.

Alice. Alice is a 3-D programming environment that makes it easy to create an animation for telling a story, playing an interactive game, or creating a video to share on the web. It is used as a tool to introduce students to programming on a computer. Alice uses a graphic, drag-and-drop interface. It's available as a free download (www.alice.org).

autonomous robots. Autonomous robots can perform desired tasks without continuous human guidance. While some robots are directly or remotely controlled by humans who monitor their behaviors and direct them, autonomous robots follow programs written to provide directions to them contingent on situations they encounter.

axle. An axle is a stationary or rotating rod that goes through the center of a wheel/wheels or a beam. An axle, powered by a motor, turns the wheels of a vehicle or turns the vanes of a windmill.

baseplate (or plate). The thin building sheet on which LEGO pieces are affixed.

blueprints. Detailed plans that inform and direct the construction of a robot.

Bluetooth. A wireless technology that enables devices to communicate over short distances. LEGO NXT Robotics materials use Bluetooth to enable downloading a program from the computer on which it is written to the NXT processor in the robot or to send it remote instructions.

bot. The term *bot* is short for robot, often used in a name descriptive of the robot's particular function, for example, tug-of-war bot, art bot, fetch bot, gather bot, and line-follower bot.

brick. An oblong-shaped LEGO component. LEGO building pieces are called bricks, however, when talking about robots *the* brick refers to the programmable piece that holds the power and stores the programs that run LEGO robots. A programmable brick also serves as a robot's core element, where connections to motors and sensors can be made. An RCX brick is generally integrated into the constructed body of the robot. A brick is the same thickness as three baseplates on top of one another.

build. The process together with the period of time involved in producing a robot is called the build.

collaborative learning. An approach to teaching and learning that focuses on learners working together on activities. This approach has much in common with constructivism, in which the social dimensions of learning help groups of students to learn.

constructivism. A theory of learning that holds that learners create meaning for themselves as a result of reflection on their own experiences.

firmware. A small program required to run an electronic device, firmware is generally fixed, unlike computer software that the user works with in a dynamic fashion. In LEGO Robotics, the brick (processor) that holds and runs the robot's program uses firmware.

FIRST LEGO League (FLL). An international organization begun in 1989 devoted to running robotic competitions. One of the most popular of the organized programs that offer robotics activities for students, FIRST LEGO League is designed to give young people opportunities to learn about robotics. FLL has a central structure that directs and supports activities, though activities are presented through a hierarchy of local events. FIRST is an acronym derived from "For Inspiration and Recognition of Science and Technology."

GEMS. An acronym for girls in engineering, math, and science, GEMS is an after-school science, math, and technology enrichment project for young women in Grades 4–8 in Minneapolis. The GEMS program is a collaboration among NASA, Augsburg College, and more than a dozen urban Minneapolis schools (www.augsburg.edu/nasa_space_grant/gems.html).

Inventor. Of the three programming levels offered by LEGO Robotics Robolab software, Inventor is level two, more advanced than Pilot (which is level one).

Investigator. Of the three programming levels offered by LEGO Robotics Robolab software, Investigator is the third and highest level. A student advances from programming as a Pilot to a more advanced Inventor, and then achieves the level of Investigator, which combines the proficiencies of the first two levels.

IR Tower. IR stands for infrared. The IR Tower is a device included with LEGO Robotics RCX Generation kits that enables students to download the robot's program from the computer on which it is created and transmit the program to the RCX brick (processor) of the robot. The tower operates on communications technology based on electromagnetic waves.

Junior FIRST LEGO League (Jr.FLL). Junior FIRST LEGO League is a newer program (begun in 2004) offered by FIRST (For Inspiration and Recognition of Science and Technology), the umbrella organization for the FIRST Robotics and FIRST LEGO League (FLL) programs. Jr.FLL is offered to accommodate students ages 6 through 9 who are too young to participate in FLL.

LEGO. LEGO materials are popularly provided to students and young people for play, experimentation, and learning activities and is the name of the provider that produces and sells these materials. LEGO components are construction materials that provide a platform for activities that focus on designing and constructing things. LEGO bricks, interlocking construction modules, are the basis of LEGO materials. Among the many varieties of LEGO materials are LEGO Robotics materials.

LEGO Education. The Division of the LEGO Group devoted to educational applications and sales of LEGO products.

LEGO Mindstorms for Schools. LEGO Mindstorms (also spelled MINDSTORMS) for Schools are kits that contain the same materials as in other LEGO Robotics packages, though the quantities of components and parts are specific to the needs of students and teachers in schools.

LEGO Robotics. The term LEGO Robotics refers to the LEGO materials and practices of using them to construct robots. LEGO Robotics materials are durable, small scale, and relatively low cost. LEGO Robotics are favored by schools, hobbyists, and parents because of their practicality, and they work similarly to more expensive, full-scale robotics materials used by scientists and businesspeople.

LEGO Robotics Kits. Packaged collections of LEGO Robotics materials are called LEGO Robotics Kits. Generally, these include the materials needed to build many possible types of one robot. The kits include such items as robot body construction pieces, connectors, the "brick" or processor, motors, and sensors. Numerous varieties of kits over the years bear the LEGO name. While LEGO Robotics materials may be purchased singly, beginners appreciate that each kit includes preselected parts, instructions, and the storage bin the kit comes in.

metacognition. Understanding one's own thought processes. After a class robotics session, when students discuss how they solved a design or programming problem, they are engaging in metacognition.

Mindstorms NXT. This programmable LEGO Robotics kit comes with the NXT-G programming software. Mindstorms NXT was preceded by LEGO Mindstorms and followed by LEGO Mindstorms NXT 2.0.

narrative procedure. See procedural narrative.

NXT. Pronounced and spelled by some as "NEXT," NXT is a newer generation of LEGO Robotics materials developed after the original RCX Generation, which used standard LEGO building blocks. NXT components have a more modern, streamlined look, and the programmable NXT's processor (brick) is more powerful than its RCX predecessor.

NXT-G. NXT-G is a programming software that is intended for use with the NXT generation of LEGO Robotics materials.

NXT Generation of LEGO Robotics. In the NXT Generation of LEGO Robotics materials, the robot's onboard processor (brick) is labeled "NXT."

object-based programming. Object-based programming is a simplified system of computer programming in which graphic objects—or icons—are used instead of a character-based language. By assembling a series of these graphic objects in sequence, students produce programs to direct the robot.

Photoshop Elements. Photoshop Elements is Adobe's more affordable version of its photo-editing software Photoshop.

Picasa. Google's free, downloadable photo-editing software (http://picasa.google.com).

Pilot. The popular Robolab software used to program LEGO Robots. Pilot 1 is the most basic and most commonly used of Robolab's programming levels. See the Robolab site (www.technologystudent.com/robo1/robex.htm) for specific information on Pilot 1, Pilot 2, Pilot 3, and Pilot 4.

plate. The thin building baseplate on which LEGO pieces are affixed.

platform. The hardware and/or software that serves as the foundation of a computer's operating system or application program. The word "environment" is used synonymously with platform.

Power Puzzle. In 2007 the FIRST LEGO League's challenge competition was to see which team could construct the most efficient Power Puzzle. The challenge was designed as a way for students to learn about alternative energy and featured tasks such as moving power lines, evaluating/choosing fuel sources, and planting trees.

procedural narrative/narrative procedure. A written description of the process by which something is achieved, created, or accomplished. Similar to a recipe or a "how to" manual, a procedural narrative is sequential, describing the order in which steps were or are to be taken and the details of each step, so that someone else can replicate the entire process.

processor. A computing device or portion of a computing device that is dedicated to understanding (processing) data and/or carrying out the instructions of a program. In LEGO Robotics, the RCX or NXT microprocessor (brick) is the robot's processor.

programming. The process of writing digital instructions for a robot. In LEGO Robotics, students use object-based programming on computers to tell the robot what to do. The program is transmitted to the bot's brick, where it is stored.

project-/problem-based learning. Teaching and learning driven by the students' need to solve a problem or design a project that culminates in the creation of a product or performance. Examples of such products are robots, science projects, art exhibits, and musical performances.

RCX. The first popular generation of robotics materials from LEGO was named RCX. The RCX platform uses standard LEGO construction bricks/blocks that snap together (unlike the NXT generation of materials) and the yellow, programmable RCX brick.

Robofest. An annual autonomous robotics competition focusing on STEM (science, technology, engineering, and math) learning for students in Grades 5–12 and college students. Robofest challenges teams of students to design, build, and program robots to compete in a variety of categories in two age divisions. Robofest is a registered trademark of Lawrence Technological University, Southfield, Michigan (www.robofest.net).

Robolab. One of the most popular pieces of software developed for use with LEGO Robotics. Robolab is object-based programming, using icons to build diagrams as a method of writing programs that control the robots. Robolab has progressive programming levels, so that some students may work on a simple, basic level, and others may move on to more difficult programs, such as those that incorporate data collection.

robot. A mechanical device or machine designed to assist humans in their work or to do their work for them. Some robots (or bots) are humanoid, that is, they resemble humans. However, the majority of real-world robots are built to perform their functions in the most efficient ways; that is, their forms follow their functions (and most real-world robots are stationary).

RobotC. RobotC is a programming language for LEGO Robotics adapted from the computer programming language "C." For more information, see www.robotc.net/download/nxt.

robotics challenge. A robotics *challenge* is a type of robotics-based learning activity in which students are given a problem or a series of problems to solve by designing and operating a robot.

rotation sensor. The rotation sensor counts the number of revolutions the motor makes. In programming a brick, instead of directing the robot to go for a certain length of time, the rotation sensor allows the programmer to direct the bot to go for a specific number of revolutions before it stops. (In the RCX LEGO platform, the rotation sensor is separate from the motor; in LEGO's NXT platform, the rotation sensor is incorporated into the motor.)

rubrics. A student learning and achievement assessment instrument generally written in the form of a table or a graphic organizer. Rubrics list the various criteria by which students' work will be assessed with a point value for each criterion. Rubrics are a popular alternative method of assessment, closely associated with project-based and portfolio-based student work. Rubrics are used to assess work that cannot be evaluated by traditional testing. RubiStar (http://rubistar.4teachers.org) is a free tool to help teachers create rubrics.

screencast video. A screencast video is a movie that shows the changes a user sees on his/her computer monitor (screen) over time, along with audio explanations of the unfolding action.

screenshot. A screenshot is an immobile picture of a computer's monitor (screen).

sensors. In robotics, sensors are devices that are added to the robot to collect data or to enable the bot to sense certain stimuli. Common sensors used in LEGO Robotics are the touch sensor, light sensor, sound sensor, and ultrasonic sensor.

SD card. An SD card (a secure digital memory card), also called flash memory, is a small data storage device. The SD card can be inserted directly into computers and other devices or can be accessed via detachable SD card readers.

STEM. An acronym formed from the subject names science, technology, engineering, and mathematics, STEM is a popular organizing principle for instruction in these areas. Advocates for STEM instruction believe that these areas' strong interrelationships justify their teaching and learning in integrated fashion.

storytelling. Storytelling (also called digital storytelling) is a popular approach to teaching and learning literacy skills and content in related areas. Storytelling draws connections between the ancient art of telling stories and formal instruction and frequently requires students to conduct research, make outlines (sometimes using storyboarding), write stories based on their research, and give oral presentations.

USB cable. A USB cable is a type of cable and connector used to enable communication between computers and processors and peripheral or attached devices (i.e., a LEGO Robotics brick and a robot's motor). USB cables are also made for cameras to transfer photos to a computer. The abbreviation "USB" is formed from the words "unified (or universal) serial bus."

USB port. All newer model computers have a USB port enabling a USB portable hard drive to be connected to the computer's operating system.

WeDo Robotics kits. A newer generation of LEGO Robotics materials, WeDo Robotics kits are specifically designed to accommodate the learning needs of young children, especially those for whom RCX or NXT materials may be too difficult or advanced.

APPENDIX D

NETS for Students, Teachers, and Administrators

LEGO Robotics is a body of materials, resources, and practices, as well as an extended community of learners and practitioners. It offers a multitude of opportunities for teachers and administrators and leaders to approach and conform to the ISTE NETS and Performance Indicators.

National Educational Technology Standards for Students (NETS•S)

All K–12 students should be prepared to meet the following standards and performance indicators.

1. **Creativity and Innovation**

   Students demonstrate creative thinking, construct knowledge, and develop innovative products and processes using technology. Students:

   a. apply existing knowledge to generate new ideas, products, or processes

   b. create original works as a means of personal or group expression

c. use models and simulations to explore complex systems and issues

d. identify trends and forecast possibilities

2. **Communication and Collaboration**

Students use digital media and environments to communicate and work collaboratively, including at a distance, to support individual learning and contribute to the learning of others. Students:

a. interact, collaborate, and publish with peers, experts, or others employing a variety of digital environments and media

b. communicate information and ideas effectively to multiple audiences using a variety of media and formats

c. develop cultural understanding and global awareness by engaging with learners of other cultures

d. contribute to project teams to produce original works or solve problems

3. **Research and Information Fluency**

Students apply digital tools to gather, evaluate, and use information. Students:

a. plan strategies to guide inquiry

b. locate, organize, analyze, evaluate, synthesize, and ethically use information from a variety of sources and media

c. evaluate and select information sources and digital tools based on the appropriateness to specific tasks

d. process data and report results

4. **Critical Thinking, Problem Solving, and Decision Making**

Students use critical-thinking skills to plan and conduct research, manage projects, solve problems, and make informed decisions using appropriate digital tools and resources. Students:

a. identify and define authentic problems and significant questions for investigation

b. plan and manage activities to develop a solution or complete a project

c. collect and analyze data to identify solutions and make informed decisions

d. use multiple processes and diverse perspectives to explore alternative solutions

5. **Digital Citizenship**

Students understand human, cultural, and societal issues related to technology and practice legal and ethical behavior. Students:

a. advocate and practice the safe, legal, and responsible use of information and technology

b. exhibit a positive attitude toward using technology that supports collaboration, learning, and productivity

c. demonstrate personal responsibility for lifelong learning

d. exhibit leadership for digital citizenship

6. **Technology Operations and Concepts**

Students demonstrate a sound understanding of technology concepts, systems, and operations. Students:

a. understand and use technology systems

b. select and use applications effectively and productively

c. troubleshoot systems and applications

d. transfer current knowledge to the learning of new technologies

National Educational Technology Standards for Teachers (NETS•T)

All classroom teachers should be prepared to meet the following standards and performance indicators.

1. Facilitate and Inspire Student Learning and Creativity

Teachers use their knowledge of subject matter, teaching and learning, and technology to facilitate experiences that advance student learning, creativity, and innovation in both face-to-face and virtual environments. Teachers:

a. promote, support, and model creative and innovative thinking and inventiveness

b. engage students in exploring real-world issues and solving authentic problems using digital tools and resources

c. promote student reflection using collaborative tools to reveal and clarify students' conceptual understanding and thinking, planning, and creative processes

d. model collaborative knowledge construction by engaging in learning with students, colleagues, and others in face-to-face and virtual environments

2. Design and Develop Digital-Age Learning Experiences and Assessments

Teachers design, develop, and evaluate authentic learning experiences and assessments incorporating contemporary tools and resources to maximize content learning in context and to develop the knowledge, skills, and attitudes identified in the NETS·S. Teachers:

a. design or adapt relevant learning experiences that incorporate digital tools and resources to promote student learning and creativity

b. develop technology-enriched learning environments that enable all students to pursue their individual curiosities and become active participants in setting their own educational goals, managing their own learning, and assessing their own progress

c. customize and personalize learning activities to address students' diverse learning styles, working strategies, and abilities using digital tools and resources

d. provide students with multiple and varied formative and summative assessments aligned with content and technology standards and use resulting data to inform learning and teaching

3. Model Digital-Age Work and Learning

Teachers exhibit knowledge, skills, and work processes representative of an innovative professional in a global and digital society. Teachers:

a. demonstrate fluency in technology systems and the transfer of current knowledge to new technologies and situations

b. collaborate with students, peers, parents, and community members using digital tools and resources to support student success and innovation

c. communicate relevant information and ideas effectively to students, parents, and peers using a variety of digital-age media and formats

d. model and facilitate effective use of current and emerging digital tools to locate, analyze, evaluate, and use information resources to support research and learning

4. Promote and Model Digital Citizenship and Responsibility

Teachers understand local and global societal issues and responsibilities in an evolving digital culture and exhibit legal and ethical behavior in their professional practices. Teachers:

a. advocate, model, and teach safe, legal, and ethical use of digital information and technology, including respect for copyright, intellectual property, and the appropriate documentation of sources

b. address the diverse needs of all learners by using learner-centered strategies and providing equitable access to appropriate digital tools and resources

c. promote and model digital etiquette and responsible social interactions related to the use of technology and information

d. develop and model cultural understanding and global awareness by engaging with colleagues and students of other cultures using digital-age communication and collaboration tools

5. Engage in Professional Growth and Leadership

Teachers continuously improve their professional practice, model lifelong learning, and exhibit leadership in their school and professional community by promoting and demonstrating the effective use of digital tools and resources. Teachers:

a. participate in local and global learning communities to explore creative applications of technology to improve student learning

b. exhibit leadership by demonstrating a vision of technology infusion, participating in shared decision making and community building, and developing the leadership and technology skills of others

c. evaluate and reflect on current research and professional practice on a regular basis to make effective use of existing and emerging digital tools and resources in support of student learning

d. contribute to the effectiveness, vitality, and self-renewal of the teaching profession and of their school and community

National Educational Technology Standards for Administrators (NETS•A)

All school administrators should be prepared to meet the following standards and performance indicators.

1. Visionary Leadership

Educational Administrators inspire and lead development and implementation of a shared vision for comprehensive integration of technology to promote excellence and support transformation throughout the organization. Educational Administrators:

- a. inspire and facilitate among all stakeholders a shared vision of purposeful change that maximizes use of digital-age resources to meet and exceed learning goals, support effective instructional practice, and maximize performance of district and school leaders
- b. engage in an ongoing process to develop, implement, and communicate technology-infused strategic plans aligned with a shared vision
- c. advocate on local, state, and national levels for policies, programs, and funding to support implementation of a technology-infused vision and strategic plan

2. Digital-Age Learning Culture

Educational Administrators create, promote, and sustain a dynamic, digital-age learning culture that provides a rigorous, relevant, and engaging education for all students. Educational Administrators:

- a. ensure instructional innovation focused on continuous improvement of digital-age learning
- b. model and promote the frequent and effective use of technology for learning
- c. provide learner-centered environments equipped with technology and learning resources to meet the individual, diverse needs of all learners
- d. ensure effective practice in the study of technology and its infusion across the curriculum

e. promote and participate in local, national, and global learning communities that stimulate innovation, creativity, and digital-age collaboration

3. Excellence in Professional Practice

Educational Administrators promote an environment of professional learning and innovation that empowers educators to enhance student learning through the infusion of contemporary technologies and digital resources. Educational Administrators:

a. allocate time, resources, and access to ensure ongoing professional growth in technology fluency and integration

b. facilitate and participate in learning communities that stimulate, nurture, and support administrators, faculty, and staff in the study and use of technology

c. promote and model effective communication and collaboration among stakeholders using digital-age tools

d. stay abreast of educational research and emerging trends regarding effective use of technology and encourage evaluation of new technologies for their potential to improve student learning

4. Systemic Improvement

Educational Administrators provide digital-age leadership and management to continuously improve the organization through the effective use of information and technology resources. Educational Administrators:

a. lead purposeful change to maximize the achievement of learning goals through the appropriate use of technology and media-rich resources

b. collaborate to establish metrics, collect and analyze data, interpret results, and share findings to improve staff performance and student learning

c. recruit and retain highly competent personnel who use technology creatively and proficiently to advance academic and operational goals

d. establish and leverage strategic partnerships to support systemic improvement

e. establish and maintain a robust infrastructure for technology including integrated, interoperable technology systems to support management, operations, teaching, and learning

5. Digital Citizenship

Educational Administrators model and facilitate understanding of social, ethical, and legal issues and responsibilities related to an evolving digital culture. Educational Administrators:

a. ensure equitable access to appropriate digital tools and resources to meet the needs of all learners

b. promote, model, and establish policies for safe, legal, and ethical use of digital information and technology

c. promote and model responsible social interactions related to the use of technology and information

d. model and facilitate the development of a shared cultural understanding and involvement in global issues through the use of contemporary communication and collaboration tools

Index

C

F

P

Q

R

S